THE
AFRO-AMERICAN
SHORT STORY

Recent Titles in
Bibliographies and Indexes in Afro-American and African Studies

Black-Jewish Relations in the United States: A Selected Bibliography
Compiled by Lenwood G. Davis

Black Immigration and Ethnicity in the United States: An Annotated Bibliography
Center for Afroamerican and African Studies, The University of Michigan

Blacks in the American Armed Forces, 1776-1983: A Bibliography
Compiled by Lenwood G. Davis and George Hill

Education of the Black Adult in the United States: An Annotated Bibliography
Compiled by Leo McGee and Harvey G. Neufeldt

A Guide to the Archives of Hampton Institute
Compiled by Fritz J. Malval

A Bibliographical Guide to Black Studies Programs in the
United States: An Annotated Bibliography
Compiled by Lenwood G. Davis and George Hill

Wole Soyinka: A Bibliography of Primary and Secondary Sources
Compiled by James Gibbs, Ketu H. Katrak, and Henry Louis Gates, Jr.

Afro-American Demography and Urban Issues: A Bibliography
Compiled by R. A. Obudho and Jeannine B. Scott

Afro-American Reference: An Annotated Bibliography of Selected Resources
Compiled and edited by Nathaniel Davis

THE
AFRO-AMERICAN
SHORT STORY

A Comprehensive,
Annotated Index
with Selected Commentaries

Compiled by Preston M. Yancy

Bibliographies and Indexes in Afro-American and African Studies, Number 10

GREENWOOD PRESS
Westport, Connecticut • London, England

Library of Congress Cataloging-in-Publication Data

Yancy, Preston M., 1938-
 The Afro-American short story.

 (Bibliographies and indexes in Afro-American and
African studies, ISSN 0742-6925 ; no. 10)
 Includes indexes.
 1. Short stories, American—Afro-American authors—
Bibliography. 2. Short stories, American—Afro-American
authors—Indexes. 3. Short stories, American—
Afro-American authors—History and criticism.
4. Afro-Americans in literature—Bibliography.
I. Title. II. Series.
Z1229.N39Y36 1986   016.813'01'08896   85-27132
[PS153.N5]
ISBN 0-313-24355-7 (lib. bdg. : alk. paper)

Library of Congress Catalog Card Number: 85-27132
ISBN: 0-313-24355-7
ISSN: 0742-6925

First published in 1986

Greenwood Press
A division of Congressional Information Service, Inc.
88 Post Road West
Westport, Connecticut 06881

Printed in the United States of America

The paper used in this book complies with the
Permanent Paper Standard issued by the National
Information Standards Organization (Z39.48-1984).

10 9 8 7 6 5 4 3 2 1

To the memory of Preston M. Yancy, Sr., to "Mama," Ivey, "Bob," Robert, and especially to Marilyn.

CONTENTS

ACKNOWLEDGMENTS

        Several institutions and individuals rendered valuable
assistance to this undertaking. Virginia Union University
granted me leave time. The National Endowment for the
Humanities funded the Summer Seminar for College Teachers
during which the study was begun. The United Negro College
Fund selected me for its Strengthening the Humanities Faculty
Program Grant--funded by the Andrew W. Mellon Foundation--for
Academic Year 1981-82, the summer of 1983, the summer of 1984
and the Fall Semester of Academic Year 1984-85.
        The following libraries and library staffs were very
helpful: The Samuel W. Williams Collection at the Atlanta
(Georgia) Public Library; The Trevor Arnett and Robert
Woodruff Libraries at Atlanta University, Atlanta, Georgia;
The Robert Woodruff Library, Emory University, Atlanta,
Georgia; The William J. Clark Library, Virginia Union
University, Richmond, Virginia; the libraries at Yale
University, New Haven, Connecticut; The Richmond (Virginia)
Public Library, and the library at Virginia State University,
Petersburg, Virginia.
        I am indebted to the following individuals: Professors
Ruby T. Bryant, E. D. McCreary, and William H. Owens of
Virginia Union University, Professor Chester M. Hedgepeth of
The University of Maryland Eastern Shore, and Professor
Thomas A. Greenfield of Bellamine College. These colleagues
recommended me for the grants I received. Dean Samuel K.
Roberts and President David T. Shannon of Virginia Union
University nominated me for grants and fellowships. Professor
Michael Cooke of Yale University accepted me for his Summer
Seminar for College Teachers in 1980 and made useful
suggestions for the study.

INTRODUCTION

The objective of this book is to provide both a comprehensive reference to modern Afro-American short stories and some analysis and commentary on modern black short fiction. Over 850 stories by approximately 300 authors are included. The book fills the need for an extensive study of Afro-American short fiction during this period. This work provides considerable data on the black short story of the period 1950-1982.

There are several useful anthologies and collections containing stories published between 1950 and 1982, and this book employed most of them. This study takes the next step beyond the necessary practice of collecting stories in anthologies and collections; it provides an extensive guide to many of the stories published in anthologies, collections, and periodicals during the period considered.

Short stories by black Americans are relevant to scholars and students in several academic areas. These stories serve a number of functions for their readers. First, Afro-American short stories are literary works which are parts of the bodies of Afro-American and American literature. Second, much of the fiction written by black Americans offers insight into the issues that concern blacks at given periods in time. Beyond the concerns of the various aspects of the black experiences, Afro-American writers in this genre have used it to entertain their readers, to express themselves, to earn money, to promote causes, ideas, and philosophies, and to do all the other things other short story writers have employed the genre to do.

The emphasis was placed on stories written by black citizens of the United States. However, a few stories are included by authors who are not black Americans. In some instances this is because the stories appear in publications aimed primarily at black readers, and the authors' ethnicities are not given. In other instances the authors are blacks who are not citizens of the United States—but who write about aspects of Afro-American life.

Part One, "Chronology," is a listing of the stories by the year of publication and alphabetically within each year. An index code precedes each story. The index code cross references the Chronology to the Author Index and the Title Index. An asterisk immediately before the story title indicates stories for which there are commentaries in Part Three. For example:

52-6. *"Heaven to Hell." Hughes, L.

Index code 52-6 indicates that this is the sixth story listed for 1952 in Part Two; the asterisk indicates that there is a commentary on this story in Part Three.

52-7. "Little Old Spy." Hughes, L.

This is the seventh story listed for 1952. No commentary is in Part Three, as no asterisk appears before the title.

Part Two, "Anthologies and Collections" is a bibliographical listing of the anthologies and collections used for this study. The anthologies and collections are listed in a standard bibliographical format. A list of the stories in each work follows each bibliographical entry. The following are examples of anthology and collection entries respectively:

Chapman, Abraham, ed. Black Voices: An Anthology of Afro-American Literature. New York: The New American Library, 1968.
    "McDougal." Frank London Brown
    "To Da-duh in Memoriam." Paule Marshall
    "Neighbors." Diane Oliver

Gaines, Ernest J. Bloodline. New York: W. W. Norton Co., 1963.
    "A Long Day in November"/"The Sky Is Gray"/"Three Men"/"Bloodline"/"Just Like a Tree."

Stories are listed in the order of their appearance unless a note indicates some other kind of listing.

Part Three, "Commentaries," consists of analyses/commentaries/critiques of selected stories in accordance with traditional literary genres: comedy, epic, tragedy, tragicomedy, and unresolved struggle, as well as generally accepted types of Afro-American literature: celebrative-commemorative, militant, protest, personal experience, and universal concerns.

There have been a number of efforts to categorize Afro-American literature. In Down Home: The Pastoral Impulse in Afro-American Short Fiction (New York: Putnam, 1975), Robert A. Bone views the Afro-American short fiction from its beginnings through the Harlem Renaissance--1800-1930--as being pastoral, anti-pastoral, or picaresque. However, Bone's categorization is criticized as being too general and too simplistic in Darwin T. Turner's review of Down Home in American Literature 48(3), November 1976. In Negro Voices

in American Fiction (New York: Russell and Russell, 1965)
Hugh M. Gloster uses the terms southern realism, propaganda,
Harlem realism, proletarian fiction, and folk realism.
 Charles L. James discusses the folk tradition, the
plantation tradition, the abolitionist tradition, protest,
and dissent in From the Roots: Short Stories by Black
Americans (New York: Dodd, Mead, 1973). Arthur P. Davis and
Saunders Redding write of accommodation, protest, integration,
and Black Nationalism in Cavalcade: Negro American Writing
from 1760 to the Present (Boston: Houghton Mifflin, 1971).
Mercer Cook and Stephen Henderson describe militant black
literature in The Militant Black Writer in the United States
and Africa (Madison: University of Wisconsin Press, 1969).
     The categories used to classify Afro-American literature
in this study are defined as follows: Celebrative-commemorative works promote positive views of black culture and the
black experiences without apology or complaint. Negative
aspects of the black experiences and of race and race relations are subordinate in celebrative works. In the personal
experience category the story has ramifications, primarily,
for the characters in the stories, but can be extended
beyond the personal, becoming universal in scope. The black
protest story cries out against situations and circumstances--
usually racial discrimination, while militant stories involve
black resistance to forces viewed as oppressive. The Commentaries section also includes a note on the role of race
relations in each story.
     An asterisk immediately before story titles in the
Chronology and the Title Index indicates the stories which
appear in the Commentaries section.
     The Author Index is an annotated bibliography in
alphabetical sequence by author's last name. Birth and death
dates are given when possible. At the beginning of the index
on page 76, five sources which contain information on Afro-
American authors are cited which give information on many
authors included in the index. When an author is included in
one or more of the sources, numbers corresponding to the
appropriate source(s) will follow the author's name. All the
short stories published between 1950 and 1982--which could be
located--are listed alphabetically in the authors' entries.
The point of view is given for selected stories. All other
sources that could be identified for each story are cited.
A brief description is given for selected stories. The index
code cross references the stories to the Chronology. For
example:

Hughes, Langston. (1902-1967) (2) (3) (4) (5)
    "African Morning." Third person. In Laughing To Keep from
    Crying, Hughes; Brothers and Sisters, A. Adoff, ed.;
    Something in Common, Hughes.
         A twelve year old interracial child lives with his white
         British father after the death of his black African
         mother. 52-1.

     Every effort was made to find dates for all of the
authors. However, a study which is this inclusive contains

works by "minor" authors as well as a few established
authors--who are listed in a number of reference works--for
whom no dates are available. In addition to checking the
reference works on page 76 to determine which authors were
listed in those works, checks for all authors--for whom no
dates could be found--were made in Index to Black American
Writers in Collective Biographies, Dorothy W. Campbell,
editor and Who's Who among Black Americans, William C. Matney,
editor.

The Title Index is an alphabetical listing of the stories.
An asterisk precedes those stories which are in the Commentaries section. The index code cross references the stories in
the Title Index to the stories in the Chronology.

THE
AFRO-AMERICAN
SHORT STORY

PART ONE
CHRONOLOGY

1950
   50-1. *"Abraham and the
   Spirit." Shockley, A. A.
   50-2. "Betrayal." Bowen, T.
1951
   51-1. "The Outing."
   Baldwin, J.
   51-2. *"See How They Run."
   Vroman, M. E.
1952
   52-1. "African Morning."
   Hughes, L.
   52-2. "Big Meeting."
   Hughes, L.
   52-3. "Djapie and His Magic Dwarf." des Pres,
   F. T.
   52-4. "Exodus." Baldwin,J.
   52-5. *"God Bless America."
   Killens, J. O.
   52-6. *"Heaven to Hell."
   Hughes, L.
   52-7. "Little Old Spy."
   Hughes, L.
   52-8. "Mysterious Madame
   Shanghai." Hughes, L.
   52-9. "Name in the Papers."
   Hughes, L.
   52-10. "Never Room with a
   Couple." Hughes, L.
   52-11. "On the Road."
   Hughes, L.
   52-12. "On the Way Home."
   Hughes, L.
   52-13. *"One Friday Morning." Hughes, L.
   52-14. "Powder-White
   Faces." Hughes, L.

1952
   52-15. *"Professor."
   Hughes, L.
   52-16. "Pushcart Man."
   Hughes, L.
   52-17. "Rouge High."
   Hughes, L.
   52-18. "Roy's Wound."
   Baldwin, J.
   52-19. "Sailor Ashore."
   Hughes, L.
   52-20. "Sarotoga Rain."
   Hughes, L.
   52-21. "Slice Him Down."
   Hughes, L.
   52-22. "Something in Common." Hughes, L.
   52-23. "Spanish Blood."
   Hughes, L.
   52-24. "Tain't So."
   Hughes, L.
   52-25. "The Tale - A West
   Indian Folk Story."
   des Pres, F. T.
   52-26. "Tragedy at the
   Baths." Hughes, L.
   52-27. *"Trouble with the
   Angels." Hughes, L.
   52-28. *"Who's Passing for
   Who." Hughes, L.
   52-29. "Why You Reckon."
   Hughes, L.
1953
   53-1. "The Beautician."
   Barron, E.
1954
   54-1. *"Audrey." Dunham,K.
   54-2. "The Valley Bet-
   ween." Marshall, P.

1954
   54-3. "The-Valley-Where-
   the-Sun-Never-Shines."
   des Pres, F. T.
1956
   56-1. "Anancy and the Mon-
   goose." des Pres, F. T.
   56-2. "A Coupla Scalped
   Indians." Ellison, R.
   56-3. "How Le Machoquette
   Was Changed into a
   Tornado." des Pres, F. T.
1957
   57-1. "The Need to Understand." Demond, A. S.
   57-2. "Sonny's Blues."
   Baldwin, J.
1958
   58-1. *"Come Out the Wilderness." Baldwin, J.
   58-2. "Has Anybody Seen Miss
   Dora Dean." Petry, A.
   58-3. *"Thank You M'am."
   Hughes, L.
1959
   59-1. "Big Boy." Anderson, A.
   59-2. "Blueplate Special."
   Anderson, A.
   59-3. "The Checkerboard."
   Anderson, A.
   59-4. *"Comrade." Anderson, A.
   59-5. "Dance of the Infidels." Anderson, A.
   59-6. *"The Dozens." Anderson, A.
   59-7. "A Fine Romance."
   Anderson, A.
   59-8. "Lover Man." Anderson, A.
   59-9. "Old Man Maypeck."
   Anderson, A.
   59-10. "Schooldays in North
   Carolina." Anderson, A.
   59-11. "Signifying." Anderson, A.
   59-12. "A Sound of Screaming." Anderson, A.
   59-13. "Susie Q." Anderson,
   A.
   59-14. "Sweet Town." Bambara, T. C.
   59-15. "Talisman." Anderson,
   A.
   59-16. "Think." Anderson, A.
1960
   60-1. "A Chance Meeting."
   Colter, C.
   60-2. *"Mississippi Ham
   Rider." Bambara, T.C.
   60-3. "Soul Clap Hands
   and Sing." ("Barba-
   dos") Marshall, P.
   60-4. "This Morning,
   This Evening, So
   Soon." Baldwin, J.
1961
   61-1. "Barbados." ("Soul
   Clap Hands and Sing.")
   Marshall, P.
   61-2. "Beginning." Vail,
   B.
   61-3. "Brazil." Marshall,
   P.
   61-4. "British Guiana."
   Marshall, P.
   61-5. *"Brooklyn." Marshall, P.
   61-6. "A Good Season."
   Williams, J. A.
   61-7. "John Henry on the
   Mountain." Gores, J.
   61-8. *"Liars Don't Qualify." Edwards, J.
   61-9. "The Lookout."
   Colter, C.
   61-10. "McDougal." Brown,
   F. L.
   61-11. "The Mob." Gores,
   J.
   61-12. "Murder at Fork
   Junction." Anderson, A.
   61-13. "Out of the Hospital and under the Bar."
   Ellison, R.
   61-14. "Overnight Trip."
   Colter, C.
   61-15. "Sorrow for a Midget." Hughes, L.
   61-16. "A Special Kind of
   Courage." Reid, A.
1962
   62-1. "Blues for Pablo."
   Stewart, J.
   62-2. "Bruzz." Thompson,
   S.
   62-3. *"Chiterlings for
   Breakfast." Mighty, J.
   G.
   62-4. "Corinna." Reid, A.
   62-5. "Cry for Me." Kelley, W. M.

1962
62-6. "The Death of Tommy
   Grimes." Meaddough,
   R. J., III.
62-7. "End of a Rest."
   Mack, T. L.
62-8. *"Enfranchisement."
   Campbell, J. E.
62-9. "Lennie." Smith, D.
62-10. "The Line of Duty."
   Olsen, P.
62-11. "A Little Ordinary."
   Ingram, A.
62-12. "A Matter of Time."
   Brown, F. L.
62-13. "Mother Dear and
   Daddy." Edwards, J.
62-14. "The Mountain."
   Hamer, M. J.
62-15. *"The Night of the
   Senior Ball." Reid, A.
62-16. *"The Only Man on
   Liberty Street. Kelley,
   W. M.
62-17. *"The Picture Prize."
   Shockley, A. A.
62-18. "Pollution." Lomax,
   S. P.
62-19. *"Reena." Marshall,P.
62-20. "The Rescue." Colter,
   C.
62-21. "Son in the After-
   noon." Williams, J. A.
62-22. "Strike." Rive, R.
62-23. "The Summer of My
   Sixteenth Year, A Remi-
   niscence." Demond, A.S.
62-24. "Trees Past the
   Window." Barker, M.
1963
63-1. "The Almost White
   Boy." Motley, W.
63-2. *"And Shed a Murderous Tear." Reid, A.
63-3. *"The Beach Umbrella."
   Colter, C.
63-4. "Beautiful Light and
   Black Our Dreams."
   King, W.,Jr.
63-5. *"Bloodline." Gaines,
   E. J.
63-6. "Coffee for the Road."
   La Guma, A.
63-7. "Come Home Early
   Chile." Dodson, O.
63-8. *"The Convert."

Bennett, L. J.
63-9. "The Democrat."
   Kalish, R. A
63-10. *"Direct Action."
   Thelwell, M.
63-11. "The Eagle the
   Dove and the Black-
   bird." Dumas, H.
63-12. "Early Autumn."
   Hughes. L.
63-13. "Eric Was Eric."
   Burroughs, M.
63-14. "I Need Your Love
   So Bad." Dalton, F. E.
63-15. "Just Like a Tree."
   Gaines, E. J.
63-16. "The Life of Lin-
   coln West." Brooks, G.
63-17. "The Marchers."
   Dumas, H.
63-18. "Miss Muriel."
   Petry, A.
63-19. *"Never Alone in
   the World." Hernton,
   C. C.
63-20. "The One Upstairs."
   Gores, J.
63-21. *"Rat Joiner Routs
   the Klan." Poston, T.
63-22. "Revolt of the An-
   gels." Clarke, J. H.
63-23. "Rock Church."
   Hughes, L.
63-24. "Saint Paul and the
   Monkeys." Kelley, W. M.
63-25. "The Screamers."
   Jones, L. (Baraka, A.)
63-26. "Singing Dinah's
   Song." Brown, F. L.
63-27. *"The Sky Is Gray."
   Gaines, E. J.
63-28. "Tales of Child-
   hood." Williams, J. A.
63-29."The Winds of
   Change." Hairston, L.
1964
64-1. "Aggie." Kelley, W.M.
64-2. "The Ancient Book."
   Brown, F. L.
64-3. Black Bottom."
   Collins, P.
64-4. "Bottle of Ship."
   Flannery, J. S.
64-5. "Brother Carlyle."
   Kelley, W. M.

1964

64-6. *"Christmas and the Great Man." Kelley, W.M.
64-7. "Community of Victims." Thelwell, M.
64-8. "Connie." Kelley, W.M.
64-9. "The Cut Throat." Randall, D
64-10. "Direct Action." Hart, N.
64-11. "The Distributors." Dumas, H.
64-12. "The End of Jamie." Martin, K. K.
64-13. "Enemy Territory." Kelley, W. M.
64-14. "Getting Acquainted." Bims, H.
64-15. *"A Good Long Sidewalk." Kelley, W. M.
64-16. *"Goodbye Baby Boy." Rivers, C. K.
64-17. *"The Harlem Rat." Jones, J. H.
64-18. "The Life You Save." Kelley, W. M.
64-19. *"A Long Day in November." Gaines, E. J.
64-20. "Mary's Convert." Colter, C.
64-21. *"Monday Will Be Better." Shockley, A. A.
64-22. *"The Most Beautiful Legs in the World." Kelley, W. M.
64-23. "Not Exactly Lena Horne." Kelley, W. M.
64-24. "The Peacemaker, A Fantasy." Westbrook, G.
64-25. "The Poker Party." Kelley, W. M.
64-26. "Rapport." Colter, C.
64-27. "Sarah." Hamer, M. J.
64-28. *"The Servant Problem." Kelley, W. M.
64-29. "So Quaint (A Fable)." Alba, N.
64-30. "Some Get Wasted." Marshall, P.
64-31. *"A Sound of Crying." Cornwell, A. R.
64-32. "A Visit to Grandmother." Kelley, W. M.
64-33. "Wedding Day." Watkins, G. R.
64-34. "What Shall We Do

with the Drunken Sailor." Kelley, W.M.

1965

65-1. "Any Other Reason." Gray, A. J.
65-2. "Blackberry Pit." Hamilton, B.
65-3. "Both My Girls." Diggs, J.
65-4. "The Bug Feeder." Holt, L.
65-5. "The Crossing." Dumas, H.
65-6. "A Dangerous Thing." Mitchell, K. J.
65-7. "The Day the World Almost Came to an End." Crayton, P.
65-8. "The Game." King, W. Jr.
65-9. "Gift." Bluitt, B.
65-10. *"Going To Meet the Man." Baldwin, J.
65-11. "Health Service." Oliver, D. A.
65-12. *"Home X and Me." Bates, A. J.
65-13. "Incident on a Bus." Randall, D.
65-14. "Jacob's Dilemma." Robinson, L.
65-15. "James Washburn." Simmons, B. C.
65-16. "Klactoveedsedstene." Russell, C.
65-17. "Life with Red Top." Fair, R.
65-18. "Lord Randall." Fox P.
65-19. "Luck of the Mestizo." Jones, E. S.
65-20. "The Man Child." Baldwin, J.
65-21. *"The Negrophile." Russell, C. E.
65-22. "A New Mirror." Petry, A.
65-23. "Now That Henry Is Gone." Riley, C.
65-24. "O'Grady Says." White, J.
65-25. "One Mexican." Bims, H.
65-26. "Quietus." Russell, C.
65-27. "Reaching Is His

1965
Rule." "Knight, E.
65-28. "The Rockpile." Baldwin, J.
65-29. "The Satin-Back Crepe
Dress." Alba, N.
65-30. "Ten Minutes at the
Bus Stop." Burke, R.
65-31. "To the Fair." Wolf,
H. R.
65-32. "Walker in the Dust."
Sweet, E.
65-33. "Yes We Can Sing."
Greenlee, S.
1966
66-1. "Adjo Means Goodbye."
Young, C. A.
66-2. "And Save a Round for
Jamie Brown." Cornwell,
A. R.
66-3. "The Apostle." Ful-
ler, H.
66-4. "Between the Summers."
Cornwell, A. R.
66-5. "Black for Dinner."
Colter, C.
66-6. "Bright and Mournin'
Star." Thelwell, M.
66-7. "Bus No. 51." Bluitt,B.
66-8.*"Chinese Food."
Rivers, C. K.
66-9. "A Day's Living." Armstead, D.
66-10. "A Gift." Colter, C.
66-11. "Grandma's Game."
Williams, R.
66-12. "The Hammar Man."
Bambara, T. C.
66-13. "The Hatcher Theory."
Shepherd, D.
66-14. "Ice Tea." Adams, A.
66-15. *"Judah's a Two Way
Street Running Out."
Barris, J.
66-16. *"Karen's Spring."
Greenfield, E.
66-17. "The Last Supper."
Barksdale, R. K.
66-18. "A Love Song for
Seven Little Boys Called
Sam." Fuller, C. H.
66-19. "My Father, My Bottom, My Fleas," Knight,
E.
66-20. "Navy Black." Wil-
liams, J. A.

66-21. *"Neighbors." Oli-
ver, D. A.
66-22. "Niggers Don't
Cry." Williams, T.
66-23. "Noblesse Oblige."
Greenfield, E.
66-24. "A Scary Story."
Alba, N.
66-25. "The Senegalese."
Fuller, H. W.
66-26. "Shoe Shine Boy."
Randall, D.
66-27. "The Sign." Green-
lee, S.
66-28. "Summer Sunday."
Greenlee, S.
66-29. "Ten to Seven."
Fields, J.
66-30. "Traffic Jam."
Oliver, D. A.
66-31. "United States
Congressman." Bims, H.
66-32. "The Unresolved
Denouement." Brown, W.
66-33. "Victoria." Ran-
dall, D.
66-34. "The Wall." Davis,
G.
66-35. *"Will the Circle
Be Unbroken." Dumas,H.
1967
67-1. "Afternoon into
Night." Dunham, K.
67-2. *"Ain't No Use in
Crying." Shockley, A.
67-3. "The Alternative."
Baraka, A. (Jones, L.)
67-4."Answers in Pro-
gress." Baraka, A.
(Jones, L.)
67-5. "Aspiration." Brookins, M. S.
67-6. "Autumn Leaves."
Greenlee, S.
67-7. "Beyond Chicago
Someone Sleeps." ("On
Trains.") James, A.
(McPherson, J. A.)
67-8. "Blackbird in a
Cage." Rodgers, C.
67-9. "Brownstone Blues."
Anthony, P.
67-10. "A Chase (Aligh-
iere's Dream)." Bara-
ka, A. (Jones, L.)
67-11. *"Daddy Was a Num-

1967

bers Runner." Meriwether, L. M.

67-12. "The Death of Horatio Alger." Baraka, A. (Jones, L.)

67-13. "Desire Is a Bus." Esslinger, P. M.

67-14. "Duel with the Clock." Edwards, J.

67-15. "The Engagement Party." Boles, R.

67-16. "The Equalizer Supreme." Fields, J.

67-17. "The Firing Squad and the Afterlife." Lucas. W. F.

67-18. *"The Funeral." Shockley, A. A

67-19. *"Going Down Slow." Baraka, A. (Jones, L.)

67-20. "The Gold Fish Monster." Crayton, P.

67-21. "Heroes Are Gang Leaders." Baraka, A. (Jones, L.)

67-22. "A House Divided." Taylor, J. A.

67-23. "Houseboy." Myers, W.

67-24. "An Interesting Social Study." Hunter, K.

67-25. "Junkie Joe Had Some Money." Milner, R.

67-26. *"Like a Piece of the Blues." Davis, G.

67-27. "The Longest Ocean in the World." Baraka, A. (Jones, L.)

67-28. *"The Machine." Smith, J. W.

67-29. "Maggie of the Green Bottles." Bambara, T. C.

67-30. "A Man in the House." Colter, C.

67-31. "The Migraine Workers." Petry, A.

67-32. *"Mint Julep Not Served Here." Oliver, D.A.

67-33. "Miss Luhester Gives a Party." Fair, R.

67-34. "Mother to Son." Rivers, C. K.

67-35. *"A New Day." Wright, C.

67-36. "New Sense." Baraka, A. (Jones,L.)

67-37. "New Spirit." Baraka,

A. (Jones, L.)

67-38. "The Newcomer." ("Mister Newcomer.") Bullins, E.

67-39. "Night in Chicago." Sandiata, S.

67-40. "No Body   No Place." Baraka, A. (Jones, L.)

67-41. "Not Your Singing Dancing Spade." Fields, J.

67-42. "Now and Then." Baraka, A. (Jones, L.)

67-43. *"Old Blues Singers Never Die." Johnson, C. V.

67-44. "'On,' The Charms of Harry Jones." de Joie, N.

67-45. "On the Next Train South." Knight, E.

67-46. *"The Other Side of Christmas." Meaddough, R. J.

67-47. "Playing with Punjab." Bambara, T. C.

67-48. *"The Red Bonnet." Patterson, L.

67-49. *"The Revolt of the **Evil Fairies.**" Poston, T.

67-50. "Salute." Baraka, A. (Jones, L.)

67-51. "Somebody." Johnson, D.

67-52. "Song of Youth." Myers, W.

67-53 *"The Stick Up." Killens, J. O.

67-54. *"The Storekeeper." Bullins, E.

67-55. "A Story for Claustrophobiacs." Mahoney, B. and Hampton,J.

67-56. *"Support Your Local Police." Bullins,E.

67-57. "Talking Bout Sonny." Bambara, T. C.

67-58. *"That She Would Dance No More." Smith, J. W.

67-59. "Through Leanness and Desire,"Sloan,D.L.

67-60. "To Da-duh in Memoriam." Marshall, P.

1967
67-61. *"To Hell with dying." Walker, A.
67-62. "Uncle Tom's Cabin: Alternate Ending." Baraka, A. (Jones, L.)
67-63. "Unfinished." Baraka, A. (Jones, L.)
67-64. "The Wise Guy." White, J.
67-65. "Words." Baraka, A. (Jones, L.)

1968
68-1. *"An Act of Prostitution." McPherson, J. A.
68-2. "All the Lonely People." McPherson, J. A.
68-3. "The Bag Man." King, W., Jr.
68-4. "Cheesy Baby!" Holmes, R. E.
68-5. "Chicken Hawk's Dream." Young, A.
68-6. "The Confessions of George Washington." Holred, F. T.
68-7. "Debut." Hunter, K.
68-8. "The Dentist's Wife." Kelley, W. M.
68-9. "The Diary of an African Nun." Walker, A.
68-10. "The Double Triangle." Bryant, G.
68-11. *"Frankie Mae." Smith, J.W.
68-12. "The Game." Reams,C.
68-13. "Gold Coast." McPherson, J. A.
68-14. "A Happening in Barbados." Meriwether, L.
68-15. "Hue and Cry." McPherson, J. A.
68-16. "The Hypnotist." Bamberg, E. G.
68-17. "The Hypochondriac." Fields, J.
68-18. "Jolof." Richardson, F. D.
68-19. "The Large End of the Strop." Meriwether,L.
68-20. "Listen to the Wind Blow." King, W., Jr.
68-21. "The Manipulators." Bambara, T. C. (Cade,T.)
68-22. "A Matter of Vocabulary." McPherson, J.A.

68-23. "A New Place." McPherson, J. A.
68-24. "Of Cabbages and Kings." McPherson, J.A.
68-25. "On Trains." ("Beyond Chicago Someone Sleeps.") McPherson,J.A.
68-26. "One Way or Another." Chideya, C. M.
68-27. "Private Domain." McPherson, J. A.
68-28. "Rain God." ("Echo Tree.") Dumas, H.
68-29. *"A Revolutionary Tale." Giovanni, N.
68-30. "Sins of the Fathers." Jacobs, M. K.
68-31. *"A Solo Song for Doc." McPherson, J. A.
68-32. "South from Nowhere." McKnight, N.
68-33. "Strong Horse Tea." Walker, A.
68-34. "Sursum Corda (Lift Up Your Hearts.)" White, E.
68-35. "Tell Martha Not To Moan." Williams, S. A.
68-36. *"Three Men." Gaines, E. J.
68-37. *"Train Whistle Guitar." Murray, A.
69-1. "Ain't That a Groove." Cobb, C.
69-2. "Black Daedalus Dreaming." Wilson, F.M.
69-3. "The Bouncing Game." Bates, A. J.
69-4. "A Ceremony of Innocence." Bates, A. J.
69-5. *"The Committee." Wilmore, S. R.
69-6. "The Contrabande." Anderson, S. E.
69-7. "Dear Sis." Bates,A. J.
69-8. "Dinner Party." Bates, A. J.
69-9. *"End of the Affair." Shockley, A. A.
69-10. "The Entertainers." Bates, A. J.
69-11. "The Fighter." Myers, W.
69-12. "Fon." Dumas, H.
69-13. "A Friend for a

1969

Season." Harrison, D.

69-14. *"Harlem on the Rocks." Hairston, L.

69-15. *"How Long Is Forever." Myers, W.

69-16. "I Remember Omar." Jackson M.

69-17. "I'm Going to Move Out of This Emotional Ghetto." Lee, A.

69-18. "Little Jake." Bates, A. J.

69-19. "Loimos." White, E.

69-20. "Lost Note." Bates, A. J.

69-21. "The Magic Word." Henderson, S.

69-22. "Marigolds." Collier, E.

69-23. *Moma." Lee, A.

69-24. "Not Anymore." Greenfield, E.

69-25. "The Numbers Writer." Pharr, R. D.

69-26. "Of Acidia." White, E.

69-27. "Poppa's Story." Meaddough, R. J.

69-28. "The Return of the Spouse." Bates, A. J.

69-29. "Runetta." Bates, A.J.

69-30. "The Shadow between Them." Bates, A. J.

69-31. "Silas." Bates, A. J.

69-32. "Sinner Man Where You Gonna Run To." Neal, L.

69-33. "The Soul's Sting." Cabbell, E. J.

69-34. "A Statistic Trying To Make It Home." Rodgers, C.

69-35. "Stonewall Jackson's Waterloo." Murray, A.

69-36. *"To Be a Man." Shockley, A. A.

69-37. "The Top Hat Motel." Moreland, C. K.

69-38. *"The Willie Bob Letters." Wilson, T.

1970

70-1. "The Addict." De-Ramus, B.

70-2. "After the Ball." Colter, C.

70-3. "All Day Long."

Angelous, M.

70-4. "Alownne." Mondesire, J. W.

70-5. "Ark of Bones." Dumas, H.

70-6. "The Block." Lee, A.

70-7. "A Boll of Roses." Dumas, H.

70-8. "Boy (A Short Story in Allegory Form)." Cumbo, K. M.

70-9. "Bumper's Dream." Kelley, W. M.

70-10. *"Cotton Alley." Crayton, P.

70-11. "The Day Little Mose Spoke." McMillan, H. L.

70-12. "Double Nigger." Dumas, H.

70-13. "Dream Panopy." Greenfield, E.

70-14. "Echo Tree." ("Rain God.") Dumas, H.

70-15. "The Figure Eight." Williams, J. A.

70-16. "The Figurines." Bertha, G.

70-17. "Four Moments in Time." Richardson, F.D.

70-18. "Girl Friend." Colter, C.

70-19. "A Great Day for a Funeral." Williams,E.G.

70-20. "A Harlem Farewell." Ahmed, A. B.

70-21. "A Harlem Game." Dumas, H.

70-22. "The Harlem Teacher." Freeman, L.

70-23. *"Harlem Transfer." Walker, E. K.

70-24. "A Harsh Greeting." Gray, D.

70-25. "Hoom." Pritchard, N. H.

70-26. "Let Me Hang Loose." Howard, V.

70-27. *"The Library." Giovanni, N.

70-28. "Miss Nora." Patterson, L.

70-29. "Moot." Colter, C.

70-30. "Nefertiti." Hunter, C.

70-31. "Nightmare."

1970

Williams, E. G.
70-32. "No Great Honor."
Fields, J.
70-33. "NUT-BROWN: A Soul
Psalm." Goss, C.
70-34. "Porky." Clemmons,C.G.
70-35. *"The President."
Shockley, A. A.
70-36. "Randalene Ain' t No
Baby." Sanders, M. B.
70-37. "Rehabilitation and
Treatment." Martinez, J.
70-38. "Remembrances of a
Lost Dream." Williams.E.G.
70-39. *"The Ride." Lee, A.
70-40. "Rough Diamond."
Killens, J. A.
70-41. "A Separate but Equal
Heaven." Wells, O. R.
70-42. "Sketch in Blue."
Higgs, E. V.
70-43. "Soldier Boy." An-
derson, S. E.
70-44. "Sonny's Seasons."
Greenlee, S.
70-45. *"Strawberry Blonde,
That Is." Burroughs, M.
70-46. "Strike and Fade."
Dumas, H.
70-47. "Stuff."Hemsley, H.
70-48. "Three Parables."
Marvin X.
70-49. "A Time To Mourn."
Knight, E.
70-50. "To Love a Man."
Lee, A.
70-51. "A Tooth for an Eye."
Greenfield, E.
70-52. "An Untold Story."
Colter, C.
70-53. "The Victims."
Price, E. C.
70-54. "A Wandorobo Masai."
Melford, L.
70-55. "Watching the Sun-
set." Coleman, W.
70-56. "Wednesday." Amini,J.
70-57. *"The Welcome Table."
Walker, A.
70-58. "The Welfare Check."
Jones, G.
70-59. "With Malice Afore-
thought." Lofton, C. A.
70-60. "Zamani Goes to Market." Feelings, M. L.

1971

71-1. "After Saturday
Night Comes Sunday."
Sanchez, S.
71-2. "Alienation." Lee,A.
71-3. "The Anticlimax."
Jackman, O.
71-4. "The Blue of Mad-
ness." Kemp, A.
71-5. *"Blues Ain't No
Mockin' Bird." Bambara,
T. C.
71-6. *"Crying for Her
Man." Shockley, A. A.
71-7. "DANDY, or Astride
the Funky Finger of
Lust." Bullins, E.
71-8. "The Drive." Bul-
lins, E.
71-9. "Esther." Robin-
son, R.
71-10. *"Etta's Mind."
Gant, L
71-11. *"The Faculty Par-
ty." Shockley, A. A.
71-12. "The Fare to Crown
Point." Myers, W.
71-13. "Glass Rain." Angelous, M.
71-14. "The Going On."
Myer, W.
71-15. "He Couldn't Say
Sex." Bullins, E.
71-16. "The Helper." Bul-
lins, E.
71-17. "Honor among Thie-
ves." Hunter, K.
71-18. "The Hungered One."
Bullins, E.
71-19. "I Ain't Playing,
I'm Hurtin'." ("Goril-
la My Love.") Bambara,
T. C.
71-20. "In New England
Winter." Bullins, E.
71-21. "In the Wine Time."
Bullins, E.
71-22. "Is She Relevant."
Shockley, A. A.
71-23. "Just a Little More
Glass." Fair, R.
71-24. "Kiss the Girls for
Me." White, W.
71-25. "Legacy." Walker,
E. K.
71-26. "Like It Is."

1971

Banks, B.
71-27. "Mama Hazel Takes to Her Bed." ("My Man Bovanne.") Bambara, T. C.
71-28. "A Man Is a Man." Lee, A.
71-29. "The March." Colter,C.
71-30. "Marchover." Appling, W.
71-31. "The Messenger." Bullins, E.
71-32. "Mister Newcomer." ("The Newcomer.") Bullins, E.
71-33. "Moon Woman, Sunday's Child." Welburn, R.
71-34. *"Mother Africa." Petry, A.
71-35. "November." Anderson, M. H. (Holland, M. K.)
71-36. "Package Deal." Butterfield, S.
71-37. "The Pilgrims." Mccluskey, J. M.
71-38. "THE RALLY or Dialect Determinism." Bullins, E.
71-39. "Raymond's Run." Bambara, T. C.
71-40. "The Reluctant Voyage." Bullins, E.
71-41. "The Return: A Fantasy." Jones, G.
71-42. "A Right Proper Burial." Richardson, A. I.
71-43. "Rites Fraternal." Barber, J.
71-44. "The Savior." Bullins, E.
71-45. "Second Line/Cutting the Body Loose." Ferdinand, V. (Salaam, K. Y.)
71-46. "The Seed of a Slum's Eternity." Priestley, E.
71-47. "Sinbad the Cat." Collier, E.
71-48. "Something-To-Eat." Smith, J. W.
71-49. "A Sudden Trip Home in the Spring." Walker,A.
71-50. "Taking Grits for Granted." Henderson, G.
71-51.*"Travel from Home." Bullins, E.
71-52. "Waiting for Her Train." Lee, A.
71-53. "Wake Me Mama." Bates, A. J.
71-54. "Winona Young Is a Faceless Person." Brown, S.
71-55. "The Witness." Petry, A.
71-56. "A Word about Justice." Muller-Thym, T.

1972

72-1. "The American Dream." Thomas, F. L.
72-2. *"Antonio Is a Man." Lee, A.
72-3. *"Arthur." Mathis, S. B.
72-4. "Basement." Bambara, T. C.
72-5. "Black on Black: A Political Love Story." Mayfield, J.
72-6. "A Black Woman's Monologue." Davis, A.J.
72-7. "Bubba." Myers, W.
72-8. "Cecil." Kilgore, J. C.
72-9. "Claudia."Jackson,F
72-10. "Cold Ben, New Castle." Beckham, B.
72-11. "The Enemy." Franklin, J. E.
72-12. "The Fake Picasso." De Ramus, B.
72-13. "The Flogging." Milner, R.
72-14."A 'For God and Country' Thing Circa 1940." Oliver, J. B.
72-15."A Gift for Mama." Hunter, M. J.
72-16. *"Gorilla My Love." ("I Ain't Playing I'm Hurtin'.") Bambara,T.C.
72-17. "Happy Birthday." Bambara, T. C.
72-18. "Home Is Much Too Far To Go." Davis, G.
72-19. "How I Got Into the Grocery Business, Hunter, K.
72-20. "Huntin'." Nyx, M.
72-21. "I Wanna Be Sumpin'." Smith, S.
72-22. "Intrusion." Greenfield, E.

1972
72-23. "The Johnson Girls."
Bambara, T. C.
72-24. "The Lesson." Bam-
bara, T. C.
72-25. "A Life Story." Major, C.
72-26. "The Long Sell."
Walker, V. S.
72-27. "Love Knot." Crit-
tenden, A. R.
72-28. "A Love Song for
Wing." Fuller, C. H.
72-29. "Maude." Gladden,F.A.
72-30. "My Man Bovanne."
("Mama Hazel Takes to
Her Bed.") Bambara, T.C.
72-31. "Ndugu from Touga-
loo." Self, C.
72-32. "Not We Many." Cooper, C. J.,Jr.
72-33. "The Physics Teacher." Southerland, N.
72-34. "The Ray." Milner,R.
72-35. "Remember Him a Outlaw." De Veaux, A.
72-36. "Roman Times."
Jones, S.
72-37. "Rufus." Roach, R.
72-38. "See What Tommorow
Brings." Thompson, J. W.
72-39. "Silas Canterbury."
Coombs, O.
72-40. "Sonny's Not Blue."
Greenlee, S.
72-41. "The Survivor." Bambara, T. C.
72-42. *"Sweet Potato Pie."
Collier, E.
72-43. "T Baby." Patter-
son, L.
72-44. "Testimonial." Hankins, P.
72-45. "That Girl from
Creektown." Meriwether,L.
72-46. "The Valley of the
Shadow of Death." Les-
ter, J.
72-47. "Walk wid Jesus."
Rodgers, C.
72-48. "The Washtub."
Banks, B.
72-49. "Willie T. Washington's Blues." Crawford,M.
1973
73-1. "Beanie." Anderson,M.H.

73-2. "Blues for Little
Prez." Greenlee, S.
73-3. "Boodie the Player."
Heard, N. C.
73-4. "Brooklyn - A Semi-
True Story." Murray,S.M.
73-5. "The Child Who Fa-
vored Daughter." Wal-
ker, A.
73-6. "Entertaining God."
Walker, A.
73-7. "Ernie Father." Ma-
this, S. B.
73-8. *"Everyday Use."
Walker, A.
73-9. "The Faithful."
McPherson, J. A.
73-10. "A Few Fact Filled
Fiction of African
Reality." Joans, T.
73-11. "The Flowers."
Walker, A.
73-12. "For Once in My
Life (A Short State-
ment)." Smart-Grosven-
ors, V. M. (Grosvenors,
V. M.)
73-13. "The Forget-for-
Peace- Program." Herve',
J. W.
73-14. "Freedom." White,W.
73-15. "The Gift of Mer-
cilessness." Wardlow,
E. X. L.
73-16. "God and Machine."
Baraka, A. (Baraka,I.A.)
73-17. "Great God Stebbs."
Davis, A.
73-18. "Gums." Myers, W.
73-19. "HE & SHE or LUV
Makes You Do Foolish
Things." White, T.
73-20. "Her Sweet Jerome."
Walker, A.
73-21. "Jevata." Jones, G.
73-22. "Love Song on South
Street." Evans, D.
73-23. "Mama Pritchett."
Bright, Hazel V.
73-24. "Mother Wit versus
the Sleet Medallion
Fleet." Brown, W.
73-25. "Nairobi Nights."
McCluskey, J. A.
73-26. "Of Fathers and
Sons." Toure, A. M.

1973
73-27. "The Plot To Bring
Back Dunking." Fields, J.
73-28. "Points of Refer-
ence." Williams, G. M.
73-29. "Put Ya Feet on a
Rock." Brown, T.
73-30. "Really, Doesn't
Crime Pay?" Walker, A.
73-31. "The Revenge of Hannah Kemhuff." Walker, A.
73-32. "Rosa Lee Loves Bennie." Wilkerson, B. S.
73-33. "Roselily." Walker,A.
73-34. "A Sense of Secu-
rity." Jones, G.
73-35. "Sister Bibi." Sa-
laam, K. Y.(Ferdinand, V.
73-36. "Soldiers." Southerland, E.
73-37. "A Special Evening."
Shockley, A. A.
73-38. *"Story of a Scar."
McPherson, J. A.
73-39. "Sun and Flesh."
Clarke, S.
73-40. *"Ten Pecan Pies."
Major, C.
73-41. "Tender Roots."
Banks, B. C.
73-42. "Tricks." Tibbs, D.
73-43. "The Way of Shadows."
Jones, S.
73-44. "We Drink the Wine
in France." Walker, A.
73-45. "When You Dead You
Ain't Done." Bright, H.V.
73-46. "You've Come a Long
Way Baby." Gant, L.
1974
74-1. "Beans." Taylor, G.
74-2. "Courtney Go Huntin'."
Warniz, C.
74-3. "The Crossing." Cherry, E.
74-4. "The First Day (A Fable after Brown)." Wal-
ker, A.
74-5. "For You There Is Only
the Dancing." Perry, R.
74-6. "Give Us this Day."
Reid, A.
74-7. "Intruder." Kent,G.E.
74-8. "Jo Jo Banks and the
Treble Clef." Reid, A.
74-9. "Juanita." Stiles,T.J.

74-10. "The Long Night."
Bambara, T. C.
74-11. "Never Show Your
Feelings, Boy." Guar-
dine, L. J.
74-12. "Only Clowns Pass-
ing Through."Taylor,J.A.
74-13. "The Saga of Pri-
vate Julius Cole."
Shockley, A. A.
74-14. "Send for You Yes-
terday, Here You Come
Today." Smart-Grosve-
nors, V. M.
74-15. "Suffer Little
Children." Davis, A. I.
74-16. "Way To Go Home."
Greenfield, E.
1975
75-1."The Americanization
of Rhythm." Stewart, J.
75-2. "Bloodstones." Ste-
wart, J.
75-3. "Brother Isom."
("Isom.") Spillers, H.
75-4. *"Central Standard
Time Blues."Rodgers,C.M.
75-5. "Convergence." Tor-
res, B.
75-6. "A Credit to the
Race." Hudson, W.
75-7. "Early Morning."
Stewart, J.
75-8. "Emancipation." King,
W., Jr.
75-9. "A Few Hypes You
Should Be Hip to by
Now." Brown, C.
75-10. "Going Home." Har-
rison, D.
75-11. "The Harlem Mice."
Bullins, E.
75-12. "A Hole They Call a
Grave." Baldwin, J. A.
75-13. "In the Winter Of."
Stewart, J.
75-14. *"Julia." Stewart,J.
75-15. "Letter to a Would-
be Prostitute." Ste-
wart, J.
75-16. "Light through the
Ivy." Brooks, S.
75-17. "Me and Julius."
Perry, R.
75-18. "Not a Tear in Her

1975
Eye." Moss, I.
75-19. *"One Time." Rod-
gers, C.
75-20. *"The Pre-Jail Party."
Stewart, J.
75-21. "Rabbit, Rabbit,
You're Killing Me."
Black, I. J.
75-22. "Rag Sally." Cuthber-
son, J. O.
75-23. "56 Ravine Avenue."
Mitchell, G.
75-24. "Rendezvous with
G. T." Duncan, P.
75-25. *"Ricky." Collier,E.
75-26. "Satin's Dream."
Stewart, J.
75-27. "Social Work." Ma-
jor, C.
75-28. "Spaces." Jones, G.
75-29. "Stick Song." Ste-
wart, J.
75-30. "Strength." Taylor,G.
75-31. "Sukkie's Song."
Sutton, C. D.
75-32. "Thalia." Dumas, H.
75-33. "That Old Madness -
1974." Stewart, J.
75-34. "The Third Step in
Caraway Park." Evans, M.
75-35. "White Rat." Jones,G.
75-36. "The World Is Wide,
The World Is Small."
Barrow, B.
75-37. "Youngblood." Evans,D.
1976
76-1. "Absence." Sherrod, L.
76-2. "After Europe the
First Time." Cjohnathan,
E. C.
76-3. "Another Life."
Coombs, O.
76-4. "Aunt Melia's Visit:
Memories from the '40s."
Jefferson, S.
76-5. "Boots." Anderson,M.H.
76-6. "Bridal Shower." Marcus, L.
76-7. "Contact." Duncan, P.
76-8. "Early Morning Calls."
Lawson, J.
76-9. "Eulogy for a Public
Servant." Lee, A.
76-10. "The Funeral." An-
derson, M. H.

76-11. "Gone after Jake."
Anderson, M. H.
76-12. "The Grief." Anderson, M. H.
76-13. "Harvest." Jones,
E. P.
76-14. "Inertia." Ecleua,
T. O.
76-15. "The Lie." Wil-
liams, M.
76-16. "Mama." Oliver, K.
76-17. "Manton Street
Blues." Wingate, S. V.
76-18. "The Mermaid."
Okore, O.
76-19. "Momma's Child."
Anderson, M. H.
76-20. "The Mute." Ander-
son, M. H.
76-21. "Needin'." Smith,
R. K.
76-22. "Negra." Monoz, A.
76-23. "Ralph's Story."
Hawkins, O.
76-24. "The Real Meaning
of Understanding."
Anderson, M. H.
76-25. "The Return of
Tarkwa." Obinkaram, T.
76-26. "Reunion."
O'Brien, T.
76-27. "Roll Call." Law-
son, J. M.
76-28. "A Sense of Pride."
Watkins, O.
76-29. "Shopping Trip."
Campbell, B. B.
76-30. "The Sizing Tree."
Anderson, M. H.
76-31. "Sunday School."
Woods, D.
76-32. "Survivor's Row."
Steele, S.
76-33. "Terror." Wolf, S.
76-34. "Thickets." Ander-
son, M. H.
76-35. "Waiting for
Beale." De Ramus, B.
76-36. "Water." Bray, R.
76-37. "What Goes Around."
Shelton, P. L.
76-38. "When Baby Got Go-
ing." Anderson, M. H.
76-39. "Witchbird." Bam-
bara, T. C.
1977

1977

77-1. "Advancing Luna - and Ida B. Wells." Walker,A.

77-2. "Alice." White, P.C.

77-3. "All of Us and None of You." Davenport, S.B.

77-4. "The Apprentice." Bambara, T. C.

77-5. "Asylum." Jones, G.

77-6. "Betrayal." Moore, C.

77-7. "Bless the Dead." Jackson, N.

77-8. "Broken Field Running." Bambara, T. C.

77-9. "Christmas Eve at Johnson's Drugs N Goods." Bambara, T. C.

77-10. "Clarissa's Problem." Harrison, D.

77-11. "Cleaning out the Closet." Jackson, M.

77-12. "The Coke Factory." Jones, G.

77-13. *"Elbow Room." McPherson, J. A.

77-14. *"A Far Piece." Curry, G.

77-15. "Friends." Carole,J.

77-16. "A Girl's Story." Bambara, T. C.

77-17. "Giving Honor to God." James, R.

77-18. "The Granddaughter." Marshall, S. R.

77-19. "I Am an American." McPherson, J. A.

77-20. "I Can Stand a Little Rain." Myers, V.

77-21. *"If That Mockingbird Don't Sing."Mack,D.

77-22. "Impotence."O'Neal,R.

77-23. "Just Enough for the City." McPherson, J. A.

77-24. "A Lament."Spillers,H.

77-25. "The Last Chew." Braswell, J.

77-26. "Lead Role." Vickens, J.

77-27. "Legend." Jones, G.

77-28. "A Loaf of Bread." McPherson, J. A.

77-29. "A Matter of Breaking Free." Chaney, B. N.

77-30. "Medley."Bambara,T.C.

77-31. "Mississippi Remembered." Perry, R.

77-32. "Monday Morning." Manns, A.

77-33. "Moonlight and Mississippi."Perry, R.

77-34. "The More Things Change." Shockley,A.A.

77-35. "No Time for Geting Up." Burks, E.

77-36. "Not on Sunday." Alakaye, I.

77-37. "The Organizer's Wife." Bambara, T. C.

77-38. "Payment on Account." Comiskey, M.H.

77-39. "Persona."Jones,G.

77-40. "Problems of Art." McPherson, J. A.

77-41. "A Quiet Place for the Summer." Jones,G.

77-42. "Reward."Solomon,P.

77-43. "The Roundhouse." Jones, G.

77-44. "The Sea Birds Are Still Alive." Bambara, T. C.

77-45."A Sense of Story." McPherson, J. A.

77-46. "The Silver Bullet." McPherson, J. A.

77-47. "Spectator."Prior, J. A.

77-48. "Still Waters." Duncan, P.

77-49. "The Story of a Dead Man."McPherson,J.A.

77-50. "Sunset Boogie." Williams, D. A.

77-51. "Talk O' The Town." Kensey, B. L.

77-52. "A Tender Man." Bambara, T. C.

77-53. "Three Girls." Robinson, J.

77-54. "Thursday Reckoning." Talley, M.

77-55. "Unkept Promises." Shaw, E. S.

77-56. "Unwanted."Bailey, L. K.

77-57. "Version 2." Jones,G.

77-58. "Waiting for September." Burns, K.

77-59. "What Are Friends For." Douglass, G.

77-60. *"Why I Like Country Music." McPherson,

1977
J. A.
77-61. "Why Mother." Wil-
liams, K.
77-62. "Widows and Orphans."
McPherson, J. A.
77-63. "A Woman's Man."
Moss, G.
77-64. "The Women." Jones, G.
77-65. "Your Poems Have
Very Little Color in
Them." Jones, G.
1978
78-1. "All Because of Emi-
ly." Slaughter, E.
78-2. "The Anniversary
Story." Simpson, J. C.
78-3. "Baptism 1945." Williams, L. G.
78-4. "The Bird Cage."
White, P. C.
78-5. "Blood Sisters." Boyer, J. W.
78-6. "A Day in the Life of
Civil Rights." Spillers, H.
78-7. "First Comes Touch."
Lauderdale, B.
78-8. "Gestures." d Pate, A.
78-9. "I Could Rest For-
ever." Jackson, M.
78-10. "I Remember Bessie."
Moss, G., Jr.
78-11. "Just Give Me a Little Piece of the Sun."
Smith, C.
78-12. "Laurel." Walker, A.
78-13. "Lubelle Berries."
Thomas, J. C.
78-14. "Marilyn." Major, C.
78-15. "Miriam." Greene, B. G.
78-16. "oh she gotta head
fulla hair." Shange, N.
78-17. "The Riddles of Egypt Brownstone." De
veaux, A.
78-18. "Small Victories."
Stewart, J.
78-19. "A Time in Septem-
ber." Childress, J.
78-20. "Unfinished Canvas."
Caldwell, R. E.
78-21. "The Vigil." Adonis,
J. C.
78-22. "The Vision of Fe-
lipe." Myers, W. D.
1979

79-1. "aw babee, you so
pretty." Shange, N.
79-2. "Carrie: A New World
Ritual." Robinson, B. H.
79-3. "Color the World."
Rawls, M. A.
79-4. "Dark Hyacinth."
Barbour, F.
79-5. "Devil Bird." Dumas,
H.
79-6. "Firmly Though Softly." Harris, P.
79-7. "Going Home on a
Long Cord." Rawls, M. A.
79-8. "Harlem." Dumas, H.
79-9. "In Light of What
Has Happened." Stiles.
T. J.
79-10. "Invasion." Dumas, H.
79-11. "The Lake." Dumas, H.
79-12. "Mama Load." Bam-
bara, T. C.
79-13. "A Meeting of the
Sapphic Daughters."
Shockley, A. A.
79-14. "Old Flames Die
Hard." Smith, C.
79-15. "The Rape." Shawn, K.
79-16. "Requiem for Willie
Lee." Hodges, F.
79-17. *"Rope of Wind."
Dumas, H.
79-18. "Six Days Shall
You Labor." Dumas, H.
79-19. "Thrust Counter
Thrust." Dumas, H.
79-20. "The University of
Man." Dumas, H.
79-21. "The Voice." Du-
mas, H.
79-22. "Who's Gonna Tell
Wilma." Jackson, M.
1980
80-1. "Baby's Breath."
Bambara, T. C.
80-2. "A Birthday Remem-
bered." Shockley, A. A.
80-3. "Coming into Her
Own." Mc Kissack, A. G.
80-4. "comin to terms."
Shange, N.
80-5. "Eve." Wesley, V. W.
80-6. "Fly Away Blackbird,
Fly Away Home." Thief, L.
80-7. "Gift Exchange."
Hansen, J.

1980
80-8. "Holly Craft Isn't
Gay." Shockley, A. A.
80-9. "Home To Meet the
Folks."Shockley, A, A.
80-10. "How Did I Get Away
with Killing One of the
Biggest Lawyers in the
State? It Was Easy."
Walker, A.
80-11. "The Island Lover."
Wiggins, P.
80-12. "Isom." ("Brother
Isom.") Spillers, H.
80-13. *"A Life on Beekman
Place." ("Lucielia Lou-
ise Turner.")Naylor, G.
80-14. "Love Motion."
Shockley, A. A.
80-15. "Luther on Sweet Auburn." Bambara, T. C.
80-16. "Meditations on History." Williams, S. A.
80-17. "One Going, One Staying." Hobs, D.
80-18. "One More Saturday
Night Around." Shockley,
A. A.
80-19. "The Play."Shockley,
A. A.
80-20. "Play It but Don't
Say It." Shockley, A. A.
80-21. "She Was Linda Be-
fore She Was Ayesha."
Welsh, K.
80-22. "Smells That Go Boom."
Mason, J. A.
80-23. "Spring into Autumn."
Shockley, A. A.
80-24. "These Ain't All My
Tears." Jackson, M.
1981
81-1. "The Abortion." Walker, A.
81-2. "Accross the Wide
Missouri." Wideman, J. E.
81-3. "The Beginning of
Homewood." Wideman, J. E.
81-4. "The Chinaman." Wideman, J. E.
81-5. "The Coat of Alms."
Evans, H. L.
81-6. "Coming Apart by Way
of Introduction to Lorde,
Teish, and Gardner."
Walker, A.

81-7. "Daddy Garbage."
Wideman, J. E.
81-8. *"Damballah." Wide-
man, J. E.
81-9. "Elethia."Walker,A.
81-10. "Fame." Walker, A.
81-11. "God Bless the
Cook." Welsh, K.
81-12. "Hazel."Wideman,
J. E.
81-13. "I Was Here but I
Disappeared." Brown,W.
81-14. "Just Another Sat-
urday Night." Johnson,
J. C.
81-15. "Lerna's Mother,
Verda Lee." Mays,R.Y.
81-16. "A Letter of the
Times or Should This
Sado-Masochism Be Sav-
ed." Walker, A.
81-17. "Lizabeth: The Ca-
terpillar Story."Wide-
man, J. E.
81-18. "The Lover." Walk-
er, A.
81-19. "Nineteen Fifty-
five." Walker, A.
81-20. "Passing the Word."
Neely, B.
81-21. "Petunias." Walk-
er, A.
81-22. "Porn." Walker, A.
81-23. "Rashad." Wideman,
J. E.
81-24."Solitary."Wideman,
J. E.
81-25. "The Songs of Reba
Love Jackson."Wideman,
J. E.
81-26. "Source."Walker,A.
81-27. "Tommy." Wideman,
J. E.
81-28. "The Watermelon
Story." Wideman, J. E.
81-29. "Widow Woman."Gas-
kin, J.
1982
82-1. "The Block Party."
Naylor, G.
82-2. "Cora Lee."Naylor,G.
82-3. "Dawn." Naylor, G.
82-4. "Etta Mae Johnson."
Naylor, G.
82-5. "Kiswana Brown."
("When Mama Comes To

1982
   Call.") Naylor, G.
  82-6. "Lucielia Louise Turner." ("A Life on Beekman Place.") Naylor, G.
  82-7. "Mattie Michael."
   Naylor, G.
  82-8. "The Peach Tree."
   Hudson, F. B.
  82-9. "The Two." Naylor, G.
  82-10. "When Mama Comes to
   Call." ("Kiswana Brown.")
   Naylor, G.

PART TWO
ANTHOLOGIES
AND COLLECTIONS

ANTHOLOGIES

Adoff, Arnold, ed. Brothers and Sisters: Modern Stories by
    Black Americans. New York: MacMillan, 1970.
    "Sonny's Blues." James Baldwin
    "Marigolds." Eugenia Collier
    "Cotton Alley." Pearl Crayton
    "Rain God." Henry Dumas
    "Mother Dear and Daddy," Julius Edwards
    "A Love Song for Seven Little Boys Called Sam." C. H.
    Fuller, Jr.
    "The Sky Is Gray." Ernest J. Gaines
    "The Library." Nikki Giovanni
    "The Mountain." Martin Hamer
    "African Morning." Langston Hughes
    "The Poker Party." William Melvin Kelley
    "The Death of Tommy Grimes." R. J. Meaddough, III.
    "Neighbors." Diane A. Oliver
    "Black Bird in a Cage." Carolyn Rodgers
    "The Figure Eight." John A. Williams

Baker, Houston A., Jr., ed. Black Literature in America. New
    York: McGraw Hill, 1971.
    "A Coupla Scalped Indians." Ralph Ellison
    "God Bless America." John O. Killens
    "Son in the Afternoon." John A. Williams
    "Barbados." Paule Marshall
    "Cry for Me." William Melvin Kelley

Bambara, Toni Cade, ed. Tales and Stories for Black Folks.
    Garden City, N. Y.: Doubleday, 1971.
    "Raymond's Run." Toni Cade Bambara
    "Thank You M'am." Langston Hughes
    "Train Whistle Guitar." Albert Murray
    "To Hell with Dying." Alice Walker
    "The Day the World Almost Came to an End." Pearl Crayton.
    "The Sky is Gray." Ernest J. Gaines
    "Let Me Hang Loose." Vanessa Howard
Barksdale, Richard and Keneth Kinnamon, eds. Black Writers

of America: A Comprehensive Anthology. New York: The Mac-
millan Co., 1971.
"Sonny's Blues." James Baldwin
"Barbados." Paule Marshall
"The Sky Is Gray." Ernest J. Gaines
"The Dentist's Wife." William Melvin Kelley

Chapman, Abraham, ed. Black Voices: An Anthology of Afro-
American Literature. New York: The New American Library,
1968.
"McDougal." Frank London Brown
"To Da-duh in Memoriam." Paule Marshall
"Neighbors." Diane Oliver

Chapman, Abraham, ed. New Black Voices: An Anthology of Con-
temporary Afro-American Literature. New York: New Ameri-
can Library, 1972.
"The Numbers Writer." Robert Dean Pharr
"Mary's Convert." Cyrus Colter
"Three Men." Ernest J. Gaines
"A Time to Mourn." Etheridge Knight
"A Good Long Sidewalk." William Melvin Kelley
"Bright and Mourning Star." Mike Thelwell
"Chicken Hawk's Dream." Al Young
"A Solo Song for Doc." James Alan McPherson
"A House Divided." Jeanne A. Taylor
"The Long Sell." Victor Steven Walker

Clarke, John Henrik, ed. American Negro Short Stories. New
York: Hill and Wang, 1966.
"See How They Run." Mary Elizabeth Vroman
"Exodus." James Baldwin
"God Bless America." John Oliver Killens
"Train Whistle Guitar." Albert Murray
"The Senegalese." Hoyt W. Fuller
"A Matter of Time." Frank London Brown
"Cry for Me." William Melvin Kelley
"Reena." Paule Marshall
"The Convert." Lerone Bennett
"The Winds of Change." Loyle Hairston
"The Screamers." Amiri Baraka (Leroi Jones)
"Sarah." Martin J. Hamer
"The Sky Is Gray." Ernest J. Gaines

Clarke, John Henrik, ed. Harlem. New York: New American Li-
brary, 1970.
"Roy's Wound." James Baldwin
"Revolt of the Angels." John Henrik Clarke
"A Good Long Sidewalk." William Melvin Kelley
"Some Get Wasted." Paule Marshall
"Now That Henry Is Gone." Clayton Riley
"Unfinished." Amiri Baraka (Leroi Jones)
"The Other Side of Christmas." R. J. Meaddough
"Rough Diamond." John Oliver Killens
"The Harlem Teacher." Lorraine Freeman
"All Day Long." Maya Angelou

"Daddy Was a Numbers Runner." Louise W. Meriwether
"Harlem on the Rocks." Loyle Hairston

Clarke, John Henrik, ed. <u>Harlem USA.</u> Berlin: Seven Seas
Books, 1964. reprint ed. New York: Collier Books, 1971.
(Partial listing based on secondary sources.)
"Revolt of the Angels." John Henrik Clark
"The Harlem Rat." John H. Jones
"The Winds of Change." Loyle Hairston
"Some Get Wasted." Paule Marshall

Coombs, Orde, ed. <u>What We Must See; Young Black Storytell-
ers.</u> New York: Dodd, Mead, & Co., 1971.
"Rites Fraternal." John Barber
"Second Line/Cutting the Body Loose." Val Ferdinand.
(Kalamu Ya Salaam)
"Etta's Mind." Liz Grant
"Cheesy Baby." R. Ernest Holmes
"The Blue of Madness." Arnold Kemp
"Waiting for Her Train." Audrey M. Lee
"The Pilgrims." John McCluskey
"A Word about Justice." Thomas Muller-Thyme
"The Fare to Crown Point." Walter Myers
"Miss Nora." Lindsay Patterson
"The Seed of a Slum's Eternity." Eric Priestley
"A Right Proper Burial." Alice I Richardson
"After Saturday Nite Comes Sunday." Sonia Sanchez
"Harlem Transfer." Evan K. Walker
"Sursum Corda (Lift Up Your Hearts)." Edgar White
"Kiss the Girls for Me." Wallace White

Davis, Arthur P and Saunders Redding, eds. <u>Cavalcade: Negro
American Writing from 1760 to the Present.</u> Boston: Hough-
ton Mifflin Co., 1971.
"Brooklyn." Paule Marshall
"The Only Man on Liberty Street." William Melvin Kelley
"Just Like a Tree." Ernest J. Gaines

Davis, Charles T. and Daniel Walden, eds. <u>On Being Black.</u>
Greenwich, Conn.: Fawcett Pubs., 1970
"The Only Man on Liberty Street." William Melvin Kelley
"A Solo Song for Doc." James Alan McPherson

Elam, Julia Corene, ed. <u>The Afro-American Short Story: From
Accommodation to Protest.</u> Ann Arbor , Mich.: University
Microfilms, 1971.
"Exodus." James Baldwin
"Neighbors." Diane A. Oliver
"The Almost White Boy." Willard Motley
"To Be a Man." Ann Allen Shockley
"A Sound of Crying." Anita R. Cornwell (This story is
not in the anthology; the editor comments on the story.)
"Black Daedalus Dreaming." Freddie M. Wilson
"The Convert." Lerone Bennett (This story is not in the
anthology; the editor comments on the story.)
"Sonny's Blues." James Baldwin

"Direct Action." Mike Thelwell
"The Magic Word." Stephen Henderson
"Cry for Me." William Melvin Kelley

Emanuel, James A, and Theodore Gross, eds, Dark Symphony:
   Negro Literature in America. New York: The Free Press,
   1968.
   "Sonny's Blues." James Baldwin
   "Train Whistle Guitar." Albert Murray
   "Son in the Afternoon." John A. Williams
   "Brazil." Paule Marshall
   "The Sky Is Gray." Ernest J. Gaines
   "Cry for Me." William Melvin Kelley

Hayden, Robert, David J Burrows, and Frederick R. Lapides.
   Afro-American Literature: An Introduction. New York:
   Harcourt, Brace, Jovanovich, 1971.
   "Sonny's Blues." James Baldwin
   "On Trains." James Alan McPherson

Hill, Herbert, ed. Soon One Morning: New Writing by American
   Negroes 1940 - 1962. New York: Alfred A. Knopf, 1963.
   "Miss Muriel." Ann Petry
   "Rock Church." Langston Hughes
   "Out of the Hospital and under the Bar." Ralph Ellison
   "The Life of Lincoln West." Gwendolyn Brooks
   "Come Home Early Chile." Owen Dodson
   "Singing Dinah's Song." Frank London Brown
   "Rat Joiner Routs the Klan." Ted Poston
   "The Almost White Boy." Willard Motley
   "The Beach Umbrella." Cyrus Colter

Hughes, Langston, ed. The Best Short Stories by Negro Wri-
   ters. Boston: Little Brown and Co., 1967.
   "Thank You M'am." Langston Hughes
   "The Revolt of the Evil Fairies." Ted Poston
   "The Beach Umbrella." Cyrus Colter
   "The Almost White Boy." Willard Motley
   "Afternoon into Night." Katherine Dunham
   "Come Home Early Chile." Owen Dodson
   "The Stick Up." John O. Killens
   "The Checkerboard." Alston Anderson
   "See How They Run." Mary Elizabeth Vroman
   "The Blues Begins." Sylvester Leaks
   "Son in the Afternoon." John A. Williams
   "Singing Dinah's Song." Frank London Brown
   "Duel with the Clock." Junius Edwards
   "Barbados." Paule Marshall
   "The Day the World Almost Came to an End." Pearl Crayton
   "An Interesting Social Study." Kristin Hunter
   "A New Day." Charles Wright
   "Quietus." Charles Russell
   "Mother to Son." Conrad Kent Rivers
   "A Long Day in November." Ernest J. Gaines
   "Miss Luhester Gives a Party." Ronald Fair
   "The Death of Tommy Grimes." R. J. Meaddough, III.

"Old Blues Singers Never Die." Clifford Vincent Johnson
"The Only Man on Liberty Street." William Melvin Kelley
"Beautiful Light and Black Our Dreams." Woodie King, Jr.
"The Red Bonnet." Lindsay Patterson
"Direct Action." Mike Thelwell
"The Engagement Party." Robert Boles
"To Hell with Dying." Alice Walker

James, Charles L., ed. From the Roots: Short Stories by Black
   Americans. New York: Dodd, Mead & Co., 1973.
   "Come out the Wilderness." James Baldwin
   "The Two Worlds." James C. Lyman
   "Saint Paul and the Monkeys" William Melvin Kelley
   "A Long Day in November." Ernest J. Gaines
   "Uncle Tom's Cabin:Alternate Ending." Amiri Baraka (Le-
   roi Jones)
   "A Matter of Vocabulary." James Alan McPherson

Jones, Leroi (Amiri Baraka) and Larry Neal, eds. Black Fire.
   New York: William Morrow, 1969.
   "Fon." Henry Dumas
   "A Love Song for Seven Little Boys Called Sam." C. H.
   Fuller, Jr.
   "Not Your Singing Dancing Spade." Julia Fields
   "That She Would Dance No More." Jean Wheeler Smith
   "Life with Red Top." Ronald Fair
   "Sinner Man Where You Gonna Run To." Larry Neal
   "Ain't That a Groove." Charlie Cobb

King, Woody, Jr.,ed. Black Short Story Anthology. New York
   Columbia University Press, 1972.
   "A Revolutionary Tale." Nikki Giovanni
   "Frankie Mae." Jean Wheeler Smith
   "Harlem Transfer." E. K. Walker
   "DANDY or Astride the Funky Finger of Lust." Ed Bullins
   "Sonny's Not Blue.." Sam Greenlee
   "Testimonial." Paula Hankins
   "The Ray." Ron Milner
   "A Good Season." John A Williams
   "The Alternative." Amiri Baraka (Imamu Amiri Baraka)
   "Strong Horse Tea." Alice Walker
   "A Love Song for Wing." Charles H. Fuller, Jr.
   "The Convert." Lerone Bennett, Jr.
   "Not Your Singing Dancing Spade." Julia Fields
   "A Happening in Barbados." Louise M. Meriwether
   "Early Autumn." Langston Hughes
   "Just Like a Tree." Ernest Gaines
   "Not We Many." Clarence L. Cooper, Jr.
   "See What Tomorrow Brings." James W. Thompson
   "A Coupla Scalped Indians." Ralph Ellison
   "Come out the Wilderness." James Baldwin
   "The Game." Woodie King
   "The Poker Party." William Melvin Kelley
   "Liars Don't Qualify." Junius Edwards
   "The Contrabande." S. E. Anderson
   "Like a Piece of the Blues." George Davis

"The Enemy." J. E. Franklin
"Loimos." Edgar White
"The Flogging." Ron Milner

Long, Richard and Eugenia Collier, eds. Afro-American Writ-
    ing. Vol. 2. New York: New York University Press, 1972,
    "Cry for Me." William Melvin Kelley
    "The Sky Is Gray." Ernest J. Gaines
    "To Da-duh in Memoriam." Paule Marshall

Mirer, Martin, ed. Modern Black Stories. Woodbury, N. Y.:
    Barron's Educational Series, Inc., 1971.
    "The Bench." Richard Rive
    "Bruzz." Samuel Thompson
    "The Convert." Lerone Bennett, Jr.
    "The Death of Tommy Grimes." R. J. Meaddough, III.
    "Mister Courifer." A. Cosely-Hayford
    "Professor." Langston Hughes
    "Rat Joiner Routs the Klan." Ted Poston

Reed, Ishmael, ed. 19 Necromancers from Now. Garden City,
    N. Y.:Doubleday & Co., 1970.
    "Answer in Progress." Amiri Baraka (Leroi Jones)
    "Hoom." N. H. Pritchard

Sanchez,Sonia, ed. We Be Word Sorcerers: 25 Stories by Black
    Americans. New York: Bantom Books, 1973.
    "Blues Ain't No Mockin Bird." Toni Cade Bambara
    "God and Machine." Amiri Baraka (Imamu Amiri Baraka)
    "Put Your Feet on a Rock." Tiki Brown
    "Mother Wit versus the Sleet Medallion Fleet." Wesley
    Brown.
    "DANDY or Astride the Funky Finger of Lust." Ed Bullins
    "Sun and Flesh." Sebastian Clarke
    "You've Come a Long Way Baby." Liz Gant
    "Sonny's Seasons." Sam Greenlee
    "For Once in my Life (A Short Statement)." Verta Mae
    Smart-Grosvenor (Verta Mae Grosvenor)
    "Boodie the Player." Nathan C. Heard
    "A Few Fact Filled Fiction of African Reality."Ted Joans
    "Sister Bibi." Kalamu Ya Salaam (Val Ferdinand)
    "Listen to the Wind Blow." Woodie Knight, Jr.
    "Brooklyn - A Semi-true Story." Samuel M. Murray
    "Gums." Walter Myers
    "After Saturday Night Comes Sunday." Sonia Sanchez
    "Of Fathers and Sons." Askia Muhammed Toure
    "Her Sweet Jerome." Alice Walker
    "Legacy." Evan K. Walker
    "The Gift of Mercilessness." Exavier X Lowtricia Wardlow
    "Rosa Lee Loves Bennie." Brenda Scott Wilkinson

Shuman, R. Baird, ed. A Galaxy of Black Writing. Durham,N.C.
    Moore Pub. Co., 1970
    "Porky." Carole Cregory Clemmons
    "BOY (A Short Story in Allegory Form)." Kattie M. Cumbo
    "A Great Day for a Funeral." Edward G. Williams

"Nightmare." Edward G. Williams
"Remembrances of a Lost Dream." Edward G. Williams

Stadler, Quandra Prettyman, ed. Out of Our Lives: A Selection
of Contemporary Black Fiction. Washington: Howard
University Press, 1978.
"Gorilla My Love." Toni Cade Bambara
"Stonewall Jackson's Waterloo." Albert Murray
"Daddy Was a Numbers Runner." Louise Meriwether
"A Friend for a Season." Delores Harrison
"The Screamers." Amiri Baraka (Leroi Jones)
"The New Mirror." Ann Petry
"Tell Martha Not To Mourn." S. A. Williams
"Sarah." Martin J. Hamer
"Poppa's Story." R. J. Meaddough
"Three Men." Ernest Gaines
"Bright and Mournin' Star." Mike Thelwell
"Mother Dear and Daddy." Junius Edwards
"Black for Dinner." Cyrus Colter
"The Funeral." Ann Allen Shockley
"The Gold Fish Monster." Pearl Crayton

Turner, Darwin T., ed. Black American Literature - Fiction.
Columbus, Ohio: Charles E. Merrill, 1969.
"Thank you M'am." Langston Hughes
"The Only Man on Liberty Street." William Melvin Kelley
"Debut." Kristin Hunter

Washington, Mary Helen, ed. Black-eyed Susans: Classic Sto-
ries by and about Black Women. Garden City, N. Y.: An-
chor Press/Doubleday, 1975.
"Frankie Mae." Jean Wheeler Smith
"A Happening in Barbados." Louise Meriwether
"My Man Bovanne." Toni Cade Bambara
"Everyday Use." Alice Walker
"Reena." Paule Marshall
"A Sudden Trip Home in the Spring." Alice Walker

Washington, Mary Helen, ed. Midnight Birds: Stories of Con-
temporary Black American Writers. Garden City, N. Y.:
Anchor Press/Doubleday, 1980.
"Alice." Paulette Childress White
"The Riddles of Egypt Brownstone." Alexis Deveaux
"The Bird Cage." Paulette Childress White
"Laurel." Alice Walker
"Advancing Luna and Ida B. Wells." Alice Walker
"aw babee, you so pretty." Ntozake Shange
"Requiem for Willie Lee." Frenchy Hodges
"Remember Him a Outlaw." Alexis Deveaux
"Asylum." Gayl Jones
"Jevata." Gayl Jones
"Witchbird." ToniCade Bambara
"Meditations on History." Sherley Ann Williams
"comin to terms." Ntozake Shange
"Medley." Toni Cade Bambara

Watkins, Mel, ed. Black Review No 1. New York: William Mor-
     row & Co., 1972.
     "Cold Ben, New Castle." Barry Beckham
     "Travel from Home." Ed Bullins
     "Home Is Much Too Far To Go." George Davis
     "Claudia." Franklin Jackson

Watkins, Mel, ed. Black Review No. 2. New York: William Mor-
     row & Co., 1972.
     "Ndugu from Tougaloo." Charles Self
     "Silas Canterbury." Orde Coombs
     "That Girl from Creektown." Louise Meriwether
     "The Valley of the Shadow of Death." Julius Lester

Williams, John A., ed. The Angry Black. New York: Lancer
     Books, 1962.
     "Mother Dear and Daddy." Junius Edwards
     "Pollution." S. P. Lomax
     "The Line of Duty." Paul Olsen
     "Son in the Afternoon." John A. Williams

Williams, John A., ed. Beyond the Angry Black. New York:
     Cooper Square Pubs., 1969.
     "Mother Dear and Daddy." Junius Edwards
     "The Apostle." Hoyt W. Fuller
     "Pollution." S. P. Lomax
     "Line of Duty." Paul Olsen
     "Navy Black." John A. Williams
     "Adjo Means Goodbye." Carrie Allen Young

COLLECTIONS

Anderson, Alston. Lover Man. Garden City, N. Y.: Doubleday &
     Co., 1959.
     "The Checkerboard"/"The Dozens"/"Signifying"/"A Fine Ro-
mance"/"A Sound of Screaming"/"Big Boy"/"Suzie Q"/"Old Man
Maypeck"/"Schooldays in North Carolina"/"Think"/"Blueplate
Special"/"Comrade"/"Dance of the Infidels"/" Talisman"/"Lover Man."

Anderson, Mignon Holland. Mostly Womenfolk and a Man or Two:
     A Collection. Chicago: Third World Press, 1976.
     "When Baby Got Going"/"Momma's Child"/"The Sizing Tree"/
"Boots"/"Beanie"/"Thickets"/"The Real Hidden Meaning of Un-
dertaking"/"The Grief"/"November"/"Gone after Jake"/"The
Mute"/"The Funeral."

Baldwin, James. Going To Meet the Man. New York: The Dial
     Press, 1965.
     "The Rockpile"/"The Outing"/"The Man Child"/"Previous
Condition"/"Sonny's Blues"/"This Morning, This Evening, So
Soon"/"Come out the Wilderness"/"Going To Meet the Man."

Bambara, Toni Cade. Gorilla My Love. New York: Random House,
     1972.
     "My Man Bovanne"/"Gorilla My Love"/"Raymond's Run"/"The

Hammer Man"/"Mississippi Ham Rider"/"Happy Birthday"/"Playing
with Punjab"/"Talking bout Sonny"/"The Lesson"/"The Survivor"/"Sweet Town"/"Blues Ain't No Mockin' Bird"/"Basement"/
"Maggie of the Green Bottles"/"The Johnson Girls."

Bambara, Toni Cade. The Sea Birds Are Still Alive. New York:
     Random House, 1977.
     "The Organizer's Wife."/"The Apprentice"/"Broken Field
Running"/"The Sea Birds Are Still Alive"/"The Long Night/
"Medley"/" A Tender Man"/"A Girl's Story"/"Witchbird"/
"Christmas Eve at Johnson's Drugs N Goods."

Bates, Arthenia J. Seeds beneath the Snow: Vignettes from
     the South. New York: Greenwich Book Pubs., 1969, reprint
     ed. Washington, D. C.: Howard University Press, 1975.
     "Silas"/"Little Jake"/"Runetta"/"The Shadow Between
Them"/"Return of the Spouse"/"The Bouncing Game"/"Dear Sis"
/"The Entertainers"/"Home X and Me"/"Lost Note"/"Dinner
Party"/"A Ceremony of Innocence."

Bullins, Ed. The Hungered One: Early Writings. New York:
     William Morrow & Co., 1971. (Brief Sketches are omitted;
     titles are listed alphabetically, rather than in the
     order of appearance in the book.)
     "DANDY or Astride the Funky Finger of Lust"/"The Drive"/
"He Couldn't Say Sex"/"The Helper"/"The Hungered One"/"In
New England Winter"/"In the Wine Time"/"The Messenger"/"Mister Newcomer"/"THE RALLY or Dialect Determinism"/"The Reluctant Voyage"/"The Savior"/"Support Your Local Police"/"Travel from Home."

Colter, Cyrus. The Beach Umbrella. Iowa City: University of
     Iowa Press, 1970.
     "Man in the House"/"A Chance Meeting"/"The Rescue"/"The
Lookout"/"Girl Friend"/"Rapport"/"Mary's Convert"/"Black
for Dinner"/"Moot"/"Overnight Trip"/"An Untold Story"/"After
the Ball"/"A Gift"/"The Beach Umbrella."

Dumas, Henry. Ark of Bones and Other Stories. Hale Chatfield
     and Eugene Redmond, eds. Carbondale: Southern Illinois
     University Press, 1970.
     "Ark of Bones"/"Echo Tree"/"A Boll of Roses"/"The
Crossing"/"Double Nigger"/"A Harlem Game"/"Will the Circle
Be Unbroken"/"Strike and Fade"/"Fon."

Dumas, Henry. Rope of Wind: And Other Stories. New York: Ran-
     dom House, 1979.
     "The Marchers"/" The Eagle the Dove and the Blackbird"/
"Harlem"/"The University of Man"/"Rope of Wind"/"Devil
Bird"/"Invasion"/"The Lake"/"The Distributors"/"Thrust
Counter Thrust"/"Six Days You Shall Labor"/"The Voice."

Gaines, Ernest J. Bloodline. New York: W. W. Norton & Co.
     1963.
     "A Long Day in November"/"The Sky Is Gray"/"Three
Men"/"Bloodline"/"Just Like a Tree."

Hughes, Langston. <u>The Langston Hughes Reader: The Selected Writings of Langston Hughes.</u> New York: George Braziller, 1958.
"Thank You M'am"/"Patron of the Arts"/"Who's Passing for Who?"/"Something in Common"/"Spanish Blood"/"Tain't So"/"One Friday Morning"/"On the Way Home"/"Tragedy at the Baths"/"Big Meeting."

Hughes, Langston. <u>Laughing To Keep from Crying.</u> New York: Henry Holt & Co., 1952. (Some of the stories in this collection appeared in periodicals prior to 1950.)
"Who's Passing for Who?"/"Something in Common"/"African Morning"/"Pushcart Man"/"Why You Reckon"/"Saratoga Rain"/"Spanish Blood"/"Heaven to Hell"/"Sailor Ashore"/"Slice Him Down"/"Tain't So"/"One Friday Morning"/"Professor"/"Name in the Papers"/"Powder-White Faces"/"Rouge High"/"On the Way Home"/"Mysterious Madame Shanghai"/"Never Room with a Couple"/"Little Old Spy"/"Tragedy at the Baths"/"Trouble with the Angels"/"On the Road"/"Big Meeting."

Hughes Langston. <u>Something in Common and other Stories.</u> New York:Hill and Wang, 1963.
"Thank You M'am."/"Rock Church"/"Little Old Spy"/"Who's Passing for Who?"/"African Morning"/"Pushcart Man"/"Why You Reckon"/"Saratoga Rain"/"Spanish Blood"/"Heaven to Hell"/"Sailor Ashore"/"Slice Him Down"/"Tain't So"/"Professor"/"Sorrow for a Midget"/"Powder-White Faces"/"Rouge High"/"On the Way Home"/"Mysterious Madame Shanghai"/"Patron of the Arts"/"Early Autumn"/"Never Room with a Couple"/"Tragedy at the Baths"/"Trouble with the Angels"/"On the Road"/"Big Meeting"/"Something in Common."

Jones Gayl. <u>White Rat.</u> New York: Random House, 1977.
"White Rat"/"Your Poems Have Very Little Color in Them"/"The Women"/"Jevata"/"Asylum"/"Persona"/"The Coke Factory"/"The Return: A Fantasy"/"The Roundhouse"/"The Legend"/"A Quiet Place for the Summer"/"Version 2."

Jones Leroi (Amiri Baraka). <u>Tales.</u> New York: Grove Press, 1967.
"A Chase (Alighieri's Dream)"/"The Alternative"/"The Longest Ocean in the World"/"Uncle Tom's Cabin: Alternate Ending"/"The Death of Horatio Alger"/"Going Down Slow"/"Heroes Are Gang Leaders"/"The Screamers"/"Salute"/"Words"/"New Sense"/"Unfinished"/"New Spirit"/"No Body   No Place"/"Now and Then"/"Answers in Progress."

Kelley, William Melvin. <u>Dancers on the Shore.</u> Garden City, N. Y.:Doubleday & Co., 1964.
"The Only Man on Liberty Street"/"Enemy Territory"/"The Poker Party"/"Not Exactly Lena Horne"/"Aggie"/"A Visit to Grandmother"/"Saint Paul and the Monkeys"/"What Shall We Do with the Drunken Sailor?"/"Christmas and the Great Man"/"Connie"/"The Servant Problem"/"Brother Carlyle"/"The Life You Save"/"A Good Long Sidewalk"/"The Most Beautiful Legs in the World"/"Cry for Me."

McPherson, James Alan. <u>Elbow Room.</u> Boston: Little Brown &
    Co., 1977.
    "Why I Like Country Music"/"The Story of a Dead Man"/
"The Silver Bullet"/"The Faithful"/"Problems of Art"/"The
Story of a Scar"/"I Am an American"/"Widows and Orphans"/"A
Loaf of Bread"/"Just Enough for the City"/"A Sense of Sto-
ry"/"Elbow Room."

McPherson, James Alan. <u>Hue and Cry.</u> Boston: Little Brown &
    Co., 1969.
    "A Matter of Vocabulary"/"On Trains"/"A Solo Song for
Doc"/"Gold Coast"/"Of Cabbages and Kings"/"All the Lonely
People"/"An Act of Prostitution"/"Private Domain"/"A New
Place"/"Hue and Cry."

Marshall, Paule. <u>Reena and other Stories.</u> Old Westbury, N.
    Y.: The Feminist Press, 1983.
    "The Valley Between"/"Brooklyn"/"Barbados"/"Reena"/"To
Da-duh in Memoriam"/"Merle."

Marshall, Paule. <u>Soul Clap Hands and Sing.</u> Chatham, N. J.:
    The Chatham Bookseller, 1961.
    "Barbados"/"Brooklyn"/"British Guiana"/"Brazil."

Naylor, Gloria. <u>The Women of Brewster Place: A Novel in Se-
    ven Stories.</u> New York:The Viking Press, 1982.
    "Dawn"/"Mattie Michael"/"Etta Mae Johnson"/"Kiswana
Browne"/"Lucielia Louise Turner"/"Cora Lee"/"The Two"/"The
Block Party."

Petry, Ann. <u>Miss Muriel and other Stories.</u> Boston: Houghton
Mifflin Co., 1971.
    "Miss Muriel"/"The New Mirror"/"Has Anybody Seen Miss
Dora Dean?"/"The Migraine Workers"/"Mother Africa"/"The
Witness."

Shockley, Ann Allen. <u>The Black and White of It.</u> Tallahassee,
    Fla.: Naiad Press, 1980.
    "Spring into Autumn"/"Play It but Don't Say It"/"The
Play"/"Home To Meet the Folks"/"A Meeting of the Sapphic
Daughters"/"Holly Craft Isn't Gay"/"One More Saturday Night
Around"/"A Birthday Remembered"/"Love Motion"/"A Special
Evening."

Stewart, John. <u>Curving Road.</u> Chicago: University of Illinois
    Press, 1975..
    "Blues for Pablo"/"Letter to a Would-be Prostitute"/"The
Pre-Jail Party"/"Satin's Dream"/"Julia"/"Bloodstones"/"In
the Winter Of"/"That Old Madness - 1974"/"Early Morning"/
"Stick Song."

Walker, Alice. <u>In Love and Trouble.</u> Harcourt, Brace, Jovan-
    ovich, 1973.
    "Roselily"/"Really, Doesn't Crime Pay?"/"Her Sweet Je-
rome"/"The Child Who Favored Daughter"/"Everyday Use"/"The
Revenge of Hannah Kemhuff"/"The Welcome Table"/"Strong Horse

Tea."

Walker Alice. <u>You Can't Keep a Good Woman Down.</u> New York:
Harcourt,Brace, Jovanovich, 1981.
"Nineteen Fifty-five"/"How Did I Get Away with Killing
One of the Biggest Lawyers in the State? It Was Easy"/"Ele-
thia"/"The Lover"/"Petunias"/"Coming Apart"/"Fame"/"The
Abortion"/"Porn"/"Advancing Luna - and Ida B. Wells"/"Lau-
rel"/"A Letter of the Times, or Should This Sado-Masochism
Be Saved?"/"A Sudden Trip Home in the Spring."

Wideman, John E. <u>Damballah.</u> New York: Avon Books, 1981.
"Damballah"/"Daddy Garbage"/"Lizabeth: The Caterpillar
Story"/"Hazel"/"The Chinaman"/"The Watermelon Story"/"The
Songs of Reba Love Jackson"/"Accross the Wide Missouri"/
"Rashad"/"Tommy"/"Solitary"/"The Beginning of Homewood."

PART THREE
COMMENTARIES

1950

"Abraham and the Spirit." Ann Allen Shockley
Category A. Comic. Category B. Celebrative
There is no treatment of race relation in the story.

The story is humouous and light-hearted. Little Abraham will
not join the church until he feels the spirit, and the spirit
comes to everyone else, but not to Abraham. The congregation
is very anxious to leave the hot church on this hot July Sunday, and Abraham's grandmother tries in vain to get Abraham
to join the church - even though he has not felt the spirit.
Finally, Granny stabs Abraham with her hatpin, and Abraham is
sure that he has felt the spirit. So he is an eager - if
pained convert.
   "Abraham and the Spirit" is celebrative; it depicts aspects of black life and culture without apology and without
complaint. The story commemorates and celebrates black life,
and there is no indication that there are any problems associated with being black.

1951

"See How They Run." Mary Elizabeth Vroman
Category A. Epic, Tragi-comic. Category B. Celebrative,
Protest
Race is a minor factor.

Jane Richards is a young black teacher in her third year of
teaching. She teaches the third grade at a segregated southern school she has forty-three students some of whom have
famous names - "Frederick Douglass, Franklin Delano, Abraham
Lincoln, Booker T., Joe Louis, George Washington." On the
other hand C. T. Young has no first or middle names - just
initials. C. T. represents Jane's big challenge.
   Tanya Fulton represents another challenge. When Tanya
gets diptheria, Jane sees to it that she gets medical care.

Most of the other teachers refuse to help her. But when the
child dies, some of the teachers who refused to help with
the medical bills go to the funeral, and the entire faculty
contributes to the funeral wreath.

C. T. has repeated the first and second grades; he
expects to repeat the third. Nothing seems to work when Jane
tries to reach him and get him to apply himself. But when
she learns he likes to build things, she devises lessons
around building model airplanes, boats, houses, and, ships.
C. T. learns enough to pass to the fourth grade. He also
chooses the name Christopher Turner.

This story touches on the negative aspects of American
race relations and of the burdens borne by black people
when the story was written, and it gently protests against
racial injustice. The story also protests gently against
the shortcomings and misplaced values of some black teachers.
But the story very strongly celebrates the black determination to succeed. The celebrative aspects of the story are
more pronounced than the protest aspects.

Jane Richards is a aymbol of the dedicated, resilient,
resourceful, black teacher. At this level the story is epic.
Tanya's death is tragic, and this is balanced by Jane's
ability to also see the humorous aspects of life and to
laugh at them, so the story has deeply serious and very
light aspects.

                       1952

     "God Bless America." John Oliver Killens
     Category A. Tragic. Category B. Protest
     Race is a major concern.

Joe is a black soldier on his way to the Korean War. His wife
Cleo is pregnant; Cleo cannot understand why the war is
taking place, nor can she understand what black soldiers have
to fight for. Joe is trying very hard to believe that the
black soldier has a stake in fighting. Joe's friend, Luke
Robinson, is race conscious and cynical about patriotism. As
the soldiers march in segregated units march to the ship -
with the whites in the front - the band plays "God Bless
America" while the white soldiers march on board. When the
black soldiers begin to board the ship, the band plays "The
Darktown Strutters' Ball." Luke is cynically amused; Joe is
quite upset.

     "Heaven to Hell." Langston Hughes
     Category A. Comic. Category B. Personal Experience
     There is no treatment of race relations.

Amelia and her husband, Mackenzie, are in an automobile
accident. Initially, Amelia dreams that she and Mackenzie are
in heaven, but she is not happy because Nancy Smothers, a
woman she views as a rival, is also in heaven. Then she
awakens to find Nancy at her bedside. Nancy brings word that
Mackenzie is doing well. In spite of Amelia's desire to

behave well in the presence of the white nurse, she insults
Nancy. Nancy attributes the insults to the fact that Amelia
has been drugged. After Nancy leaves, Amelia frets about
whether Nancy is going home as she says she is, or if she is
going to Mackenzie's room.
This story is typical of Hughes' humor.

"One Friday Morning." Langston Hughes
Category A. Epic, Tragic. Category B. Protest
Race is a major concern.

Nancy Lee Johnson is a black high school girl who is well-
liked by the teachers and students in her predominantly
white high school. She enters a picture that she has drawn
in a scholarship competition sponsored by the Artist Club,
and her picture wins the competition. Both her white teacher
- Miss Dietrich - and her white vice principal - Miss O'Shay
- are very happy for her. Nancy Lee is proud to be American.
Then they learn that blacks are not eligible for the
scholarship competition. Miss O'Shay is quite upset; she vows
to help Nancy make America the nation it ought to be.
This story is deeply involved in the tragedy of race
relations in America. Hughes protests the negative aspects
of race relations and strongly suggests that blacks and
whites who believe in racial justice should work together to
change things. This suggestion adds an advocacy element to
the protest, making the story both protest and propaganda.
Some of Hughes' stories which deal with race relations have
white characters who believe in racial justice as - Miss
O'Shay does in this story. Both Nancy Lee and Miss O'Shay
represent blacks and whites determined to work for racial
justice; at this level they are epic figures.

"Professor." Langston Hughes
Category A. Epic, Tragic. Category B. Protest
Race is a major concern.

T. Walton Brown is a black sociology professor at a small,
black southern college. He has published a book, The Sociology of Prejudice. The book attracts the attention of the
Chandlers who are wealthy white philanthropists. The Chandlers invite Brown to dinner at their home, because they are
interested in his college and his book. The other dinner
guest is a Professor Bulwick, a white teacher at an all
white school in the city where the Chandlers live. Brown is
overly diplomatic during the evening except when he gently
reminds Bulwick that his college excludes blacks. Brown says
all the right things, and he requests funds from the Chandlers
- especially for the sociology chair which he hopes to fill.
Brown feels that if he can have an endowed chair in sociology,
he will make enough money to take his family to South America
for a summer vacation. He believes that in South America he
and his family will be able to forget they are black.
Brown leaves believing that he has impressed the Chandlers.
This story protests about race relations. The Chandlers
represent certain types of white philanthropist, and Brown

represents those blacks who behave diplomatically in order
to get money from people such as the Chandlers. Brown constantly thinks about racial injustice as he goes about his
mission. It is not clear whether Langston Hughes condemns
Brown for his actions or whether Hughes excuses Brown's
behavior because of the situation Brown confronts. It is
clear that Hughes protests the state of American race relations.

> "Trouble with the Angels." Langston Hughes
> Category A. Tragic. Category B. Protest
> Race is a major concern.

A musical with a religious theme and an all black cast is
scheduled to perform before audiences from which blacks will
be excluded in Washington D. C. Blacks from Washington appeal
to the actor who plays the role of "God" to do something. The
actor - referred to derisively as God - insists that there is
nothing he can do. One of the actors - Johnny Logan - tries
to get the other actors to strike. At first they all agree,
but by the time they get to Washington, Logan stands alone.
None of the cast is willing to strike, and Logan is arrested
for disturbing the peace.
   This story protests American race relations, and it
protests the failure of blacks - such as the actors who
refused to strike - to act against racism.

> "Who's Passing for Who." Langston Hughes
> Category A. Comic. Category B. Personal Experience
> Race is a major concern.

Three black friends - the narrator who is a writer, another
writer, and an artist meet Caleb Johnson - a black man - and
three white people - two men and a woman - in a nightclub.
The whites are from Iowa. The narrator and his friends consider Caleb and the white people he brings to Harlem bores;
they see themselves as sophisticates. The whites are impressed by the black writers and the black artist. The blacks
pretend to be nonchalant; they drop a lot of names and make
a number of statements they consider clever.
   At a nearby table, a black man begins to hit a woman who
appears to be white. One of the white men at the narrator's
table goes to the aid of the woman only to learn that the
woman is black and that the man hitting her is her husband.
The black couple - who had been fighting - then attacks
the white man from Iowa, and they are all evicted from the
nightclub.
   They go to a resturant where the blacks castigate the
man who intervened in the fight for becoming apologetic
upon learning that the woman he was defending was not white.
He gets upset and leaves. The remaining "white" couple then
"confesses" that they are really blacks who are "passing"
as whites. Everyone but Caleb is delighted, and they spend
the night "bar hopping" and behaving as if they are all
black. But when the couple leaves them they "confess" that
they are not black after all, rather they have spent the

night passing for black. The blacks are left confused.
    Some of Hughes' stories poke fun at American race rela-
tions.

1954

    "Audrey." Katherine Dunham
    Category A. Tragedy. Category B. Protest
    Race is a major concern.

The narrator is black, and Audrey is white; they are close
friends in the way in which young girls are. Their other
friends are white; Audrey, the narrator, and their other
friends eat lunch together. There are other black students at
the school - who are usually together by themselves - but the
narrator feels no real friendship for these other blacks.
    One day Audrey's aunt - from Florida - and Audrey's
mother visit the school; they learn that Audrey eats with the
narrator. Audrey's aunt suggests that the narrator ought to
be with the other blacks and that Audrey should not be so
close to the narrator. When Audrey tells the other friends
what her aunt has said and asks their opinions about it, the
narrator is so crushed she becomes ill. The narrator grows
cool toward Audrey, and their relationship becomes very
strained. At the end of the school year Audrey moves to
Florida, and the narrator wonders how long she will continue
to be pained by the experience.
    This story is about the tragedy of American race rela-
tions. Dunham protests this tragedy.

1958

    "Come out the Wilderness." James Baldwin
    Category A. Unresolved Struggle. Category B. Personal
    Experience.
    Race is a major concern.

Ruth is a black woman who lives with Paul - a white man. She
has an office job; he is an artist. They have an apartment in
Greenwich Village. Ruth believes that Paul is about to leave
her; this upsets her a great deal. Ruth came from the South
where she lived with her parents, her brother, and her two
sisters. When she was seventeen her brother surprised her in
a barn with a boy. Nothing had taken place but an ugly scene
ensued. She now blames that incident for the fact that her
brother is a thirty year old delinquent. Shortly after the
incident in the barn, Ruth ran away with a musician twenty
years her senior; she lived with him for four years.
    The only other black person at the insurance company
where she works is Mr. Davis. Davis tells Ruth that he is
being promoted and offers her the opportunity to become his
secretary. Then he invites her to lunch. He begins to grow
friendly during and after lunch, but she resents it.
    That afternoon she tries to call Paul; when he does not

answer, she goes to a bar, ponders the confusion in her life,
then she wanders aimlessly about.
    This story explores the difficulty of establishing good
racial relations, even in the context of a love affair. This
also is a very personal story about an individual struggling
with aspects of her life.

    "Thank You M'am." Langston Hughes
    Category A. Unresolved Struggle. Category B. Celebrative
    The story does not treat race relations.

Roger a young boy, tries to snatch Mrs. Luella Bates Washington Jones purse, but he slips and falls, and she gives him a
sharp kick and a good shaking. Then she takes him home, gives
him supper, learns that he is poor and on the streets fending
for himself much of the time, and she confesses that she is
ashamed of some of the things she has done. When Mrs. Jones
learns that Roger snatched her purse to get ten dollars for
some shoes, she gives him ten dollars, and he leaves. He
wants to say something more than "thank you m'am" but he
cannot even say that.
    Hughes has shown the humanity of two people who are
confronted with situations which are not ideal. There is no
white presence in the story; rather the story reflects the
ability of blacks to express humanity in the face of odds.

                           1959

    "Comrade." Alston Anderson
    Category A. Tragi-comic. Category B. Personal Experience
    Race is a major concern.

Frank DeVoe is a black American soldier stationed in Germany
towards the end of World War II. He befriends a wounded dog
and the dog becomes attached to him. The dog's original
owner - Herr Schaub discovers DeVoe has the dog and comes for
it, but Devoe has to accompany Schaub home, since the dog
will not go without DeVoe.
    When they get to Schaub's house, Schaub refers to DeVoe
by the German term for black man - Neger, and DeVoe gets
insulted. Schaub explains that Neger is derived from Niger
which is Latin for black. He explains that "nigger" - the
epithet DeVoe thought Schaub had used is a Cockney mispronun-
ciation of the German word Neger, begun by British sailors in
the seventeenth century. Schaub did not feel that blacks
should be insulted by the term. DeVoe says he will think
about what Schaub has said, and Devce returns to the post.
    Anderson mixes the humorous and the sad in this story;
he also looks at race relations in an interesting manner.

    "The Dozens." Alston Anderson
    Category A. Tragedy. Category B. Celebrative, Personal
    Experience
    Race relations are not treated.

James Washington (Mutton Head) and the narrator (Little One)
go fishing. After they have a fight because Little One "puts
Mutton Head in the dozens" i. e. insults his mother, Mutton
Head gets caught in quicksand, and Little One's efforts to
rescue him are futile. The narrator concludes the story by
saying that this incident has given him considerable distaste
for the dozens.

The celebrative aspect of this story is reflected by the
author's presentation of certain aspects of the black culture
in which James and Little One live, and by the satisfaction
they derive from living in their culture. This makes the
tragedy of James' death all the more acute.

1960

"Mississippi Ham Rider." Toni Cade Bambara
Category A. Tragi-comic. Category B. Celebrative
Race plays a major role.

The narrator - a black woman - and Neil McLoughlin - a white
man - are employed by a recording company to recruit old
black blues singers to go to New York to make some recordings.
This story tells of their efforts to make a deal with the
colorful blues singer, Mississippi Ham Rider. Rider is reluctant, but he will consider going if he can take his family
with him.

This story reflects some of the positive and negative
aspects of race relations. The story contains some humor and
some references to the tragedies some of the black singers
have experienced. The author presents certain aspects of the
southern black experience in a celebrative commemorative
context.

1961

"Brooklyn." Paule Marshall
Category A. Tragic, Unresolved Struggle. Category B.
Personal Experience
Race plays a major role.

Professor Max Berman is no longer religious, but he was
reared in the Jewish tradition. His membership in the Commu-
nist Party has cost him several teaching jobs. He is teaching
a summer course at a college in Brooklyn; he has not told the
administrators of the college about his past. Midway through
the session, the administration discovers Berman's past; he
is terminated effective the end of the session.

Berman is attracted to a black woman in his class. He
speaks to her privately about a paper she has written, and he
invites her to his country house. At first she appears frightened and she refuses. She stops attending class during the
final three weeks. But she does come to the final examination,
and she agrees to visit his country house if the invitation
is still open.

When she visits, a confrontation takes place. The student demonstrates contempt for Berman, and she experiences a new level of courage and determination. Berman feels old and defeated.

This story is related to the difficulties in establishing healthy race relations. The professor is tragic; the student's life has been difficult, but the confrontation has given her a new lease on life.

"Liars Don't Qualify." Junius Edwards.
Category A. Tragic. Category B. Protest
Race is a major concern.

Will Harris - a black man - goes to register to vote. He has recently been discharged from the army. Charlie and Sam are the white registrars; they are not pleased about Will's effort to register. Charlie and Sam grow even more agitated with Will when Will says that The Declaration of Independence is correct about all men being created equal. Will meets all the qualifications for registering, but he says he does not belong to any organization. Since he is in the Army Reserve the registrar insists that he has made a false statement; he is not allowed to register.

The tragedy of American race relations is an integral part of this story. Will accepts all of the abuse and humiliation that Charlie and Sam heap upon him, but they find a rationalization for refusing to register him. Edwards' story is clearly a protest against racial injustice.

"A Special Kind of Courage." Alice Reid
Category A. Unresolved Struggle. Category B. Personal Experience
Race relations is a major concern.

A white woman, who dates a black man, goes home with him to meet his family. She concludes that having an interracial romance requires a special kind of courage, and she doubts that they have the courage required.

1962

"Chitterlings for Breakfast." Julia Grimes Mighty
Category A. Comic. Category B. Celebrative, Personal Experience
This story presents a positive aspect of race relations.

Marge - a black woman - grew up in Wisconsin, and she learned to like chitterlings when she visited her grandmother in Alabama. Marge's mother felt that eating chitterlings projected negative stereotypes of blacks.

Marge's husband is a soldier and they are stationed in Alaska. She finds chitterlings in the commissary; she buys some. Her husband does not want any chitterlings, so she cooks them late one night when he is out. The next morning - Lola - a southern white woman comes over introduces herself,

and finally finds the courage to ask Marge if she has cooked
chitterlings the night before. Marge answers yes - defensive-
ly - expecting a complaint, but Lola has come to say that she
likes chitterlings very much, but she has lacked the courage
to cook any for fear of projecting negative stereotypes of
southerners. Lola and Marge sit down and enjoy chitterlings
for breakfast.

At one level this story is personal and humorous, but it
has wider implications. Other writers have used similar
themes to illustrate the negative consequences of over
reacting to the fear of promoting negative stereotypes. This
story presents a positive aspect of race relations.

"Enfranchisement." James E. Campbell.
Category A. Unresolved Struggle. Category B. Militant
Race is a major concern.

Marcus is a sixty-three year old southern black man who has
decided to register to vote. His wife Lucille is worried about
the consequences of his decision. Three white men come to
their house to warn them not to register, shove Lucille
around, and beat up Marcus. After they leave, Marcus feels
that he has stood up for his rights for the first time in his
life, and he is still determined to register.

Marcus' action falls in the category of legal, nonviolent,
militancy. He confronts the forces which oppress him, but his
actions are legal and nonviolent. What he does is challenge
the status quo. He has not won, nor has he lost.

"The Night of the Senior Ball." Alice Reid
Category A. Epic. Category B. Personal Experience
Race is a major concern.

The narrator of the story is a white man who had finally
danced with Cora - the only black person at his high school
Senior Ball. The incident occurred in the early 1900s, and
the question of who would dance with her had become a cruel,
racist, joke. So dancing with her was an act of courage. Cora
represents courageous blacks, because she knew that going to
the ball could prove embarrassing; it also took courage to
accept the invitation to dance. The narrator represents whites
who wish to treat blacks decently.

There are positive and negative aspects of race relations
in this story; the narrator and Cora are presented in a
positive light, while those who joke about dancing with Cora
are somewhat lacking in tolerance.

"The Only Man on Liberty Street." William Melvin Kelley
Category A. Tragic. Category B. Protest
Race is a major concern.

No men live on Liberty Street, only the interracial and black
mistresses of white men and their interracial offspring.
Jennie lives there with her mother, but one day Jennie's
white father, Maynard Herder, moves in with them.

Herder's wife and the rest of the white community put so

much pressure on Herder that he goes back home to his wife.
Before he leaves gives Jenny a medal he had won and he
urges her to go north and get married when she grows up.
    This story protests the state of race relations.

"The Picture Prize." Ann Allen Shockley
Category A. Tragic. Category B. Protest
Race is a major concern.

James Henry - a little black boy - wins first prize in the
state Children's Art Festival. His black teacher, Miss Cain,
and the white art supervisor, Miss Higgins, are very proud of
James. The award presentations are to be made in the new
Museum and Art Institute in the state capital. James' parents,
other members of his family, friends, and his classmates come
to see the awards ceremony. But they are all barred from the
Institute because blacks are only allowed in during July.
Miss Cain insists that the ceremony be moved outside, and Mr.
Rusick, Chairman of the State Art Festival Committee agrees
to move it outside. James receives his silver cup, and his
picture is unveiled. He has drawn a small naked black boy -
who stands naked at twilight, looking skyward, and crying
blood red tears.
    The tragedy of race relations is an integral part of this
story. The tragedy is all the more intense since the victim
of racism is a little boy. The author's protest is obvious.

"Reena." Paule Marshall
Category A. Unresolved Struggle. Category B. Celebrative
Certain aspects of race relations figure prominently.

The narrator - Paulie - sees Reena - christened Doreen - at
a wake.The deceased is Reena's aunt and - also - Paulie's
godmother. Reena's parents are West Indian; Reena's skin is
quite dark. Reena tells Paulie of her very interesting
experiences since they have last seen each other.
    Reena has lost a boyfriend because his parents felt her
skin was too dark. She has grown philosophical and proud
about her blackness; she feels that some black people view
blackness as evil darkness from which they must escape. Later
Reena became involved in "left wing" political activity and
was suspended from college. She also has had a romantic
relationship with a white man. She broke off the affair,
withdrew from radical politics, returned to school and
graduated. Racial discrimination prevented her from getting a
job in her field - journalism - so she took a job with the
welfare department. She hated the welfare job, because she
felt that she was invading the welfare clients' privacy.
    Later Reena married a very militant, fair skinned Afro-
-American. The marriage broke up after they had three children; Reena has been left with the burden of rearing the
children. Yet Reena is very optimistic; she feels that
life is just beginning for her. She talks of instilling
racial pride in her children and of spending some time in
Africa to see some related cultures.
    This story deals with some aspects of the racial situa-

tion in America; it is the story of a black woman's odyssey. Reena has had her trials and tribulations, yet she is very optimistic. She will make an effort to celebrate and commemorate the black experience in the future.

1963

"And Shed a Murderous Tear." Alice Reid
Category A. Epic, Unresolved Struggle. Category B.
Militant
Race relations are major concerns.

In part one of this two part story, Mrs. Lee - a white woman - tells her black maid - Innis - how sympathetic she is towards a young black man who has braved mobs to desegregate a previously segregated southern university. Innis says the student should have avoided stirring up trouble. Mrs. Lee concedes that perhaps deeply ingrained social customs are not easily changed, and Innis wonders if the student's actions will make things better for her grandson.

Mrs. Lee is married to a bigot; he becomes very upset when he learns that the company for which he works has hired a black engineer who Lee is to supervise. During the interview with the new employee - Bill Wheeler - Lee tries to intimidate Wheeler, but Wheeler refuses to be intimidated. Wheeler is hired over Lee's opposition, and Lee grudgingly adjusts to Wheeler's presence.

This story is a blend of the epic and the tragic. The James Meredith-like black student and Bill Wheeler are made of stern stuff, and they represent black determination and courage. They overcome. But their triumph is bittersweet. Wheeler maintains his sense of humor, but the tragic aspect of the situation is that the Wheelers of the world will have to contend with the Lees of the world for a long time.

The mob which would deny the black student admission to the university and Lee represent white hostility. Mrs. Lee and the forces which grant the student admission and hire Bill Wheeler represent white decency. Both the student and Wheeler challenge white racism; this is the militant aspect of the story.

"The Beach Umbrella." Cyrus Colter
Category A. Tragic. Category B. Personal Experience
There is no treatment of race relations.

Elijah likes to go to the beach and mingle; the rest of his family - his wife Myrtle, his daughter, Susan, and his son, Randall, do not care for the beach. Elijah decides that if he has a nice beach umbrella, he will become popular at the beach. But he has no money because his wife takes his pay check and gives him just a little money for gasoline and cigarettes. He decides to borrow the money for the umbrella from Randall; he buys an umbrella, and he goes to the beach and has a good time. Then he realizes that he has no way to repay his son; he tries unsuccessfully to sell the umbrella.

Elijah is a tragic character because he is the epitome of defeat and dejection. The story makes only brief references to race and does not treat race relations.

"Bloodline." Ernest J. Gaines
Category A. Unresolved Struggle. Category B. Militant
Race is a major concern.

Cooper is the interracial son of a white plantation owner – Walter Laurent – and a black woman; both parents are dead. Cooper's uncle – Frank Laurent – now owns and runs the plantation. Cooper's aunt Amelia – who is black – works for Frank. Cooper returns to the plantation and violates the social customs of the area. He asserts that Frank is his uncle, and he refuses to enter the back door of the planta- tion house. Frank send a number of blacks to bring Cooper to him forceably, but Cooper is too strong for them. Finally Frank goes to Amelia's house where Cooper is staying. Cooper explains to Frank that he – Cooper – is General Christian Laurent – the leader of the dispossessed and he has come to claim his birthright.
  Frank responds that so long as he lives, he will fight to maintain the status quo. Cooper says he will leave, but he vows to return. He tells Frank to tell Amelia that upon his return – she will not have to enter by the back way again.
  This story explores an aspect of American race relations. Cooper and Frank struggle in racial conflict. While this story has elements of fantasy, Cooper's behavior is quite militant, and Gaines makes a unique approach to the theme of dispossessed interracial offspring of prominent white men.

"The Convert." Lerone Bennett, Jr.
Category A. Tragic, Unresolved Struggle. Category B. Militant
Race is a major concern.

The Reverend Aaron Lott is the small Mississippi town's leading black minister; Booker T. Brown is Mr. Lott's deacon, and Brown is the mortician for the town's blacks. Lott de- cides to use the white waiting room of the train station when he takes a trip; Brown begs him not to risk his life in this manner, but Lott is determined. Then Brown watches from the "Colored" waiting room as the sheriff and a mob of whites kill Lott.
  The white community puts pressure on Brown to testify that the minister tried to grab the sheriff's gun when the inquest into Lott's death is held. If he lies Brown will get a loan he needs; if he tells the truth he will probably suffer economic ruin. Brown learns from his son, Russell, that most of the blacks in town are calling him an Uncle Tom and betting that Brown will lie. But Russell has bet a hundred dollars that his father will have the courage and the integrity to tell the truth. At the inquest, Brown refuses to lie; most of the blacks in town are very proud of him. Brown feels like a man even, though he has suffered financial loss, and he is jubilant about the respect that he has gained from

his son.
   This story is about one of the worst aspects of American racism. Lott's death is tragic. Lott's challenge of segregation, and Brown's refusal to lie - when whites are pressuring him - are both militant acts.

   "Direct Action." Mike Thelwell
   Category A. Comic. Category B. Militant
   Race is a major concern.

This is a humorous fantasy in which an integrated group of college students sit in the "white" toilets of a department store and put a laxative in the water fountain. The feeling of urgency the whites who need to use the toilets have causes them to use the toilets for blacks.
   This story ridicules the American racial situation, and the students take militant action against segregation.

   "Never Alone in the World." Calvin C. Hernton
   Category A. Unresolved Struggle. Category B. Protest, Militant
   Race is a major concern.

Magdelyne Dewey is a fourteen year old black girl who tries to desegregate Central High School in Little Rock, Arkansas. Her mother, Martha, does not want Magdelyne to go after Magdelyne is roughed up by a mob of whites, but her father, the Reverend Charles Dewey, wants her to go. Magdelyne makes the decision that she will go. At the school the Arkansas National Guard turns Magdelyne back. She and her parents are cursed, jeered, spat upon, and hit by objects thrown by the mob of whites surrounding the school. And the mob brutalizes an elderly white woman who tries to console Magdelyne. At that point Magdelyne feels courage grow within.
   This story deals with the tragedy of American race relations. While it is tragic that Magdelyne and her parents are turned away and while the story implies that Magdelyne is developing into a black epic heroine, the struggle is unresolved when the story ends. Magdelyne's and her father's willingness to take a legal, nonviolent stand for their rights is militant. Hernton protests about the situation.

   "Rat Joiner Routs the Klan." Ted Poston
   Category A. Comic. Category B. Protest
   Race is a major concern.

Blacks in Hopkinsville, Kentucky get very upset when they learn that the film Birth of a Nation is to be shown at the local segregated theater. When the theater manager refuses to withdraw the film, the black adults vow to boycott the theater. Rat Joiner - a comic character who appears in several of Poston's stories - lures the black projectionist away from the theater. The white theater manager - who does not know how to run the projector ruins the film.
   This story deals humorously with both black and white relations and color discrimination among Afro-Americans. The

author employs humor to protest both racial discrimination and color discrimination among blacks.

"The Sky Is Gray." Ernest J. Gaines
Category A. Epic. Category B. Celebrative
Race relations are treated.

James - the young narrator - has a toothache, and his mother takes him from the rural plantation where they live into town to get the tooth pulled. James' family is quite poor.

In the dentist's office one of the patients wonders why the Lord lets little children suffer. A man James believes is a preacher says the Lord should not be questioned. A young man who appears to James to be a college student or a teacher argues with the "preacher" and contends that everything -including God - should be questioned and that black people's problems stem from their failure to question everything. The "preacher" becomes angry, strikes the man twice and leaves.

The dentist's nurse announces that the dentist will not see any patients until the afternoon, and James and his mother walk around the town. They are cold and hungry; it begins to sleet. They go to the black section of the town and the mother buys coffee, milk, and three small cakes. Then the mother has a fight with a man in the cafe who insults her, and they leave the cafe.

On the way back to the dentist's office a white woman - who runs a store - invites James and his mother in to eat. James' mother is too proud to accept charity, so the white lady says James will have to work for the food. She has him to move two garbage cans which appear to James to be empty. After they eat James' mother buys a quarter's worth of salt meat from the store owner, but James' mother feel that she has been given too much for a quarter, so the store owner takes back half of the meat. As they return to the dentist's office, James turns up his coat collar because he is cold, but his mother tells him to turn down his collar because he is a man and not a bum.

James' mother represents the strong, proud, black woman who will not yield to poverty. The author looks a various aspects of the black experience without apology or protest; rather he celebrates and commemorates the black experience. The white store owner represents decent and compassionate white people.

1964

"Christmas and the Great Man." William Melvin Kelley
Category A. Tragic. Category B. Personal Experience
There is no treatment of race relations per se.

Peter is a college student who stays at school during the Christmas holidays. He goes to Willard's house for Christmas dinner. Willard's grandfather, Isaiah W. Robbins, is a prominent civil rights pioneer, and Peter is anxious to discuss the early days of the movement with the old man.

However, Willard's mother is so protective that Mr. Robbins
is put to bed before dinner ends. Peter is deeply disa-
pointed. As Peter prepares to return to the domitory, he goes
upstairs to get his coat and discovers that Mr. Robbins is
awake and reading. They chat briefly and Peter learns that
Mr. Robins has sensed his disappointment.

   "A Good Long Sidewalk." William Melvin Kelley
   Category A. Tragic. Category B. Personal Experience
   Race is a concern.

Carlyle Bedlow - who is black - listens to a barber shop
discussion about interracial marriage, gets his hair cut, and
goes looking for a job shoveling snow. He finds a house with
a long sidewalk and offers his services. A white woman invites him in, gives him hot chocolate, and offers him five
dollars - which is two dollars more than he would have charged - kisses him, and suggests that when he finishes - he come
back into the house and do something else for her. Carlyle is
upset at what he perceives as the woman's attempt to seduce
him. The woman - sensing his discomfort - pays him in advance
and tells him not to come back after he finishes the job.
   The next day Carlyle learns that the woman has committed
suicide. Carlyle insists that the woman was nice; his father
says she was crazy. Carlyle's mother tells him that there are
some good white people, but his father feels that the good
white people are dead.
   Kelley explores black attitudes towards whites in this
story. The barber shop conversation leads Carlyle to be wary
of seductive white women; Carlyle's father does not care for
white people. The lonely white lady is the tragic figure in
the story.

   "Goodbye Baby Boy." Conrad Kent Rivers
   Category A. Tragi-comic. Category B. Personal Experience
   Race is a concern.

Gabe a white fight manager, drinks and tries to cope with the
fact that his daughter is engaged to a black fighter whom he
manages and trains. Gabe's friend - Cora - drinks with him
and tries to console him.

   "The Harlem Rat." John H. Jones
   Category A. Tragic, Unresolved Struggle. Category B.
   Protest.
   Race relations - per se - are not treated.

Battle Young is a World War II veteran living in a rat and
roach infested slum tenement in Harlem with his wife, Belle,
and their baby - Jean. Belle urges him to find a better
place, but he contends that they are lucky to have gotten the
place they have. Battle makes three dollars per week above
the amount allowed for tenants of the housing projects. After
a rat bites Jean, Battle decides to become involved in the
tenants' organization.He had refused to join.
   While this story does not treat race relations, its

implications about the negative circumstances blacks face are
there. The Battle Youngs of the world have to struggle
against these conditions, and this is tragic. But some of
them do struggle and refuse to be defeated. The story protests such negative conditions.

"A Long Day in November." Ernest J. Gaines
Category A. Tragi-comic. Category B. Celebrative
Race is not considered.

In this story Gaines looks at rural black life through the
eyes of the young boy who narrates the story. The narrator's
mother - Amy - is upset because the boy's father - Eddie
spends all his spare time away from home driving his old car.
Amy leaves Eddie and takes the narrator - also named Eddie
and called Sonny - to her mother's house. Young Eddie slips
out and joins his father under the pretense of going to the
outdoor toilet. Eddie takes Sonny with him and goes to
Madame Toussaint - a seer - for advice. Her advice is for him
to burn his car. Eddie finally relents and burns his car, and
he and Amy are reconciled.
This story has humorous and serious aspects, and it reflects Gaines' tendency to look at rural black culture.

"Monday Will Be Better." Ann Allen Shockley
Category A. Unresolved Struggle. Category B. Protest,
Militant
Race is a major concern.

Miss Banks, a white teacher, is disturbed when the school
where she teaches is desegregated. James P. Johnson, Jr., a
black student, is assigned to her homeroom class. Miss Banks
makes no effort to protect James from abuse, and she gives
him "C" grades even though he gets "As" and "Bs" on his
papers. When Miss Banks sees James P. Johnson Sr's. name
on a list of needy persons eligible for a basket of groceries
at Thanksgiving, she decides to take her class' basket to the
Johnsons. Mrs. Johnson politely but firmly refuses the basket.
Mrs. Johnson explains that her husband lost his job
because James went to the formerly white school, and the
Johnson family was on welfare for a while. She said the
family was still struggling, but they were willing to make
the necessary sacrifices for their son. Then James and three
white members of the football team come with the news that
James has scored the winning touchdown in the game that day.
Miss Banks realizes that James has gained acceptance without
her help.
The Johnsons have epic qualities, and their experiences
are bittersweet. Initially some of the white students at the
school were hostile, but the hostility has turned to acceptance. Since Miss Banks was not contributing to the solution,
she was part of the problem. The Johnsons also exhibit
militant and protest characteristics. They stand up for that
in which they believe. They are also innocent victims of
racism.

"The Most Beautiful Legs in the World." William Melvin
Kelley
Category A. Comic. Category B. Personal Experience
Race Relations are not considered.

Hondo's fiance has the most beautiful legs in the world, but
she has an underdeveloped arm. Carlyle, Hondo's best friend,
is disturbed about the forthcoming wedding because of the
woman's deformed arm. Carlyle tries very hard to break up the
engagement but nothing works. As they drive to the wedding,
Carlyle has an accident; Hondo's efforts to get Carlyle out
of jail cause him to be late for the wedding. Carlyle's
fiance is upset; she says that Carlyle has always opposed
their marrying, and she believes that the wreck was on
purpose. Hondo calls off his wedding contending that his
buddy's efforts to break up his engagement were tolerable,
but he cannot be married to a woman who will criticize his
best buddy.

"The Servant Problem." William Melvin Kelley
Category A. Tragi-comic. Category B. Personal Experience
Race Relations are treated.

Mitchell and Tam Pierce are white and well-to-do. They have a
son - Jake - and a black maid - Opal. Opal takes care of Jake
and the house; Tam does very little except lounge around and
go out with her friends. Tam gets very upset when Mitchell
suggests that she spend more time with Jake, insisting that
supervising Opal and making sure Opal does not steal is a
full time job.
Mitchell apparently becomes attracted to Opal, because
when a date comes to pick her up, he becomes angry and
irrational, castigates her, and searches her purse for
stolen goods.

"Sound of Crying." Anita R. Cornwell.
Category A. Tragic. Category B. Protest, Militant
Race relations are central concerns.

Hal Stonecutter is expelled from college during his senior
year for civil rights activity. His parents - Amanda and Jim
- urge him to go to New York, but he returns to Mississippi.
He completes a novel he is writing and goes to town to stage
a sit-in. Amanda reads the novel and realizes that it is
autobiographical and that he plans more civil rights activity. As she runs toward town crying Hal's name, she hears the
screeching of sirens.
Since the sheriff and the deputy have warned Amanda and
Jim that no "trouble" will be tolerated and the story is set
in rural Mississippi in the 1960s, Hal probably is in considerable difficulty. This story is a protest story decrying
the treatment of black people through the thoughts of Amanda.
Hal's actions gives the story a militant aspect.

1965

"Going to Meet the Man." James Baldwin
Category A. Tragic. Category B. Personal Experience,
Militant
Race is a major concern.

Jesse is a white deputy sheriff who is deeply disturbed by
civil rights demonstrations. He has trouble becoming sexually
aroused with his wife, and he is now afraid to have sexual
relations with black women.
    A number of thoughts run through Jesse's mind as he lies
in bed with his wife - Grace. He remembers the terrible
feeling he got after he brutalized a black boy that day. The
boy is the grandson of a woman he once collected money from
when he had another job. Jesse had tried to make the boy stop
singing a disturbing song, but the boy had insisted the
singing would go on until Jesse and his kind went crazy.
Jesse is also remembering a lynching he witnessed as a small
boy. Then he becomes sexually aroused as - he had earlier in
the day in the boy's cell, and he urges his wife to love him
as she would "love a nigger."
    James Baldwin employs his imagination to explore the
white psyche. This story is an interpretation of an aspect of
American race relations, and an interpretation of how one
troubled white man responds to black militancy.

"Home X and Me." Arthenia J. Bates.
Category A. Comic. Category B. Personal experience
The story does not deal with race relations.

The narrator writes humorously about her misadventures in
her home economics class.

"The Negrophile." Carlos E. Russell
Category A. Comic. Category B. Personal Experience
Race is a concern.

Charles Evans - the black protagonist of the story - meets
Renee Silverman - a white woman - at a party. She is friendly, but he is hostile. Charlie talks about how awful the race
problem is and about how blacks have accepted white standards
and white values. Then Charlie goes home to his white wife.
    Charlie is a comic figure because Russell pokes fun at
him and because he is such a hypocrite. This story focuses on
some of the 1960s rhetoric about race relations.

                            1966

"Chinese Food." Conrad Kent Rivers
Category A. Tragi-comic. Category B. Personal Experience
The focus is on race relations.

Gerald and Helen Oliver go to a Chinese resturant. A white
drunk comes to their table and unwittingly says a number of
things that irritate them. He insists that he has been
romantically involved with Ethel Waters. He also flirts with

Helen and puts his hands on her face. They leave him at the table still talking as if they are still there.

"Judah's a Two-Way Street Running Out." Jack Burris
Category A. Tragic. Category B. Protest
The story has racial implications.

Clay looks for a job in San Francisco, and his wife Claire Mae encourages him. But he is unable to find anything. His most recent interview at an office on Judah Street is especially frustrating.
The story implies that Clay cannot find a job because he is black, and the story contains implied protest against the difficulty blacks have finding jobs.

"Karen's Spring." Eloise Greenfield
Category A. Unresolved Struggle. Category B. Personal Experience
Race is a major concern.

Karen is a black woman who is pregnant. Her white friend Phyllis is also pregnant, and they have happily anticipated becoming parents. Then Karen becomes depressed about the prospect of bringing a black baby into a racist world. Her husband tries to get her to talk about the depression he has sensed, but she refuses to talk to him about what is bothering her. She goes to visit Phyllis. Phyllis has gone into labor when Karen gets there, and Phylis is also depressed. Phyllis now has doubts about bringing a baby into such a troubled world. Karen comes out of her depression and cheers Phyllis up by telling her that they will work together to make the world a better place.
This story presents race relations in a relatively positive light; although, it notes some of the negative aspects of race relations, and Karen does begin to resent Phyliss because she is white. But the story ends on a positive note..

"Neighbors." Diane Oliver
Category A. Tragic. Category B. Protest
Race is a major concern.

The Mitchell family tries to cope with the pressure they feel when Tommy Mitchell is scheduled to be the first black student to desegregate an all white elementary school. Some of the whites in the town are hostile to desegregation. Even though police are watching the house, a bomb is exploded in the yard, and the house is damaged. The family decides to stop the desegregation effort for the present.

"Will the Circle Be Unbroken." Henry Dumas
Category A. Tragic. Category B. Militant
Race is a major concern.

The author - who is deceased - might not agree that the story is tragic. Three whites insist on entering a club for blacks only. The music played in the club is lethal to whites and the three whites die.

The story is tragic because it views racial conflict as unreconcilable; it is a militant story because it reflects the views of some black writers of the period who called for black revolution.

1967

"Ain't No Use in Crying." Ann Allen Shockley
Category A. Tragic. Category B. Protest
Race is a major concern.

Carrie Mae is a fifteen year old black girl who goes to babysit for Bust Will - a white man. But his children are not at home, and he does not want her to babysit; he wants to seduce her. When she refuses he attempts to rape her, but she fights him off and escapes. Carrie Mae's mother goes with her to report the incident to the sheriff, but the sheriff insists that there are no white men in the town capable of raping a black girl; he angrily orders them out of his office. When Carrie Mae cries, her mother tells her "ain't no use in crying. . ."

Shockley deals with one of the worst thrusts of racism; she protest against the racism.

"Daddy Was a Numbers Runner." Louise Meriwether
Category A. Tragic, Unresolved Struggle. Category B. Protest
Race is a concern.

Francie - the narrator - helps her father sell lottery numbers in Harlem during the Depression. The family consists of Francie's mother - Jessie - her father - James - and her brothers - James Jr. and Claude. The family is quite poor. James Sr. becomes a numbers runner after he loses his job. Jessie pleads with James Sr. until he agrees that she can do domestic work to help support the family. James Jr. and Claude are keeping late hours, missing school, and it is rumored that they are running with a gang.

Sukie is a little girl about Francie's age. She is Francie's best friend, but Sukie can be very mean-spirited, and she beats Francie up frequently; Francie is afraid of Sukie.

One day two white policemen come in without a warrant and begin to search. Francie is home alone when they come; James Sr. comes while they are there. The police do not find any numbers, but they arrest James Sr. for assault and battery. He shoved one of the policemen who was holding Francie. James Sr. is upset about the prospect of having a police record.

Later Jessie tells James Sr. that she has applied for welfare, and he is so angry and hurt that he cries bitter tears. Sukie has been chasing and threatening Francie for several days, but Francie's anger about her family's problems overcomes her fear of Sukie. Francie goes out, finds Sukie,

beats her badly. Now Francie understands why blacks are so
mean-spirited.

James Sr.'s spirit is broken at the end of the story, so
the story is tragic. The author protests against the negative
circumstances blacks face and racial discrimination.

"The Funeral." Ann Allen Shockley
Category A. Tragi-comic. Category B. Celebrative
Race is a minor concern.

Melissa conducts Granny's funeral just the way Granny has
requested. That night after the funeral Melissa contemplates
her own death.

Death itself is the final tragedy, but the rituals surrounding wakes and funerals illustrate the tragi-comic nature
of life. This story celebrates and commemorates aspects of
black experiences; it contains fleeting references to race,
but it does not deal with race relations.

"Going Down Slow." Amiri Baraka (Leroi Jones)
Category A. Tragic. Category B. Personal Experience
Race is not a significant concern.

Lee Crosby is married to Rachel, and he is having an affair
with Leah Purcell. He admits to Leah that he would mind if
Rachael had an affair. Then he discovers that Rachael is
having an affair with a Japanese painter named Mauro. Lew
hits Mauro in the head with a pipe and leaves without knowing
if Mauro is alive or dead. He goes to a house where some drug
addicts live and takes heroin.

This story contains only fleeting reference to race
relations; it is the story of one family's tragedy.

"Like a piece of the Blues." George Davis
Category A. Unresolved Struggle. Category B. Personal
Experience
Race is a concern.

Billy Aaron - the fifteen year old narrator of this story -
is a Methodist minister's son who argues with Rashman X - a
barber and a Muslim - a member of The Nation of Islam. Their
arguments have become so famous that people follow Billy into
the barbershop when they see him enter. Rashman attacks
Christianity while Billy defends it. Rashman tells Billy he
understands Billy's reluctance to stand against an entire
civilization.

One Sunday Billy goes to Rashman's house, but Rashman has
gone to St. Louis. Billy talks with Rashman's wife and his
daughter, Shera, and leaves. He feels closer to Rashman and
also is afraid for him, for he feels Rashman may have decided
to stand against an entire civilization. Yet he realizes that
if Rashman were there, he would not know what to say to him.

This story is related to American race relations. At the
time the story was written the Nation of Islam defined itself
as an alternative for Afro-Americans. In this story Billy is
searching for answers while Rashman appears to have settled

on a course of action.

"The Machine." Jean Wheeler Smith
Category A. Unresolved Struggle. Category B. Protest,
Militant
Race is a major concern.

Several black civil rights activists are imprisoned in the
Mississippi State Penitentiary. Jason and Chenault are the
"outsiders;" the rest are Mississippi natives. Chenault is
the leader. The white guards are mean and brutal. The guards
demand their clothing and that they work the fields. They
give up their clothing but refuse to work. The guards' response is that if they do not work they cannot eat. Willie C.
begins to whisper with a guard, and he is given a private
cell, some prison clothes, tobacco, and candy. Later Chenault
learns that Willie C. is angry because Chenault placed Willie
in charge of the mimeograph machine when Chenault concluded
that Willie lacked the ability to become a leader. Later that
night Willie C. cries and the others console him.
    This story deals with the tragedy of race relations and
with the rise of protest and militancy in the 1960s.

"Mint Juleps Not Served Here." Diane Oliver
Category A. Tragic. Category B. Militant
Race is a major concern.

The Macks - a black couple - and their son live as recluses
deep in the Forest Preserve. Mr. Mack goes to town once a
year to sell carvings he has made. The family has moved here
from Mississippi where their son - called Rabbit - was mis-
treated. Rabbit is unable to speak. One day Rosemarie Langley
- a white social worker - comes to the Mack house. Rosemarie
has deduced that Rabbit is old enough to be in school because
of the size of the snowsuit Mr. Mack bought him. Miss Langley
tells Mrs Mack she is on a friendly rather than a professional visit but that Rabbit will have to go to school. Miss
Langley's presence is deeply disturbing to Mrs. Mack - who
wants to be left alone. When Mr. Mack comes, he kills Rosemarie with a mallet, and they bury the body. We learn that
this is the fourth white "intruder" the Macks have killed.
    The Macks have taken refuge in the deep woods, and they
want no contact with society. They are the tragic victims of
the American racial situation - as are the white "intruders."
The Macks will militantly defend their little corner of the
world from outsiders.

"A New Day." Charles Wright
Category A. Tragi-comic. Category B. Protest, Militant
Race is a major concern.

Lee Mosely - a twenty-five year old black man - gets a job as
handy man for a southern white woman - Mrs. Maude T. Davies.
She curtly instructs him on his duties. He seeks to please.
Then she yells "nigger" at him, and he waits for several
minutes and after she has called three times before he asks

if she has called. Then she tells him they will get along because she likes people who think before they answer.

This story deals with American race relations in a semi-humouous vein. It cites the early stages of the emergence of black protest and militancy of the 1960s.

"Old Blues Singers Never Die." Clifford Vincent Johnson
Category A. Epic. Category B. Personal Experience
Race is a minor concern.

The narrator's father told him about the great blues singer – River Bottom. At the time the narrator was told about Bottom, Bottom was a janitor. The narrator predicted that Bottom would be rediscovered, but his father did not think that the mood of the times would permit River Bottom to get any attention again.

But when the narrator is in the army, he goes to Paris and discovers that the French have discovered Bottom, and Bottom is back on top again. The narrator relishes the opportunity to write and tell his father that Bottom has emerged again.

River Bottom is an epic representative of blues singers and their messages; there are indirect references to race relation in the story.

"The Other Side of Christmas." R. J. Meaddough
Category A. Tragic. Category B. Protest
Race is a major concern.

This story is in three parts. In the first David – nicknamed Able – who is a track star – runs a race and thinks about having been elected to be the Queen's escort at the Christmas Prom. Brenda – the Queen – is white, but she is liberal. He also thinks of Cassandra (Sandy) – a black girl whom he likes but feels is too militant. David wins the race.

In the second part a glimpse of Sandy is shown; Cassandra believes Brenda will hurt David.

In the third part, Brenda prepares for the Prom, and David picks her up and escorts her to the Prom. At the Prom David is surprised to learn that the white boy he beat in the race is to escort Brenda for the opening ceremonies. The television stations have insisted on this change. David becomes enraged, throws his shoe at the television cameras, and swears.

This story deals with race relations and primarily with their negative aspects. David experiences tragic defeat, and the author protests against racism. There is also an implied propaganda aspect of the story; the author implies that David asked for his problem because he was lacking in race consciousness.

"The Red Bonnet." Lindsay Patterson
Category A. Tragic. Category B. Protest
Race is a major concern.

Grandma Jo has never walked, but one day she gets up and

begins to walk. But she refuses to walk in the presence of
her daughter and son-in-law. One day the narrator walks to
town, and so does Grandma Jo. The narrator buys vanilla ice
cream, and Grandma Jo buys a bright red bonnet. Grandma Jo
decides to take the bus home and to treat the narrator to a
bus ride home. But she becomes exhausted in the front of the
bus; she sits in the front. The driver throws her off the
bus, and a neighbor takes her home. The whites in the town
are very angry. They come to Grandma Jo's house and berate
her. Grandma Jo's daughter retaliates by berating the whites.
      That night Grandma Jo's family's house burns. They find
the bodies of her daughter and son-in-law, but Grandma Jo's
body is never found. The narrator says he sees her some
nights sitting on the porch of the burned house wearing a
red bonnet.
      This story is about the tragedy of American race rela-
tions. Grandma Jo's walking seems symbolic of black America's
civil rights push in the 1960s. Patterson protests against
racial discrimination.

      "The Revolt of the Evil Fairies." Ted Poston
      Category A. Tragi-comic. Category B. Protest
      Race is a minor concern; color bias in the Afro-American
      community is a major concern.

The Booker T. Washington Colored Grammar School's presentation of Prince Charming and the Sleeping Beauty is the biggest social event of the year in Hopkinsville, Kentucky.
Prince Charming, Sleeping Beauty, and the Good Fairies are
always portrayed by children who are light-skinned. The
narrator is dark-skinned, and he wants very badly to be
Prince Charming. But despite his best efforts, the best role
he can get is that of the Head Evil Fairy. The narrator is
especially disappointed the year the little girl he loves -
Sarah Williams - is Sleeping Beauty, and Leonardius Wright -
whom he dislikes - is Prince Charming.
      In the second act Leonardius makes an impromtu addition
to the script and taps the Head Evil Fairy - the narrator -
on the head with his sword. Miss H. Belle LaPrade the direc-
tor of the play - quiets the narrator's protest by insisting
that the tapping added a nice touch. In the third act, when
the Head Evil Fairy and Prince Charming were to engage in
mortal combat, the narrator punches Leonardius and the Good
Faries and the Evil Fairies begin to fight: "When the curtain
rang down, the forces of Good and Evil were locked in combat.
And Sleeping Beauty was wide awake and streaking for the wings."
      After fifteen minutes they complete the play according to
the script. No one accepts the narrator's contention that he
punched Leonardius because he thought Leonardius meant to
harm him. The narrator is barred from future plays, but he
doesn't mind since he can never be Prince Charming anyway.
      This is essentially a humorous story, but there is a
tinge of sadness implied by the treatment of the dark-skinned
children. The story takes note of the state of race relations and there is some gentle sardonic protest about race
relations, but the story is essentially a protest against

color discrimination within black society.

"The Stick Up." John O. Killens
Category A. Tragic. Category B. Protest
Race is a major concern.

The narrator is walking in a park near Greenwich village
when a large white man, who is a derelict approaches him
saying, "This is a stick up!" But the man is joking; he just
wants the narrator to give him four cents. The narrator has
no change. The big, foul smelling man clings to the narrator
and will not go away; the narrator feels trapped and revolted.
The man insists that he has had problems, but he is educated
and once was prosperous.

The narrator remembers that drunk whites often seek out
blacks as if they are doing the blacks a favor by associating
with them, and the narrator begins to grow angry. When the
white man says he does not feel superior to blacks and that,
"We're all fighting together against them goddamn gooks in
Viet Nam ain't we?" - the narrator's resentment flares full
force, and he pulls away and swears at the white man. The man
starts in the narrator's direction again, but he sits on a
park bench before he reaches him. Then he mumbles about how
bad times are, "when you can't chisel four lousy pennies offa
prosperous-looking nigger." The narrator clenches his fists,
smiles a bitter smile, and goes on his way.

This story is bound up in the tragedy of race relations.
The author protests the fact that white derelects feel that
they can associate with well dressed blacks, and the story
contains implied protest against the war in Vietnam.

"The Storekeeper." Ed Bullins
Category A. Tragic. Category B. Militant
Race is a major concern.

Two blacks - the narrator and his friend Ernie - go to a
liquor store to buy beer and wine. The white store owner and
his black clerk wait on the customers. Two black prostitutes
are in line ahead of the narrator and his friend, and the
liquor store owner propositions one of the prostitutes. She
agrees to return about two in the morning. When the narrator
and Ernie get to the counter, the store owner calls them boys.
A confrontation takes place, and the store owner pulls a gun.
Another black customer - Johnson - intervenes, and the narrator and Ernie leave at Johnson's urging.

About two o'clock when the narrator and Ernie pass the
store, the prostitute is there with the storekeeper.

This story explores two aspects of race relations in
America - black female - white male relationships and the
hostility between black males and white males.

"Support Your Local Police." Ed Bullins.
Category A. Tragi-comic. Category B. Personal Experience
Race is a concern.

This story has a ring of authenticity. It is told in the first

person by a narrator who seems a lot like the author - Ed
Bullins. The narrator is a militant black playwright hitchhiking from New York to San Francisco. One of his plays is
being presented in San Francisco, and he has an ex-girl
friend there. The ex-girl friend is white and Jewish. The
narrator is not sure whether it is his play or his ex-girl
friend that is attracting him to California.

But the narrator tells people who give him rides that he
is going to San Francisco to work as a janitor and to marry
his sweetheart - "Patsy Mae." He has concluded that this
story gets a better reception than the truth would. The
narrator is picked up by a white man with a "SUPPORT YOUR
LOCAL POLICE!!!!" bumper sticker. The man is a member of the
John Birch Society who sees communists everywhere; He believes the communists are behind Dr. Martin Luther King, Jr.
The man is also a bigot.

Then he gets a ride with a black man who is a sergeant in
the army. The soldier has been in the army for twenty-seven
years; he has just re-enlisted. The sergeant seems a bit
disappointed that he is being sent to Korea when the war is
being fought in Vietnam.

The narrator implies that he could afford to fly but
hitchhiking is an enjoyable experience. The story deals with
race relations in a relatively light-hearted fashion, but
there is some mention of the negative aspects.

"That She Would Dance No More." Jean Wheeler Smith
Category A. Tragic. Category B. Protest
Race is a concern.

Ossie Lee is a poor farm worker whose wife has left him. When
he was an eight year old boy Ossie Lee's white boss whipped
him badly for allowing a chicken to be run over. After that
Ossie Lee accepted his station in a segregated world. His
wife left because he beat her; he has grown lonely.

Ossie Lee meets Minnie Pearl at a cafe where he goes to
drink; she loves to dance. They decide to get married, and
the house his boss tells them they can have is an old shack
filled with hay. The old house upsets Ossie Lee and reminds
him of his plight. Back at the cafe where he met Minnie
Pearl, he gets upset at the sight of her dancing with someone
else; he beats her. Later that night at his mother's house -
where they live temporarily - he tries hard to impregnate her
in the hope that being pregnant will cause her to lose her
ability to balance herself and her ability to dance.

Jean Wheeler Smith seeks to blame Ossie Lee's problems on
his environment. He is a powerless victim of a racist society. He can only exert power over black women. The story
protests the conditions which oppress Ossie Lee.

"To Hell with Dying." Alice Walker
Category A. Tragi-comic. Category B. Celebrative
There is only brief allusion to race relations.

Mr. Sweet Little - who is an alcoholic - chews tobacco, and
plays his guitar. He has a wife - Miss Mary - at the begin-

ning of the story; he also has a shiftless son. The narrator
- a young woman who seems very much like Alice Walker - and
her family "adopt" Mr. Sweet, especially after Miss Mary's
death. Periodically, Mr. Sweet takes to his bed to die. But
when the narrator's father says, "To hell with dying, man,
these children want Mr. Sweet!" - Mr. Sweet "revives."
    The dying and revival ritual is repeated many times
during the narrator's life. When the narrator is twenty-four
and Mr. Sweet is ninety - Mr. Sweet takes to his death bed
again. The narrator rushes home from graduate school to
revive him again. Mr. Sweet responds briefly to her presence,
but this time he dies. In the poignant conclusion the narrator says how difficult it is to accept Mr. Sweet's death. And
she realizes how much her parents have aged. She also realizes that Mr. Sweet has been her first love.
    The story touches briefly on the limitations black men of
Mr. Sweet's generation faced, but it is principally a story
which celebrates and commemorates the joys and sorrows of the
black experience. The story also has elements of the "rites
of passage" and the "coming of age" story.

1968

"An Act of Prostitution." James Alan McPherson
Category A. Tragi-comic. Category B. Protest
Race is a major concern.

This story is set in a courtroom on a Monday morning. Philomena Brown is an Italian-American prostitute who is married
to a black American man. She and her court appointed attorney
- Jimmy Mulligan, a public defender - dislike each other.
Ralph - another public defender - urges Jimmy to make Philomena look ridiculous so the judge will be in a good mood when
Ralph's client's case is called. Jimmy agrees.
    The judge - Judge Bloom - is eccentric and mean-spirited;
he does not sit; rather, he stands and paces. The first
defendant is a black alcoholic - who is in court every week -
charged with public drunkedness, loitering, and disorderly
conduct. The habitual drunkard is given five days. The next
defendant is a black soldier charged with inciting a riot and
resisting arrest. When his case is called twenty-five bearded
black men stand around the rear of the courtroom and lock
hands. The judge sends the case to a higher court.
    Philomena's case is called and Jimmy helps to make her
look ridiculous. Judge Bloom begins to smile and joke, and
the courtroom goes into an uproar. Philomena gets the maximum
sentence, and Ralph feels very good about the mood Judge
Bloom will be in for Ralph's client's case.
    Philomena Brown is a tragi-comic figure; she has laugh-
able and pitiful qualities. Some of her problems stem from
the fact that she is married to a black man and is the victim
of bias and racism. This story is a protest against the bias
and racism which victimizes Philomena Brown.

"Frankie Mae." Jean Wheeler Smith

Category A. Tragic. Unresolved Struggle. Category B.
Militant
Race is a major concern.

Old Man Brown is a black sharecropper in Mississippi who
decides to go on strike when the white boss - Mr. White
Junior - refuses to give his workers a raise. His late daughter - Frankie Mae - is the cause of Brown's decision. Frankie
Mae had been a beautiful, alert child who loved school and
refused to become discouraged even though she could not go to
school as often as she wished. Mr. White Junior had insisted
that the girl work in the fields. And there were the times
she had to nurse her mother and times when she did not have
shoes to wear, but she persisted with her lessons.
    When Frankie Mae was thirteen, she kept a record of the
expenses and income, and she contradicted Junior's statement
that her family had not made any money for the year. Junior
had been furious, and Brown had capitulated to the boss. That
broke Frankie Mae's spirits. She was never promoted again;
she began to have babies; she overate and grew fat, and she
died giving birth to her fifth child. She bled to death on
the way to a charity hospital. Junior had refused to loan
Brown the money he needed to put her in the hospital in town.
Brown strikes because of what was done to Frankie Mae.
    Frankie Mae's fate is tragic; Brown has decided to strug-
gle against his oppression. Brown has moved to a militant
stance against his oppressor. Some very negative aspects of
American race relations are central to this story.

    "A Revolutionary Tale." Nikki Giovanni
    Category A. Comic. Category B. Celebrative
    Race is treated in the story.

This is an amusing tale told by a narrator - Kim - who has
been converted to the black consciousness movement but has no
desire to go to school or to work. Faced with the alternative
of working or of going to graduate school, she applies to
graduate school and is accepted. In spite of all of her silly
efforts to get the school to change its mind and reject her,
the school urges her to come. She arrives late because she
walks, but she is welcomed to the school in spite of being
late.
    Nikki Giovanni has satirized certain aspects of the 1960s
and some of the attitudes of some blacks and some whites in
the 1960s in this story.

    "A Solo Song for Doc." James Alan McPherson
    Category A. Tragic. Category B. Celebrative, Protest
    Race is a concern.

Doc Craft is a waiters' waiter on the train diner along with
Sheik Beasley, Uncle T. Boone, Danny Jackson, and Reverend
Hendricks. After the waiters' waiters become unionized and
gain seniority, the railroad requires that they wait tables
according to a book - the "bible." At first the book conforms
to the service the waiters give, but as time passes the rules

are changed.

When Doc Craft is seventy-three efforts are made to get
him to retire, but he refuses and the contract with the
railroad and the union has no mandatory retirement clause. In
order to force him out the railroad has to catch him giving
improper service. So efforts are made to get rid of Doc, even
though he is still the best waiter. Finally, Jerry Ewald,
"The Unexpected Inspector," catches Doc in an error because
Doc does not know of the recent rule change about the way to
serve lemons.

Five months later Doc Craft freezes to death in the
Chicago railroad yards where he has wandered in a drunken
stupor. Doc Craft is a tragic figure because his only love is
taken away from him in his old age, and his spirit is crushed

The story touches on race relations in America; it contains some protest about race relations. But the story's main
thrust is to celebrate the life of the black dining car
waiters and to lament and protest Doc Craft's individual
defeat.

"Three Men." Ernest J. Gaines.
Category A. Epic, Unresolved Struggle. Category B.
Protest.
Race is a major concern.

The narrator - Procter Lewis - is a black man who gets into a
fight and hurts a man. He turns himself in. T. J. is a white
policeman who has contempt for Procter and all other blacks.
Paul is a white policeman who is decent. Procter's cellmates
are Hattie - an effeminate homosexual - and Munford Bazille -
a career petty criminal.

Munford tells Procter that the man Procter hurt - Bayou -
is dead. Procter knows that Roger Medlow - the white owner of
the plantation on which he lives - can get him released, but
Munford warns Procter that if he lets Medlow get him off,
Procter will never be a man again. Then Munford is released.

Later a young boy is brought to the cell badly beaten,
and Procter resolves that he will refuse Medlow's offer to
have him released, suffer the beatings that T. J. and those
like T. J. will inflict upon him, and go to the penitentiary.
Procter befriends the boy and attacks Hattie who is also
trying to console the boy. Then Procter has second thoughts
about going to the penitentiary, and he concludes that he
does not know what he will do when the time comes to decide.

Munford Bazille and Procter Lewis are symbolic of "bad"
black men; Munford is what Procter may become. Procter is not
sure of the course he will take; he is struggling with his
conscience. When the boy is brought to the cell beaten and
crying, Procter contemplates militant behavior in a quest for
his manhood, but he is not sure he has what militant behavior
requires. This story is closely related to some negative
aspects of American race relations.

"Train Whistle Guitar." Albert Murray
Category A. Epic. Category B. Celebrative

Race is a concern.

This story is about two little black boys - the narrator and
Little Buddy - who live in the rural South - and about the
boys' hero - Luzana Cholly. Cholly has been decorated in the
war for bravery; he has served a sentence in the penitentiary
because he injured a man in a fight. Cholly is a drifter/
gambler/hobo and the boys idolize him. So the boys decide to
run away and live Cholly's blissful existence. They will hop
a freight train and go with Cholly.
    But Cholly brings the boys back home, and he tells them
about the realities of his life. He urges them to become
educated and make him proud of them.
    Luzana Cholly represents a category of an older genera-
tion of black men who have faith in a younger generation of
blacks represented by the narrator and Little Buddy. This
story touches on aspects of American race relations, but it
is primarily a celebration and commemoration of aspects of
the black experience.

                        1969

    "The Committee." Stephen R. Wilmore
    Category A. Tragi-comic. Category B. Protest
    Race is a major concern.

The narrator is the only black member of a twelve member
committee set up to consider black riots/rebellions. The
narrator views the committee as useless. The meeting is
interrupted by a black waitress announcing lunch. When she
takes the orders, the narrator orders foods which he feels
are associated with black people by people who stereotype
blacks. The committee chairman wants hot tea, but only iced
tea is on the menu. The waitress refuses to make special
efforts to accommodate him, so the chairman decides not to
drink anything.
    The choices for dessert are butterscotch sundae, canta-
loup, and cherry pie, and the narrator asks for "honey melon."
The other committee members are puzzled, and the narrator and
the waitress are quite amused when the waitress translates
honey melon as cantaloup.
    This story is about the tragedy of American race rela-
tions. It reflects the ability of blacks to laugh and joke
under pressure, and Wilmore protests white insensitivity to
blacks.

    "End of the Affair." Ann Allen Shockley.
    Category A. Tragic. Category B. Personal Experience
    Race is a concern.

Keith is white; Nadine is his black mistress. Nadine has
learned that she is pregnant, and Keith's wife has found out
about the affair. Keith learns that Nadine is pregnant when
he comes to tell her that they must break off their affair.
After an angry argument, Nadine shoots Keith, and as they

struggle over the gun, Nadine is also shot; they both die.

"Harlem on the Rocks." Loyle Hairston
Category A. Comic. Category B. Protest
Race is a concern.

This is a humorous story about Soul Brother's nightmare. Soul
Brother is "a genuine, pure, one-hundred percent, fullblood-
ed gutbucket, black nationalist," and he dreams that he has
become good friends with Governor Arleen Willis. Gov. Willis
is a thinly veiled pseudonym for the late Mrs. Lurleen Wallace - the wife of Governor George Wallace of Alabama - who
succeeded her husband as governor when state law prohibited
his succeeding himself.
    In the dream Gov. Willis is very liberal, and she tries
to convert Soul Brother into an integrationist. Soul Brother
snaps out of the trauma his dream has caused and returns to
normal, when his landlady's psychoanalyst's diagnosis is that
Soul Brother is in the process of becoming "a nonviolent,
responsible, Negro integrationist, darling of white liberals."
    This story is humorous protest against integrationist
attitudes by a writer who promotes a black nationalism which
opposes integrationist attitudes. Race relations are alluded
to, but this story is about debate which took place within
the black community in the 1960s and the 1970s.

"How Long Is Forever." Walter Myers
Category A. Tragic. Category B. Militant
Race is a major concern.

Moses is in prison because his partner in a robbery - Jeff
Turner - killed a man. Moses testified against Jeff, but when
he came up for parole after seven years, the parole board
said no. The parole board also said no a second time, but
Moses' fellow inmates tell him he might get out the next time
if he stays out of trouble. Moses tries to stay out of trouble, but Jenkins - a racist white guard - will not leave him
alone. One day Jenkins beats Moses up and is about to sexually assault him, and Moses beats Jenkins to death. Moses is
now aware that he will probably never get out of prison.
    This story graphically illustrates one of the worst
aspects of the tragedy of American race relations.

"Moma." Audrey Lee
Category A. Epic, Tragi-comic. Category B. Celebrative
There is no treatment of race relations.

This is a touching and moving story of how a widow struggles
as a domestic worker and sells dinners on week-ends to rear
her four children. The narrator is the youngest child - Mary
Ellen. Norman is the third child; Lory is the second child,
and Davey is the oldest. Moma is able to survive the difficulties she faces and her painful feet and her calloused
hands and to provide a decent life for her children, and they
all join in to help.
    Audrey Lee implies that some of Moma's problems with

tight-fisted, mean-spirited, suspicious employers are due to
Moma's being black, but race relations are not treated.
Rather, the story emphasizes the love and the other positive
aspects of the black experience.

"To Be a Man." Ann Allen Shockley
Category A. Tragic. Category B. Protest, Militant
Race is a major concern.

Claude and Anita are a black married couple. Anita is gain-
fully employed in a bureaucratic job; she is the only black
in her office. Claude makes ten dollars a week working for
the black "Movement." He is a frustrated writer who has been
unable to sell his works; his writings are polemics which
denounce white racism.
    Anita and Claude have begun to have bitter arguments, and
she irritates him by pointing out that she finished college
and that she is the one who pays the bills, while he dropped
out of college and is now dependent upon her. He responds by
contending that she acts white, while he works with the
brothers and sisters in the struggle.
    One night Anita goes to a cocktail party; Claude refuses
to accompany her. Before she leaves they argue, then Claude
goes to a bar in the ghetto. Two white policemen come in; the
policemen are abusive and angry because a white man has been
mugged. One of the policemen roughs Claude up because he
argues and refuses to voluntarily move to the wall to be
searched. He starts to fight back, but he is hesitant and
tentative, and his response is feeble. The policeman knocks
him unconscious and leaves him in the bar.
    He tells Anita about the experience, becomes sexually
aroused, and forces her to have intercourse. Anita angrily
responds that sexual aggressiveness alone does not make a
man, and Claude's frustrations grow worse.
    This story is closely related to the tragedy of American
race relations and also to the problems black men and women
face in their relationships. Claude wants to make a militant
response to white racism but he cannot; he is defeated. This
story protests several things: Claude's behavior, Anita's
behavior, and the behavior of aspects of white society.

"The Willie Bob Letters." Freddye Wilson
Category A. Tragic. Category B. Protest
Race is a major concern.

The story of Willie Bob's death is told in three letters.
Willie Bob is shot during a riot while trying to rescue a dog
and her puppies. The first letter is written by a Jewish
pawnshop owner - Noah Silverman - who owned the dog and the
puppies. Silverman is upset because he asked Willie Bob to
save the dog and the puppies.
    The second letter is written by a racist, white policeman
- Michael J. Brogan - who feels no remorse about Willie Bob.
Another policeman shot Willie Bob; Brogan cannot understand
why the policeman who shot Willie Bob is upset. The third
letter is from Willie Bob's older sister - Ella Jo - to

Willie Bob's mother.
    The story is tragic, and Willie Bob is pathetic. The
story protests the sad state of race relations which created
the climate for Willie Bob's death.

1970

"Cotton Alley." Pearl Crayton
Category A. Tragic. Category B. Protest
Race is a concern.

The narrator tells a story about an incident she witnessed
when she was a little girl. Mister Sam worked on a garbage
truck. Every Saturday after he got paid, he drank too much
and fought Miss Pee-wee - his common law wife - while their
little daughter - Lucy Mae - stood on the porch and cried.
Sometimes Miss Pee-wee called the police who took him to
jail. All of the policemen in the town were white; Mister
Sam's family was black. After Mister Sam was arrested, the
police always called his boss who would tell them to let him
go. Then he would come home and eat supper.
    But one day when the police came, one of them hit Mister
Sam with his black-jack, and Mister Sam kept the policemen at
bay with a plank. The policemen refused to promise that they
would not beat Mister Sam any more, and he refused to put
down the plank. Finally one of the policemen approached
Mister Sam; Mister Sam hit the policeman on the hand, and the
other policeman shot and killed Mister Sam.
    This is a story about the tragedy of race relations in
America and about one of its victims. And Pearl Crayton
laments that tragedy.

"Harlem Transfer." Evan K. Walker
Category A. Tragic. Category B. Militant
Race is a concern.

The unnamed black protagonist in this story has lost a son -
presumably to drugs - and no one will do anything about it.
He has been to the police and to N.E.G.R.O. - apparently a
derisive caricature of the NAACP, but nothing has been done.
So he puts his affairs in order, and he gives his wife an
envelope containing his insurance policies and his bank
records. Then he kills the black drug dealer - the Dapper
Dude - the white policeman - Captain Bull - who has been
taking payoffs from Dapper Dude - and some more policemen.
While the shootout is in progress, he sees his wife being
interviewed on television, and he is happy to know that she
understands his actions.
    This story is closely related to the problem of being
black in America. The protagonist's loss of his son and the
protagonist's eminent capture - or death - are tragic. The
protagonist's decision to assault the forces he holds responsible for his problems and his decision to die or lose in his
own way are militant.

"The Library." Nikki Giovanni
Category A. Unresolved Struggle. Category B. Militant
Race is a concern.

The narrator goes to a library and gets books on Booker T.
Washington and W.E.B. Du Bois. The books do not satisfy the
narrator's desire to know the full truth about Afro-American
history. Then the librarian takes the narrator to a secret
section of the library. That section contains the Black
Museum which holds the Great Black Book. The book tells the
past, the present and the future. The problem is that if one
looks into the future his development is arrested, and those
who have not seen the book will not understand those who have
seen the book. The narrator looks into the future and ends up
in a circus in a cage.
     This is a parable in which Nikki Giovanni points out how
difficult it would have been to predict the events of the
1960s and 1970s.

"The President." Ann Allen Shockley
Category A. Tragic. Category B. Protest
Race is a major concern.

President William P. Howard is a black college president who
has struggled for many years to build up his institution. He
has had to endure the contempt of some white people and abuse
from some whites in order to get what he wanted for the
college. Now the black students have become involved in the
civil rights movement, and they are making demands. Dr.
Howard is confronted by John Beal and Mary Wilson who are
demanding that he "turn the school into a black school."
     The students view President Howard as an Uncle Tom; he
views them as impetuous firebrands. The president and the
students are unable to communicate, and he finally decides
to expel those students involved in the protests.
     President Howard is a tragic figure because he cannot
cope with the changing times. The absence of communications
between the president and the protesting black students
is also tragic. The story protests President Howard's values,
and it illustrates some of the different types of responses
blacks make to the racial situation in the United States.

"The Ride." Audrey Lee
Category A. Tragic. Category B. Personal Experience
There is no treatment of race relations.

The sad looking black woman on the train appears to be asleep.
Four ill-kempt children are with her. A twelve year old boy
holds an infant girl. Two small boys play in the aisles. The
passengers speculate about the condition of the mother. The
baby is crying, and the twelve year old cannot quiet her nor
can he awaken his mother. But the boy is defensive and will
not allow anyone to touch his little sister or his mother. At
the end of the line the boy tries frantically to awaken the
mother, and the conductor discovers that the woman is dead.
The twelve year old can give no information about where they

live, a father, or about anyone who will look out for them.

"'Strawberry Blonde,' That Is." Margaret Burroughs
Category A. Comic. Category B. Personal Experience
Race is a minor concern.

This is a humorous story. Mamie Plimpton runs into her high
school classmate Rosie. Rosie does not recognize Mamie because Mamie is wearing her strawberry blonde wig; both Mamie
and Rosie are black. Mamie's statements about her wig are
unintentionally funny and ridiculous.
   This story has no direct relation to the question of race
relations, but some might argue that Mamie's wig represents
her attempt to reject her blackness.

"The Welcome Table." Alice Walker
Category A. Tragic. Category B. Protest, Militant
Race is a major concern.

An old black woman goes to a white church and refuses to
leave. She is thrown out. Then Jesus comes by and tells her
to follow him. Later there is word that an old black woman
has walked herself to death, and her body has been found
beside the highway.
   This story is about the tragedy of American race relations. The author protests the fact that segregation is
enforced even in church at the time about which this story is
written The old woman's refusal to leave the church is an
early stage of militancy.

                              1971

"Blues Ain't No Mockin' Bird." Toni Cade Bambara
Category A. Epic. Category B. Militant
Race is a major concern.

The narrator tells about how she and three other black children witness her grandparents' resistance to two white men who
are filming around her grandparents' home without permission.
The white men say they are filming for the county, and the
filming is related to the food stamp program. But Grandmother
and Grandfather Cain do not wish to be filmed.
   This story is about an aspect of race relations. The
Cains are epic representations of those blacks who challenge
white intrusion.

"Crying for Her Man." Ann Allen Shockley
Category A. Unresolved Struggle. Category B. Personal
Experience
Race is a peripheral concern.

Bonnie is married to Flash. She teaches school; Flash does
very little except waste money on "get-rich-quick" schemes.
Bill collectors are calling about overdue debts, and Bonnie
is frustrated and struggling. One day after they have been

married for six months he asks her for money, and when she refuses he slaps her senseless. After she tells him where the money is they have sexual intercourse, and he leaves her there crying.

Both Bonnie and Flash talk about what it means to be a black man in a white dominated society. But whether racism is the sole cause of Flash's shortcomings is debatable. This story also deals with the problems of some black couples.

"Etta's Mind." Liz Gant
Category A. Tragi-comic. Category B. Protest
Race is a concern.

Etta and Louise are black women who go to a meeting of a woman's liberation group at Etta's insistence. Louise is married; Etta has broken up with her boyfriend because she was not sympathetic to his complaints about how badly he is treated on his job. Louise wears a natural hair style; Etta still straightens her hair.

The theme of the meeting is how terrible men are. After the meeting Etta and Louise have dinner with Eileen - the chairman of the group - and some of the other members. Etta and Louise have been the only blacks at the meeting. It is decided that Etta will represent the chapter at the city-wide meeting. Eileen has some suggestions for Etta. Eileen wants her to show how black women are especially oppressed by black men. Then after the meeting Etta and Louise see Eileen with a black man.

This story is essentially a protest against black participation in the woman's liberation movement. Louise is the character who speaks for the author; Etta's mind is confused by maladjusted white women who know nothing of the black experience but who are willing to take black men away from black women in the author's opinion.

"The Faculty Party." Ann Allen Shockley
Category A. Tragic, Unresolved Struggle. Category B.
Personal Experience
Race relations are among the concerns.

Paul Wood - who is black and who has a doctorate degree - has just become the coordinator of a new black studies program at a predominantly white college in a small predominantly white town in the Midwest. Paul and his wife Mavis attend a faculty party at the college president's house at the beginning of the year. Dave Fry is the only other teacher in the black studies program. Paul has known Dave since he taught at Howard University several years earlier when Dave was a graduate student there, but he has not seen Dave for several years.

At the party Paul encounters several problems - some new - one old. Some white faculty members doubt the academic integrity of black studies; some of the black students are very unhappy with the college; Mavis is promiscuous and unfaithful. All of this grates on Paul's nerves.

This story deals with American race relations to an

extent, but its primary focus is on one man's struggles with his problems.

"Mother Africa." Ann Petry
Category A. Tragi-comic. Category B. Celebrative. Personal Experience
Race is a concern.

Emanuel Turner is a filthy, unkempt junk dealer. One day he is given a nude statute of a woman whom he presumes to be African. His neighbors are upset about the nude statute, but Emanuel names it Mother Africa and decides to keep it. Emanuel undergoes a number of changes. He moves his junk away from Mother Africa, he plants grass, he bathes and gets a haircut and a shave. In the barber's chair he remembers the wife who died in childbirth twenty-five years earlier and how that was when he stopped taking care of himself.
    Later he discovers that his statute is actually the likeness of a Caucasian woman, and he sells it.
    This story reflects some of life's lighter aspects and some of its more serious aspects. Emanuel reflects on the difficulties of being black although race relations are not a part of the story.

"Travel from Home." Ed Bullins
Category A. Tragic. Category B. Personal Experience. Militant
Race is a concern.

Two blacks - Red and the narrator, Chuck - leave a dice game to chase and mug a white man. After they return to the game to talk about their exploits, the police come and chase them away, but the police do not search them. Chuck goes away frequently, and his response to questions about where he goes is that he does not go far enough.
    This is a story that indicates that blacks are sometimes the perpetrators of ugly racial incidents.

1972

"Antonio Is a Man." Audrey Lee.
Category A. Unresolved Struggle. Category B. Militant, Protest
Race is a major concern.

Antonio belongs to the new breed of black man protesting injustice and discrimination. His wife Marcy wants to leave the South and go to California. Antonio is determined to fight for justice where he is. Antonio has grown a beard and let his hair grow long; this upsets his mother, but Antonio will not shave or cut his hair short, for his beard and long hair are symbols of his manhood. Since Antonio is the only man on his job who protests discrimination, he gets the least desirable assignments. Antonio is a strong, proud, black man standing alone.

Race relations are an integral part of this story. The author's stance is one of protest, for she describes those who discriminate as evil. Antonio stands on the border between protest and militant action. So far he has only spoken up for what he believes and done symbolic things, but it is probable that he will act because he is a man.

"Arthur." Sharon Bell Mathis
Category A. Epic, Unresolved Struggle. Category B. Celebrative
Race is a concern.

Arthur does not dress the way those who say they are black revolutionaries dress. His friend - Booker - who is about to change his name to Ayize - chides Authur for not wearing dashikis and for not being attuned to the revolution. But Arthur is making lis contribution in another way. He is taking care of his widowed, mentally ill mother, and he is trying to prepare his little brother - Bubba - for the revolution by encouraging Bubba to be black and proud, to be aware of Africa, and to wear dashikies. Arthur cautions Bubba not to denigrate children who do not openly express their blackness, since they may have a kind of blackness different from Bubba's. That applies to Arthur too since Arthur's blackness is different from Booker's.

The story mentions the state of American race relations. The author feels it is necessary to promote black consciousness, and the author views black revolutionaries in a positive light. There is no black and white interaction in the story.

Arthur could very well be despondent about his lot, but he is not. Rather he acts positively and maintains his good humor. Since it is clear that the author wants Arthur to be a symbol, he has epic qualities even though his struggle is not done. And since Arthur's and the author's view of the black experience is upbeat, the story is celebrative.

"Gorilla My Love." Toni Cade Bambara
Category A. Tragi-comic. Category B. Personal Experience
Race relations are not treated.

The narrator is Hazel - a little girl who does not like deception. She has always called her uncle "Hunca Bubba;" his name is Jefferson Winston Vale. Hazel illustrates her distaste for deception by recalling that when the movie theater did not show Gorilla My Love which had been advertised, she protested to the manager and demanded her money back.

Now Hazel, her Granddaddy Vale, Baby Jason - her brother, and her uncle are riding in a car. Jefferson is excited about a woman he loves and plans to marry. Hazel reminds him that several years ago he promised to wait until Hazel grew up and to marry her. She rejects his plea that he had only been teasing and cries pitiful tears; Baby Jason weeps with her.

This story is more comic than tragic. It is also a "cute" story. Hazel is hurt and serious about losing the man she expected to marry. In time she will be able to laugh at the humor of the incident. Now she is inconsolable.

"Sweet Potato Pie." Eugenia Collier
Category A. Comic. Category B. Celebrative
Race relations are not treated.

Buddy - the narrator - is a college professor. Charlie is
Buddy's older brother and protector; Charlie drives a cab in
New York. Buddy is the only member of the family who was able
to get an education, and Charlie is very proud of Buddy.
     After Buddy has dinner at Charlie's apartment, Charlie's
wife - Bea - gives Buddy the leftover sweet potato pie, and
Charlie drives Buddy back to his hotel. At the hotel Charlie
demands the brown paper bag containing the pie. He insists
that Buddy is <u>somebody</u> and that it would be inappropriate
for Buddy to take a brown paper bag into the lobby of a nice
hotel. Buddy reluctantly surrenders his pie and walks through
the hotel lobby. When he looks back, Charlie is following him
carrying his brown paper bag of sweet potato pie.
     This is a delightful story about a family's love and
affection and about their struggles. Buddy is the fulfillment
of the family's aspirations because he has managed to become
<u>somebody</u>. While this story does not deal with race, it cele-
brates some positive aspects of the black experience.

1973

"Everyday Use." Alice Walker
Category A. Comic. Category B. Celebrative
Race is a concern.

The narrator of this story is the mother of two daughters -
Maggie and Dee. Dee has changed her name to Wangero Leewanika
Kemanjo. Maggie and her mother live in a rural area. Maggie
is plain and unlettered; the mother is a big strong woman
capable of doing work usually done by men. Dee has always had
style and a determination to succeed. She has become educated
and moved to town.
     Dee comes to visit. She brings a man with her, and her
mother wonders what their relationship is, but the question
is not discussed. Dee is dressed in a bright, colorful, long,
dress; she is wearing her hair in a natural style, and she
emphasizes her name change. Dee's mother calls Dee's companion Hakim-a-Barber for short, because she cannot pronounce
his full name. Both Dee and Hakim claim to have rejected
white culture and to have adopted their version of black
culture.
     After dinner Dee wants to collect some of her mother's
possessions. She takes a butter churn top and the dasher. She
also wants two quilts that her grandmother, mother, and aunt
made, but her mother tells her that she has promised the
quilts to Maggie for a wedding present. This upsets Dee
because she says Maggie will put the quilts to everyday use.
Dee would hang them as art, but Maggie will use them on the
bed. Maggie is willing to give the quilts to Dee, but their

mother says no and that there are other quilts Dee can have.
Dee rejects the other quilts because they have been machine
stitched and stalks out to the car. When their mother and
Maggie come out to the car to say goodbye, Dee tells them
that they do not understand their heritage and the new day
for black people. Dee and Hakim leave and the narrator and
Maggie sit and enjoy their snuff until bedtime.

In this story the narrator reacts humorously to some of
the behavior of some blacks during the 1960s and 1970s. The
story is indirectly related to race relations, but its main
thrust is a humorous, satiric, celebration and commemoration
of the black experience.

"Story of a Scar." James Alan McPherson
Category A. Tragic. Category B. Personal experience
Race is a minor concern.

The narrator meets a woman in a doctor's office; she has a
long, ugly scar on her face. She tells him the story of how
she got the scar. She had worked in the post office and met
Billy Crawford - a serious, studious man - much like the
narrator. She and Billy had gone together for a time - against the advice of her friend - Red Bone - who viewed Billy as
strange.

Finally at Red Bone's urging, she began to show some
interest in Teddy Johnson. One morning there was a confrontation, and Billy had cut her badly and stabbed Teddy.

This story has some humorous spots, but it is basically
tragic. McPherson - a Pulitzer Prize winner - skillfully
unfolds the story. The story alludes to race but does not
focus on race relations.

"Ten Pecan Pies." Clarence Major
Category A. Tragi-comic. Category B. Celebrative
Race and race relations are not concerns.

It is Christmas time at the Flower home. Grady Flower is an
old, crippled man in a wheelchair. His wife is Thursday;
their granddaughter - Gal - and their grandsons - Grew, B.B.,
and Moses - live with them. Everything is in order for cook-
ing a delicious Christmas feast except Grady insists that the
pecans gathered for the pecan pies are his, and he will not
part with them. The Flower's son - Slick John - tries to
reason with the old man, but he remains adamant and cantan-
kerous.

Finally, after Thursday points out that some of the pies
are gifts for the needy and after she reminds Grady of the
enjoyment he once received from a gift of books, he relents
and Christmas dinner can be completed.

Grady's condition and his state of mind are tragic, but
his antics are comic, and the moods of all the other characters are festive and happy. So the story is tragi-comic. And
the happy characters take the black experience so naturally
that there is no suggestion that any other experience exists.

1975

"Central Standard Time Blues." Carolyn M. Rodgers
Category A. Tragic. Category B. Militant
Race is a major concern.

The narrator is a black woman travelling from Cleveland to
Chicago. An off duty bus driver sits in the seat in front of
her and tries to be friendly with her, and she tries to be
cold and hostile to him. When he sits next to her so two
people can sit together in his seat, she is quite upset. When
the people who have taken the off duty driver's seat get to
their destination and he moves - she is quite relieved. This
experience reminds her of all the black women who have suffered abuse at the hands of white men, and she is glad she
behaved as she did. Yet she also feels anger, frustration,
humiliation, and sadness.
    The tragedy of American race relations is an integral
part of this story. And while the narrator wishes she had
acted more militantly than she did, her mind-set - if not her
overt actions - was militant.

"Julia." John Stewart
Category A. Unresolved Struggle. Category B. Militant
Race is a major concern.

Julia is at a civil rights rally. The four singers on the
stage from the Student Nonviolent Coordinating Committee are
black, but everyone in the audience is white except Julia.
Julia's mind is flooded with thoughts. She misses her boyfriend, General, very much. She resents her white friend
Marcia and the other whites. She feels the desire to kill -
which is contrary to her upbringing. At the rally's end Julia
refuses to stand when they sing "We Shall Overcome."
    This story is about race relations and one woman's strug-
gle with the problems of race relations.

"One Time." Carolyn Rodgers
Category A. Tragic. Category B. Protest, Personal Exper-
ience
There is no treatment of race relations.

Linda Palmer counsels girls who are in a job training program
for high school dropouts. She has to expel Bernice Robinson
and Marlene Cleveland from the program because they are
pregnant. Bernice has had a baby before, but Marlene got
pregnant the first time she had intercourse. This is a sad
situation for all three characters.

"The Pre-Jail Party." John Stewart
Category A. Unresolved Struggle. Category B. Personal
Experience
There is no treatment of race relations.

Satin Bellamy - a prostitute - goes to a party being held for
another prostitute - Fannie Mae - who has been sentenced to

jail for soliciting. Satin buys Fannie Mae a nice clock.
Satin wishes that her lover - Fundi - were at the party with
her. After she dances with a stranger and allows him to
become intimate with her, she and the stranger have a violent bloody fight.
      This story deals with problems and difficulties which
arise out of human relationships; race and race relations are
not considered.

      "Ricky." Eugenia Collier
      Category A. Epic, Unresolved Struggle. Category B.
      Personal Experience
      Race relations and race are not treated.

Viola takes in the homeless, eleven year old Ricky, but Ricky
is a very disturbed and troubled child. After he has gotten
into a lot of trouble, she decides that she cannot keep him,
and he is sent to Boy's Village. When she refuses to let him
visit her for Christmas, he runs away. Then Viola regrets
very much that she lacked the love to cope with Ricky and
that she has not permitted him to visit. At the end of the
story he comes to her apartment.
      Ricky and Viola represent two types of blacks. Ricky is a
homeless, disturbed, little black boy. Viola is a sensitive
caring black woman who tries with limited resources.
      There is occasional allusion to race relations, but they
are not concerns in the story.

                              1977

      "Elbow Room." James Alan McPherson
      Category A. Epic. Category B. Personal Experience
      Race is a major concern.

Both an editor and a narrator tell a story - as McPherson
uses an experimental approach. Paul Frost - who is white -
marries Virginia Valentine - who is black. The first person
narrator - who is black - interacts with them. Paul and
Virginia struggle to cope with Paul's father's opposition to
the marriage. They also struggle with the problems attendant
to an interracial marriage.

      "A Far Piece." Georgia Curry
      Category A. Tragic, Unresolved struggle. Category B.
      Personal Experience
      Race relations are not treated.

Tomica - a ten year old girl - goes from Florida to South
Carolina to live with her Aunt Blossom when her mother -
Catherine Evangeline Stephenson, called Babe - is murdered by
Tomica's father - Babe's lover. Tomica is very frightened and
distraught. Aunt Blossom is a very strong willed woman who
does not want too many tears shed. The day after the funeral
Tomica goes to the cemetary alone to say goodbye in her own
way.

"If That Mockingbird Don't Sing." Donna Mack
Category A. Tragic. Category B. Protest
Race is not a central concern.

Melba Wright's husband left her with their two children -
Chrystal Mae and Ronald. She went on welfare; later she
found a job at a training school for mentally and physically
handicapped children. She becomess very involved in her job,
and she has very little time for her children.
    When Ronald is killed in a fire, Chrystal Mae runs away
because she hates her mother for neglecting them; Melba moves
to the training school.
    At the beginning of the story two cockroaches are threat-
ened by fire; one escapes - one is burned to death. This
incident is a metaphor for Melba's children. A girl at the
institution called Birdie has chattered every day that Melba
has been there. On the first day Melba moves to the institution, Birdie is silent for the entire day. This is symbolic
of the disruption of Melba's orderly world.

"Why I Like Country Music." James Alan McPherson
Category A. Comic. Category B. Celebrative, Personal
Experience
There are brief allusions to race.

The narrator claims to like country music because of the
humorous events that led to his getting to do a square dance
with Gweneth Lawson - a fourth grade classmate - on whom he
had a crush.

                            1979

"Rope of Wind." Henry Dumas
Category A. Tragic. Category B. Protest
Race and race relations are major concerns.

Johnny B. - a black youth - watches some white men lynch a
black man.

                            1980

"A Life on Beekman Place." ("Lucielia Louise Turner.")
Gloria Naylor
Category A. Tragic. Category B. Personal Experience
Race is not a concern.

Lucielia and Eugene have a problem marriage. He comes and
goes. They have a daughter - Serena - who is born while he is
away. He returns when Serena is about two months old. When
Lucielia gets pregnant again, Eugene is upset; she has an
abortion to try to please him. Then Serena dies in an accident several months later and Lucielia is crushed. The marriage is probably destroyed now.

1981

"Damballah." John Edgar Wideman
Category A. Tragic. Category B. Protest, Militant
Race is a major concern.

A slave - Orion - refuses to be broken, fights the master,
appears nude before the mistress, and is brutally killed.

AUTHOR INDEX

NOTE: Reference works which contain biographical data are cited for selected authors. The references cited are indicated as follows:

(1) Bailey, Leonard P. Broadside Authors and Artists. Detroit: Broadside Press, 1974.

(2) Fairbanks, Carol and Eugene A. Engeldinger. Black American Fiction: A Bibliography. Metuchen, N. J.: Scarecrow Press, 1975.

(3) Kallenback, Jessamine S. Index to Black American Literary Anthologies. Boston: G. K. Hall, 1978.

(4) Margolies, Edward and David Bakish. Afro-American Fiction, 1853-1976. Detroit: Gale Research Co., 1979.

(5) Rush, Theressa Gunnels, Carol Fairbanks Myers, and Esther Spring Arata. Black American Writers Past and Present. Metuchen, N. J.: Scarecrow Press, 1975.

Example. "Amini, Johari. (1935-   ) (1) (2) (5)" indicates Johari Amini was born in 1935; biographical data on her may be found in references (1), (2), and (5) above.

Adams, Alvin. (2) (5)
"Ice Tea." First person. In Negro Digest 15(5), March 1966.
A poor black boy works on a farm and has his first iced tea. 66-14.

Adonis. J. C.
"The Vigil." Third person. In Essence 9(7) November 1978.
A man and his wife react to the death of their only son and to each other's reactions. 78-21.

Ahmed, Akbar Balagoon.
"Harlem Farewell." Third person. In Liberator 10(2), February 1970.
Blacks and whites in the United States reach a hostile

point of no return; civil war results. Two black guer-
rillas fight the now all white United States Army.
77-20.

Alakaye, Imagunla.
"Not on Saturday." Third person. In Essence 8(5), September 1977.
    A lonely man talks about his experiences and feelings.
    77-36.

Alba, Nanina. (1917-1968) (1) (2) (3) (5)
"The Satin-Back Crepe Dress." First person. In Negro
Digest 14(7), May 1965.
    A decent white woman responds compassionately to the
    death of the mother of a mentally retarded black boy.
    65-29.
"A Scary Story." First person. In Negro Digest 15(9),
July 1966.
    A white man is unable to forgive his brother for
    marrying a black woman, and he reacts to the brother's
    return home to the South for their father's funeral.
    66-24.
"So Quaint." (A Fable). First person. In Negro Digest
13(4), February 1964.
    A white woman views blacks as quaint and rejects the
    racism of her white neighbors. 64-24.

Amini, Johari. (1935   ) (1) (2) (5)
"Wednesday." Third person. In Black World 19(8), June 1970.
    A young woman reacts to a note from her lover that he
    is leaving; he has threatened to leave before. 70-56.

Anderson, Alston. (1924-   ) (2) (3) (4) (5)
"Big Boys." First person. In Lover Man, Anderson.
    Two men have a razor fight. Later, after it appears
    that they have renewed their friendship, they have
    another confrontation. 59-1.
"Blueplate Special." First person. In Lover Man, Anderson.
    A harried waiter tries to take the orders of fourteen
    people in a resturant in Brooklyn. 59-2.
"The Checkerboard." First person. In Lover Man, Anderson;
The Best Short Stories by Negro Writers, Hughes, ed.
    This story gives a young boy's view of his family which
    consists of a tolerant father, a nagging mother, and an
    older brother. 59-3.
"Comrade." First person. In Lover Man, Anderson.
    A black soldier who is in Germany towards the close of
    World War II befriends a wounded dog; he and the dog
    become inseparable. When the dog's owner comes to claim
    the dog, the owner and the soldier discuss a misunder-
    standing about Latin and German words meaning black and
    the corruptions of those words. 59-4.
"Dance of the Infidels." First person. In Lover Man,
Anderson.
    The narrator befriends a fellow music lover. Later they
    smoke marijuana, and the friend uses heroin. 59-5.

"The Dozens." First person. In <u>Lover Man</u>, Anderson.
Two young friends go fishing. After they fish, talk,
"play the dozens," and fight, one is trapped in quick-
sand, and the other attempts a rescue. 59-6.
"A Fine Romance." First person. In <u>Lover Man</u>, Anderson.
A woman sits next to a man on a train and dreams of
having an affair with him. 59-7.
"Lover Man." First person. In <u>Lover Man</u>, Anderson.
Brother Jessup, a deacon, gives up his church office
and "preaches" a farewell "sermon." 59-8.
"Murder at Fork Junction." First person. In the <u>New Yorker</u>
October 21, 1961, pp. 188-192.
This is a humorous spoof of detective stories. 61-12.
"Old Man Maypeck." First person. In <u>Lover Man</u>, Anderson.
A mulatto ex-slave has inteeresting memories and inter-
esting ideas. 59-9.
"Schooldays in North Carolina." First person. In <u>Lover</u>
<u>Man</u>, Anderson.
The narrator describes his experiences at a black
academy located in a white section of a small southern
town. 59-10.
"Signifying." First person. In <u>Lover Man</u>, Anderson.
A man and a woman with strong attractions to each
other as well as strong conflicts with each other,
begin to date. 59-11.
"A Sound of Screaming." First person. In <u>Lover Man</u>,
Anderson.
A young woman is pregnant for a prominent church member
whose wife has only been dead for a month. Abortion
appears to be the solution. 59-12.
"Suzie Q." First person. In <u>Lover Man</u>, Anderson.
The attractive young woman for whom the narrator lusts,
turns out to be much more than he bargained for. 59-13.
"Talisman." First person. In <u>Lover Man</u>, Anderson.
Talisman is a brand of tobacco that two customers have
urged a store owner to stock. But the store owner and
the two customers get so interested in the salesman's
female companion, they all forget the tobacco. 59-15.
"Think." In <u>Lover Man</u>, Anderson.
This is a short story in dialogue form. A man is very
interested in meeting a friend's attractive lady
friend; the friend finally takes him to her house.
59-16.

Anderson, Mignon Holland. (2) (4) (5)
"Beanie." Third person. In <u>Freedomways</u> 13(4), Fall 1973;
<u>Mostly Womenfolk and a Man or Two</u>, Anderson.
This is a story about a little black girl and her
mother and attitudes about black and white dolls. 73-1.
"Boots." In <u>Mostly Womenfolk and a Man or Two</u>, Anderson.
A little girl is surprized and shocked to learn that
she is "colored." 76-5.
"The Funeral." Third person. In <u>Mostly Womenfolk and a</u>
<u>Man or Two</u>, Anderson.
A girl goes to the funeral of a boy who has died of
sickle cell anemia and tries to comfort the dead boy's

grandfather. 76-10.
"Gone after Jake." Third person. In <u>Mostly Womenfolk and</u>
<u>a Man or Two</u>, Anderson.
   An undertaker goes through a storm to get the body of
   a friend. 76-11.
"The Grief." Third person. In <u>Mostly Womenfolk and a Man</u>
<u>or Two</u>, Anderson.
   A black slave kills a black man who refuses to be a
   slave. 76-12.
"Momma's Child." First person. In <u>Mostly Womenfolk and a</u>
<u>Man or Two</u>, Anderson.
   A child "speaks" from the womb. 76-19.
"The Mute." First person. In <u>Mostly Womenfolk and a Man or</u>
<u>Two</u>, Anderson.
   Part I. A white abolitionist buys a mute slave woman,
   who can pass for white, and he buys a male slave whose
   blackness is apparent. The abolitionist tells the
   slaves he will free them. Part II. The Abolitionist and
   the male slave fight for the affections of the mute
   slave woman. 76-20.
"November." First person. In <u>Freedomways</u> 11(3), Summer
1971 (by Mignon K. Holland); <u>Mostly Womenfolk and a Man or</u>
<u>Two</u>, Anderson.
   A young girl discovers that the body her father is
   embalming is that of a friend. 71-35.
"The Real Meaning of Undertaking." Third person. In <u>Mostly</u>
<u>Womenfolk and a Man or Two</u>, Anderson.
   A black undertaker has a confrontation with a white
   sheriff. 76-24.
"The Sizing Tree." Third person. In <u>Mostly Womenfolk and a</u>
<u>Man or Two</u>, Anderson.
   This is a four part story that deals with the death of
   a woman after she has a baby and of the folklore in the
   region where the woman lived. 76-30.
"Thickets." First person. In <u>Mostly Womenfolk and a Man or</u>
<u>Two</u>, Anderson.
   A soldier tries to cope with fear and racism in Viet-
   nam 76-34.
"When the Baby Got Going." First person. In <u>Mostly Women-</u>
<u>folk and a Man or Two</u>, Anderson.
   A woman speculates on when her child was conceived.
   82-10.

Anderson, S. E. (1943-   ) (2) (3) (5)
   "The Contrabande." Third person. In <u>Black Arts, Anthology</u>
   <u>of Black Creations</u>; <u>Black Short Story Anthology</u>, W. King,
   Jr. ed.
      In a combat setting, a man tries to move through enemy
      territory to get to his own lines. 69-6.
   "Soldier Boy." Third person. In <u>Black World</u> 19(8), June
   1970.
      A black American soldier in Vietnam finds rapport with
      a Viet Cong soldier and alienation from white Ameri-
      cans. 70-43.

Angelou, Maya. (1928-   )

"All Day Long." In Harlem, J. H. Clarke, ed.
   A twelve year old orphan boy comes to Harlem to live
   with his aunt. She treats him well, but he hears disturbing things about her profession. 70-3.
"Glass Rain." First person. In Essence 1(9), January 1971.
   The white doll that the black narrator is forbidden to
   play with takes on a life of its own in her fantasy,
   and that leads to tragedy.

Anthony, Paul. (5)
   "Brownstone Blues." Third person. In Liberator 7(3),
   March 1967.
      A heroin addict loses his brother and his sweetheart.
      67-9.

Appling, Wynn.
   "Marchover." Third person. In Liberator 11(3), March 1971.
      In this story, which uses language similar to that in
      the King James version of the Bible, the protagonist's
      concerns about black deprivation and white racism lead
      to better conditions for blacks. 71-30.

Armstead, Dolores.
   "A Day's Living." In Negro Digest 15(8), June 1966.
      A poor, single, black woman with a child to support
      accepts food and money from a white man who has made
      advances towards her. 66-9.

Bailey, Lois K.
   "Unwanted." First person. In Essence 8(7), November 1977.
      A girl, who is a juvenile delinquent, discusses her
      sad life. 77-56.

Baldwin, James. (1924-   ) (2) (3) (4) (5)
   "Come out the Wilderness." Third person. In Mademoiselle
   March 1958; Black Short Story Anthology, W. King, Jr.,
   ed.; Going To Meet the Man, Baldwin.
      A black woman, who lives with a white artist, reflects
      on the confusion which surrounds her life. 58-1.
   "Exodus." Third person. In American Mercury vol. 75;
   American Negro Short Stories, J. H. Clarke, ed.; The
   Afro-American Short Story, J. C. Elam, ed.
      A woman leaves her old, dying mother and her brother in
      the South and goes to New York. She will never return
      to the South. 52-4.
   "Going To Meet the Man." Third person. In Going To Meet
   the Man, Baldwin.
      Civil rights activities trouble a white deputy sheriff.
      They remind him of a lynching he witnessed as a child,
      and they affect his sexuality. 65-10.
   "The Man Child." Third person. In Going To Meet the Man,
   Baldwin.
      This is a strange story about four people - a man, his
      wife, his son, and his best friend. 65-20.
   "The Outing." Third person. In New Story, 1951; Going To
   Meet the Man, Baldwin.

The annual church outing provides the backdrop for
viewing black religious experience and ritual, tension
between father and son, and homosexual attractions.
51-1.
"The Rock Pile." Third person. In Going To Meet the Man,
Baldwin.
    This is a story about a boy and his relationship to his
    half brother, his mother, and his stepfather. 65-28.
"Roy's Wound." In New World Writing No. 2; Harlem, J. H.
Clarke, ed. 52-18.
"Sonny's Blues." First person. In Partisan Review; Bro-
thers and Sisters, A. Adoff, ed. Going To Meet the Man,
Baldwin; Dark Symphony, J. A. Emanuel and T. Gross, eds.;
Black Writers of America, R. Barksdale and K. Kinnamon,
eds.; The Afro-American Short Story. J. C. Elam, ed.;
Afro-American Literature: An Introduction, R. Hayden, D.
J. Burrows, and F. R. Lapides, eds.
    A man tries to cope with his brother's heroin use and
    with the meaning of his brother's music. 57-2.
"This Morning, This Evening, So Soon." First person. In
Atlantic Monthly, September 1960; Going To Meet the Man,
Baldwin.
    A black actor - singer has become rich and famous, and
    he has lived in France for eight years. Now he prepares
    to return to the United States with his Swedish wife
    and their son. 60-4.

Baldwin, Jo Ann. (2)
"A Hole They Call a Grave." First person. In Black World
24(8), June 1975.
    A teenage girl tells a gruesome story about an old
    lady's death. 75-12.

Bambara, Toni Cade. (1939-   ) (2) (3) (4) (5)
"The Apprentice." First person. In The Sea Birds Are Still
Alive, Bambara.
    A young woman follows a community organizer around.
    77-4.
"Baby's Breath." First person. In Essence 11(5), September
1980.
    A young man tries to cope with several frustrated
    romances that ended when his lovers had abortions over
    his objections. 80-1.
"Basement." First person. In Gorilla My Love, Bambara.
    A girl talks about another girl - who is her friend -
    and about the friend's mother. The friend exaggerates;
    the friend's mother reacts violently to her daughter's
    allegations of sexual harrassment. 72-4.
"Blues Ain't No Mocking Bird." First person. In Another I/
Eye; Redbook 138(6), April 1972; Gorilla My Love, Bambara;
We Be Word Sorcerers, S. Sanchez, ed.
    This story gives a girl's view of the way her proud,
    resourceful grandparents resent being considered candi-
    dates for food stamps. 71-5.
"Broken Field Running." First person. In The Sea Birds Are
Still Alive, Bambara.

The narrator is a teacher in a "freedom school." The
narrator and another teacher take some students on a
field trip. 77-8.
"Christmas Eve at Johnson's Drugs N Goods." First person.
In The Sea Birds Are Still Alive, Bambara.
A young girl working in a small black owned store talks
about her personal problems and about the small dramas
that go on in the store. 77-9.
"A Girl's Story." Third person. In The Sea Birds Are Still
Alive, Bambara.
A girl who is involved with a liberation school has her
first menstrual period. 77-16.
"Gorilla My Love." ("I Ain't Playing, I'm Hurtin'.")
First person. In Gorilla My Love, Bambara; Out of Our
Lives, Q. P. Stadley, ed.
The narrator is a determined little girl who reacts
negatively to deception. She becomes very upset when
her uncle says he is getting married. He promised to
marry her several years earlier, and she took him
seriously. 72-16.
"The Hammer Man." First person. In Negro Digest 15(4),
February 1966; What's Happening; Gorilla My Love, Bambara.
A girl talks about the actions of a boy thought to be
crazy. 66-12.
"Happy Birthday." Third person. In What's Happening;
Gorilla My Love, Bambara.
A little girl is unhappy about the events that occur on
her birthday. 72-17.
"I Ain't Playing, I'm Hurtin'." ("Gorilla My Love.") First
person. In Redbook 140(1), November 1971. 71-19.
See "Gorilla My Love."
"The Johnson Girls." First person. In Gorilla My Love,
Bambara; Essence 3(9), June 1973.
Five women talk about men in general and about one of
the women's problems with her boyfriend. 72-23.
"The Lesson." First person. In Gorilla My Love, Bambara.
A young girl reacts to a woman's efforts to get ghetto
children to question social and racial inequities.
72-24.
"The Long Night." Third person. In Black World 23(8), June
1974; The Sea Birds Are Still Alive, Bambara.
This story is about a young woman's experiences and
thoughts when police come to her neighborhood during a
riot and when police break into her apartment. 74-10.
"Luther on Sweet Auburn." First person. In First World
2(4), 1980.
A woman - who has been a social worker - meets a man in
Atlanta whom she knew as a gang leader in New York
about fifteen years earlier. 80-15.
"Maggie of the Green Bottles." First person. In Prairie
Schooner, Winter 1967/68; Gorilla My Love, Bambara.
A young girl talks about her grandmother who was a
spiritualist with odd behavior. 67-29.
"Mama Hazel Takes to Her Bed." ("My Man Bovanne.") In
Black World 20(12), October 1971. 71-27.
See "My Man Bovanne."

"Mama Load." First Person. In Redbook 154(1) November 1979.
   A divorced woman lives with her daughter and her very unusual ex mother-in-law. 79-12.
"The Manipulators." Third person. In Liberator 8(8), August 1968.
   Two black women reflect on how to get what they want out of life. One is willing to ingratiate herself to a powerful woman. The other has managed to get a fellow-ship to a predominantly white university. 68-21.
"Medley." First person. In Midnight Birds, M. H. Washington, ed.; The Sea Birds Are Still Alive, Bambara.
   A woman - who is very experienced - talks about a love affair, a business arrangement, her daughter, her friends, and her marriages. 77-30.
"Mississippi Ham Rider." First person. In. The Massachusetts Review, Summer 1960; Gorilla My Love, Bambara.
   The narrator is a black woman who is employed by a record company to go to Mississippi with a white male record company employee to try to persuade a black blues singer to go to New York to sing. 60-2.
"My Man Bovanne." ("Mama Hazel Takes to Her Bed.") First person. In Gorilla My Love, Bambara; Black-eyed Susans, M. H. Washington, ed.
   An older woman reflects on and reacts to some of the contradictions in the "black revolution." 72-30.
"The Organizer's Wife." First person. In The Sea Birds Are Still Alive, Bambara.
   People struggle to keep valuable land. 77-37.
"Playing with Punjab." First person. In Liberator 7(2), February 1967; Gorilla My Love, Bambara.
   The narrator is a street wise, young black girl who talks about a black loan shark and hustler who becomes involved with a white community organizer. 67-47.
"Raymond's Run." First person. In Tales and Stories for Black Folks, Bambara, ed.; Redbook 137(2), June 1971; Gorilla My Love, Bambara.
   A little girl talks about running the fifty yard dash during May Day activities, and she talks about her retarded little brother and a little girl who is her rival in the race. 71-39.
"The Sea Birds Are Still Alive." Third person. In The Sea Birds Are Still Alive, Bambara.
   A number of types of peoples with interesting stories travel together in a boat. 77-44.
"The Survivor." Third person. In Gorilla My Love, Bambara.
   Thoughts run through a woman's mind as she has a baby. 72-41.
"Sweet Town." First person. In Verdome, January 1959; Gorilla My Love, Bambara.
   A fifteen year old girl's boyfriend comes to tell her he is going away. 59-14.
"Talking Bout Sonny." First person. In Liberator 7(6), June 1967; Gorilla My Love, Bambara.
   People talk about Sonny after he stabs his wife. 67-57.
"A Tender Man." Third person. In The Sea Birds Are Still

Alive, Bambara.
   A black man – with a white ex wife and – an interracial
   child whom he does not see often – establishes a relationship with a black woman who is very concerned about
   his child. 77-52.
"Witchbird." First person. In Essence 7(5), September
1976; The Sea Birds Are Still Alive, Bambara; Midnight
Birds, M. H. Washington, ed.
   An ambitious woman struggles to realize her dreams. She
   also struggles with a relationship with a man with a
   "witchbird" laugh. 76-39.

Bamberg, Estelle G.
"The Hynotist." First person. In Phylon 29(4), Fourth
Quarter, 1968.
   A hypnotist passes for white and causes a bigot to
   wish to be black. 68-16.

Banks, Brenda. (1947-   ) (2) (5)
"Like It Is." Third person. In Black World 20(8), June
1971.
   A musician seeks to cope with the death of his
   girlfriend. 71-26.
"Tender Roots." Third person. In Black World 22(9), July
1973.
   This is a two part story which views the thoughts and
   experiences of two lovers who have separated. 73-41.
"The Washtub." Third person. In Black World 21(9), July
1972.
   A man gets revenge against a woman who constantly
   borrows from him. 72-48.

Baraka, Amiri (Leroi Jones). (1934-   ) (2) (3) (4) (5)
"The Alternative." Third person. In Tales, Jones (Baraka);
Black Short Story Anthology, W. King, Jr. ed.
   This story gives a view of the late night activities in
   a black male college dormitory. 67-3.
"Answers in Progress." First person. In Tales, Jones
(Baraka); 19 Necromancers from Now, I. Reed, ed.
   Spacemen seek jazz recordings. 67-4.
"A Chase (Alighieri's Dream)." First person. In Tales,
Jones (Baraka).
   A victim of a chase responds. 67-10.
"The Death of Horatio Alger." First person. In Tales,
Jones (Baraka).
   This is a story of a snowball fight. 67-12.
"God and Machine." First person. In We Be Word Sorcerers,
S. Sanchez, ed.
   This is a complex story; it appears to be an interpre-
   tation of the relationship between man and machine.
   73-16.
"Going Down Slow." Third person. In Tales, Jones (Baraka).
   A man who is having an affair – reacts violently to
   the discovery that his wife is also having an affair.
   67-19
"Heroes Are Gang Leaders." First person. In Tales, Jones

(Baraka)
  A very ill man imagines himself to be a writer and a
  philosopher. 67-21.
"The Longest Ocean in the World." Third person. In Tales,
Jones (Baraka). 67-27.
"New Sense." First person. In Tales, Jones (Baraka).
  A black man gets a new set of values. 67-36.
"New Spirit." First person. In Tales, Jones (Baraka).
  This is a story about the response to a girl's death.
  67-37.
"No Body   No Place." First person. In Tales, Jones
(Baraka).
  This is a complex imaginative reflection on the nature
  of things. 67-40.
"Now and Then." First person. In Tales, Jones (Baraka).
67-42.
"Salute." First person. In Tales, Jones (Baraka).
  Reading has an interesting effect on an airman station-
  ed in Puerto Rico. 67-50.
"The Screamers." First person. In American Negro Short
Stories, J. H. Clarke, ed.; Tales, Jones (Baraka); Out of
Our Lives, Q. P. Stadley, ed.
  A musician greatly excites a crowd in a dance hall.
  63-25.
"Uncle Tom's Cabin: Alternate Ending." Third person. In
Tales, Jones, (Baraka).
  A school teacher asks a question about a little black
  boy. 67-62.
"Unfinished." First person. In Tales, Jones (Baraka);
Harlem, J. H. Clarke, ed.
  This is a story about scenes and actions in an about a
  bar in Harlem. 67-63.
"Words." First person. In Tales, Jones (Baraka).
  A "prodigal son" returns to Harlem and philosophizes
  about life. 67-65.

Barber, John. (2) (3) (5)
  "Rites Fraternal." Third person. In What We Must See,
  O. Coombs, ed.
    A white man from the North eats with a black Missis-
    sippi sharecropper and talks of freedom and democracy.
    71-43.

Barbour, Floyd.
  "Dark Hyacinth." Third person. In Essence 10(4), August
  1979.
    A black woman - who is an artist - loves two women
    and a man. 79-4.

Barker, Mildred.
  "Trees Past the Window." Third person. In Negro Digest
  12(1), November 1962. 62-24.

Barksdale, Richard K. (1915-   ) (2) (3) (5)
  "The Last Supper." In Phylon 27(1), First Quarter 1966.
    A young woman who is Italian-American, tries to cope

with her mother who is ill, contrary, and senile.
66-17.

Barron, Eve.
"The Beautician." Third person. In <u>Phylon</u> 14(1), First
Quarter, 1953.
Clara - the beautician - reacts to a number of frustra-
tions. 53-1.

Barrow, Bari. (2)
"The World Is Wide, The World Is Small." Third person. In
<u>Black World</u> 26(7), May 1975.
Black soldiers discover a man with African ancestry
among German and Italian prisoners of war. 75-36.

Bates, Arthenia J. (1920-   ) (2) (4) (5)
"The Bouncing Game." Third person. In <u>Seeds beneath the
Snow</u>, Bates.
A son, whose father has always bailed him out of trouble learns that the check his father gave him to cover
a "bounced" check has also "bounced." When he confronts
the old man, he discovers that his father has tired of
bailing him out of trouble. 69-3.
"A Ceremony of Innocence." Third person. In <u>Seeds beneath
the Snow</u>, Bates.
A young woman - who has become a Black Muslim - visits
her elderly cousin - who is the "Mother of the Church."
The old woman is upset about her young kinswoman's
change of faith, but she is happy to see her. 69-4.
"Dear Sis." First person. In <u>Seeds beneath the Snow</u>,
Bates.
A sister corresponds with her brother who has left
school and joined the Navy at age sixteen. 69-7.
"Dinner Party." Third person. In <u>Seeds beneath the Snow</u>,
Bates.
This is a humorous story about a black boy whose white
employer insists on feeding him - even though the
employee does not want to eat. The boy is reluctant to
eat because he belongs to a black organization that
forbids its members to eat certain foods in the pre-
sence of whites. 69-8.
"The Entertainers." First person. In <u>Seeds beneath the
Snow</u>, Bates.
The conversation of two elderly cousins provides enter-
tainment for the other passengers on a bus. 69-10.
"Home X and Me." First person. In <u>Negro Digest</u> 14(11),
September 1965.
A young girl decides to become a home economics (home
X) teacher after her sister talks about what goes on in
the class. 65-12.
"Little Jake." Third person. In <u>Seeds beneath the Snow</u>,
Bates.
Little Jake's mother is determined to make him <u>some-
body</u>; he is uncooperative. 69-18.
"Lost Note." Third person. In <u>Seeds beneath the Snow</u>,
Bates.

A grandmother attempts to condition her grandson to
cope with a racist society in the wake of the murder
of Emmett Till. 69-20.

"Return of the Spouse." Third person. In Seeds beneath
the Snow, Bates.
This story deals with the evolution of a marriage that
is subjected to considerable stress over a period of
about a dozen years. 69-28.

"Runetta." Third person. In Seeds beneath the Snow, Bates.
This is the story of a girl - Runetta - born out of
wedlock - and of Runetta's and her mother's hopes for
Runetta. 69-29.

"The Shadow between Them." Third person. In Seeds beneath
the Snow, Bates.
This is a story about a woman's cold charity and her
suspicious nature. 69-30.

"Silas." Third person. In Seeds beneath the Snow, Bates.
Silas' father has a strange notion of manhood. When
a bully picks on Silas, a minister intervenes; the
minister is killed. Then Silas tries to act like a
"man." 69-31.

"Wake Me Mama." Third person. In Black World 20(9), July
1971.
A middle class black person tries to relate to blacks
living in a rural ghetto. 71-53.

Beckham, Barry. (1944   ) (2) (3) (4) (5)
"Cold Ben, New Castle." In Black Review Number 1, M.
Watkins, ed.
Four hunters are involved in a Mexican stand-off with
four lions, and one hunter - Ben - reflects on the
situation. 72-10.

Bennett, Lerone, Jr. (1928-   )
"The Convert." First person. In Negro Digest 12(3), Jan-
uary 1963; The Afro-American Short Story, J. C. Elam, ed.;
American Negro Short Stories, J. H. Clarke, ed.; Black
Short Story Anthology, W. King, Jr., ed.; Modern Black
Stories, M. Mirer, ed.
The Reverend Aaron Lott goes into the white waiting
room of the train station in his small Mississippi town
in the early 1960s. His deacon - Booker T. Brown -
urges him not to try to desegregate the train station.
As Deacon Brown watches from the "colored" waiting
room, the sheriff and a mob of whites kill Lott. At the
inquest into the minister's death the question is
whether Brown will tell the truth. 63-8.

Bertha, Gus. (3) (5)
"The Figurines." Third person. In Liberator 10(10), Octo-
ber 1970.
This is a story of a family in trouble. 70-16.

Bims, Hamilton.
"Getting Acquainted." Third person. In Negro Digest 13(6),
April 1964.

This is an "owl and pussycat" type of "boy meets girl"
story. 64-14.
"One Mexican." Third person. In Liberator 5(12), December
1965.
A pregnant black woman - who has been assaulted by a
white man is urged to prosecute. Her lawyers are two
black men who fret about the lack of black consciousness and courage; the woman is not sure she should
prosecute. 65-25.
"United States Congressman." Third person. In Negro Digest
15(5), March 1966.
A black boy, working on a beach patronized by prominent
white people, sees a congressman shoot a snake. 66-31.

Black, Isaac J. (2) (3) (5)
"Rabbit, Rabbit You're Killing Me." First person. In
Black World 24(8), June 1975.
A teenage boy - who loves a girl - is upset when an-
other boy claims to have seduced the girl. 75-21.

Bluitt, Ben.
"Bus No. 51." First person. In Negro Digest 15(7), May
1966.
A white man becomes terribly upset when he is confronted with the possibility that Jesus may have been black.
66-7.
"Gift." First person. In Negro Digest 14(7), May 1965.
This is a satirical monologue by a prejudiced white man
about an encounter he had with a black man. 65-9.

Boles, Robert. (1943-   ) (2) (3) (4) (5)
"The Engagement Party." First person. In The Best Short
Stories by Negro Writers, L. Hughes, ed.
A man reacts to his engagement party, to his doubts
about his love for his fiancee, and to his attraction
to the caterer's daughter. 67-15.

Bowen, True.
"Betrayal." Third person. In Phylon 11(1), First Quarter,
1950.
A young black boy - apparently the only black student
in a music class - and a white girl in the class are
attracted to each other. She promises to invite him to
her Christmas party, but neither of them understand the
state of race relations at the time. 50-2.

Boyer, Jill Witherspoon. (1947-   )
"Blood Sisters." First person. In Essence 9(6), October
1978.
A dark skinned girl with wooly hair begins to feel
estranged from her close friend who has light skin and
straight hair. 78-5.

Braswell, John.
"The Last Chew." Third person. In Essence 7(9), January
1977.

A woman returns home after having lived in the city for
a long time. 77-25.

Bray, Rosemary.
"Water." First person. In Essence 7(7), November 1976.
A young woman is on a date with her boyfriend when
another man propositions her. 76-36.

Bright, Hazel V. (2) (5)
"Mama Pritchett." First person. In Black World 22(12),
October 1973.
A white woman has an encounter with a spiritualist.
73-23.
"When You Dead, You Ain't Done." First person. In Black
World 22(3), January 1973.
A "dead" narrator talks about the afterlife in the
spirit world. 73-45.

Brookins, Melvin S.
"Aspirations." First person. In Liberator 7(12), December
1967.
A young boy is impressed by a "hustler," and he is
attracted to the "hustler's" lady friend. 67-5.

Brooks, Gwendolyn. (1917-   ) (2) (3) (4) (5)
"The Life of Lincoln West." First person. In Soon One
Morning, H. Hill, ed.
This is a short story about a little boy everyone views
as ugly. 63-16.

Brooks, Suzanne.
"Light through the Ivy." Third person. In Essence 6(3),
July 1975.
A girl - who is born out of wedlock - tries to cope
with life, her mother, her stepfather, her half sister,
and her half brothers. 75-16.

Brown, Cecil. (1937-   ) (2) (3) (4) (5)
"A Few Hypes You Should Be Hip to by Now." First person.
In The Black Scholar 6(9) June 1975.
A black confidence man is very disturbed, because
several black con artists he knows are superior to
him. 75-9.

Brown, Frank London. (1927-1962) (2) (3) (4) (5)
"The Ancient Book." Third person. In Negro Digest 13(5),
March 1964.
A woman flees the hungry, threatening rats in the
condemned building where she lives and goes out into a
snow storm. She takes refuge in a bar where an old man
offers to sell her a book on African heritage for a
dollar. 64-2.
"A Matter of Time." Third person. In American Negro Short
Stories, J. H. Clarke, ed.
A man suffers deep depression after being laid off
from work. 62-12.

"McDougal." Third person. In <u>Phoenix</u> Magazine, Fall 1961;
<u>Black Voices</u>, A. Chapman, ed.
> A white trumpet player - married to a black woman -
> tries to cope with difficulties. 61-10.

"Singing Dinah's Song." First person. In <u>Soon One Morning</u>,
H. Hill, ed.; <u>The Best Short Stories by Negro Writers</u>,
L. Hughes, ed.
> "Daddy-o," a machine operator, comes to the plant where
> he works acting very strangely. He insists that the
> machine on which he works is his personal possession.
> 63-26.

Brown, Samm. (2) (5)
"Winona Young Is a Faceless Person." Third person. In
<u>Black World</u> 20(10), August 1971.
> A young woman comes to understand why her husband
> joined an underground movement to avenge blacks brutal-
> ized by whites. 71-54.

Brown, Tiki. (2) (5)
"Put Ya Feet on a Rock." Third person. In <u>We Be Word</u>
<u>Sorcerers</u>, S. Sanchez, ed.
> A little girl's efforts to get to school is filled
> with adventure. 73-29.

Brown, Wesley. (1945-   ) (5)
"I Was Here, but I Disappeared." First person. In <u>Essence</u>
11(10), February 1981.
> A man tries to cope with having his relationship with a
> woman break up and with having a good friend undergo
> considerable change. 81-13.

"Mother Wit versus the Sleet Medallian Fleet." First
person. In <u>We Be Word Sorcerers</u>, S. Sanchez, ed.
> This is a tall tale about an old black "cunjure" woman
> and taxicabs in New York and Harlem. 73-24.

"The Unresolved Denouement." Third person. In <u>Liberator</u>
6(12), December 1966.
> A young black man, his wife and four children are
> trapped in a life of poverty. His white employer has
> little sympathy for him. 66-32.

Bryant, Girard.
"The Double Triangle." Third person. In <u>Liberator</u> 8(1),
January 1968.
> A man - who is sterile and who has a heart condition -
> cheats on his wife and abuses his body. Then he dis-
> covers that his wife is pregnant. 68-10.

Bullins, Ed. (1935-   ) (2) (3) (4) (5)
"DANDY, or Astride the Funky Finger of Lust." Third person In <u>Black Short Story Anthology</u>, W. King, Jr. ed.;
<u>The Hungered One</u>, Bullins; <u>We Be Word Sorcerers</u>, S. San-
chez, ed.
> This is a story of adolescent sex and lust. 71-7.

"The Drive." Third person. In <u>The Hungered One</u>, Bullins.
> A drive around Southern California leads to a number of

interesting incidents. 71-8.
"The Harlem Mice." Third person. In <u>Black World</u> 24(8),
June 1975.
    A black mouse, a brown mouse, and a tan mouse try to
    get cheese out of a trap in this fable. 75-11.
"He Couldn't Say Sex." Third person. In <u>The Hungered One</u>,
Bullins.
    The protagonist is a wanderer and a wonderer. He cannot
    understand why his sexually active mother does not want
    sex mentioned; he wonders what his father was like.
    71-15.
"The Helper." Third person. In <u>The Hungered One</u>, Bullins.
    A man helps a family move out of an apartment. 71-16.
"The Hungered One." Third person. In <u>The Hungered One</u>,
Bullins.
    In this fantastic horror story a man finds a strange
    and vicious bird and tries to take it home. 71-18.
"In New England Winter." First person. In <u>The Hungered
One</u>, Bullins.
    While the narrator and two other men rob a finance
    company, the narrator's thoughts drift to a love affair
    he had during a winter season in New England. 71-20.
"In the Wine Time." First person. In <u>The Hungered One</u>,
Bullins.
    A boy loves a young woman. There is no physical con-
    tact she just smiles at him until one day they talk.
    71-22.
"The Messenger." First person. In <u>The Hungered One</u>, Bul-
lins.
    A man has two roommates. One roommate has an unorthodox
    religious perspective. 71-31.
"Mister Newcomer." ("The Newcomer.") In <u>The Hungered One</u>,
Bullins. 71-32.
    See "The Newcomer."
"The Newcomer." ("Mister Newcomer.") First person. In
<u>Liberator</u> 7(10), October 1967.
    A man meets a woman at night school. 67-38.
"The RALLY or Dialect Determinism." Third person. In <u>The
Hungered One</u>, Bullins.
    This is a story about a meeting of a group promoting a
    philosophy. 71-38.
"The Reluctant Voyage." First person. In <u>The Hungered One</u>,
Bullins.
    This is a strange story about a man forced to take an
    ocean voyage. 71-40.
"The Savior." Third person. In <u>The Hungered One</u>, Bullins.
    This is a strange story of a ritualistic kidnapping.
    71-44.
"The Storekeeper." Third person. In <u>Negro Digest</u> 16(7),
May 1967.
    A white storekeeper propositions a black prostitute and
    has a confrontation with two black youths. Another
    black man intercedes to restore peace. 67-54.
"Support Your Local Police." First person. In <u>Negro Digest</u>
17(1), November 1967; <u>The Hungered One</u>, Bullins.
    A relatively famous author hitchhikes around the coun-

try and relates his experiences. 67-56.
"Travel from Home." First person. In <u>The Hungered One</u>,
Bullins; <u>Black Review Number 1</u>, M. Watkins, ed.
Two blacks leave a dice game, mug a white man, and
return to the dice game. 71-51.

Burke, Ruth.
"Ten Minutes at the Bus Stop." Third person. In <u>Negro
Digest</u> 14(3), January 1965.
Two white policemen in a southern town - where segregation customs continue to be observed after segregation
laws have changed - realize that a black man and a
white woman are going to New York together on the bus.
65-30.

Burks, Earline.
"No Time for Getting Up." First person. In <u>Essence</u> 8(5),
September 1977.
A young girl frets over the threats of a stronger,
mean little girl to beat her up. 77-35.

Burns, Kay.
"Waiting for September." Third person. In <u>Essence</u> 8(4),
August 1977.
An eighteen year old young lady goes to college; she
worries about what will happen to her relationship with
her boyfriend who remains at home. 77-58.

Burris, Jack.
"Judah's a Two-Way Street Running Out." Third person. In
<u>Negro Digest</u> 15(3), January 1966.
A Black man desperately searches for a job in San
Francisco. 66-15.

Burroughs, Margaret. (1917-   ) (1) (2) (3) (5)
"Eric Was Eric." First person. In <u>Negro Digest</u> 13(1),
November 1963.
The narrator talks about an eccentric artist and some
of his escapades. 63-13.
"Strawberry Blonde, That Is." First person. In <u>Black World</u>
19(9), July 1970.
In this satirical sketch a woman talks about her straw-
berry blonde wig. 70-45.

Butterfield, Stephen.
"Package Deal." First person. In <u>Liberator</u> 11(3), March
1971.
This is a very short story about a world in which
everyone needs a life support system. 71-36.

Cabbell, Edward J.
"The Soul's Sting." First person. In <u>Phylon</u> 30(4), Fourth
Quarter, 1969.
A Black musician in Harlem - who is a refugee from the
South and who no longer attends church - befriends a
black youth who has just come to Harlem from the South.

        69-33.

Cade, Toni (Toni Cade Bambara).
    "The Manipulators." 68-21. See Bambara, Toni Cade.

Caldwell, R. E.
    "Unfinished Canvas." First person. In Essence 9(7), Novem-
    ber 1978.
        A woman's accomplishments cause her to outgrow a
        relationship. 78-20.

Campbell, Be Be.
    "Shopping Trip." First person. In Essence 7(6), October
    1976.
        A woman drives all over town shopping for bargains at
        various grocery stores and having a number of amusing
        encounters. 76-29.

Campbell, James E. (2) (5)
    "Enfranchisement." Third person. In Freedomways 2(2),
    Spring, 1962.
        A sixty-three year old black man - who is determined to
        register to vote - is beaten by three white men. 62-8.

Carole, Joan.
    "Friends." Third person. In Essence 8(3), July 1977.
        This is a sad story of the mistress of a married man.
        77-15.

Chaney, Betty Norwood.
    "A Matter of Breaking Free." Third person. In Essence
    8(1), May 1977.
        A woman and her husband oppose busing and decide to
        send their daughter to an all black alternative school.
        This brings the woman into conflict with her mother;
        her mother has a long term commitment to desegregation.
        77-29.

Cherry, Eileen.
    "The Crossing." Third person. In Black World 22(1),
    November 1974.
        Two relationships exist. Coincidentally the four people
        involved in the two relationships are thrown together.
        74-3.

Chideya, Cynthia M.
    "One Way or Another." First person. In Liberator 8(10),
    October 1968.
        A black woman contemplates rearing her daughter alone
        after her militant black husband is killed in Vietnam.
        68-26.

Childress, Janus.
    "A Time in September." Third person. In Essence 8(9),
    January 1978.
        Two lonely senior citizens meet at a senior citizens

center. 78-19.

Cjonathan, Eon Chontay.
"After Europe the First Time." First person. In Essence
6(12), April 1976.
   A young woman is involved with a married man. On a trip
   to Europe she misses him. 76-2.

Clarke, John Henrik. (1915-   ) (2) (3) (4) (5)
"Revolt of the Angels." Third person. In Freedomways 3(3),
Summer, 1963.
   A man relates a story to two co workers to illustrate
   that it is possible for a drunk to reform and become a
   pillar of his community. 63-22.

Clarke, Sebastian. (2)
"Sun and Flesh." Third person. In We Be Word Sorcerers,
S. Sanchez, ed.
   A man dreams about some of his experiences and feel-
   ings. 73-39.

Clemmons, Carole G. (1945-   ) (1) (3) (5)
"Porky." Third person. In A Galaxy of Black Writing,
R. B. Shuman, ed.
   A girl - who lives with her sick aunt and her uncle -
   experiences growing pains. 70-34.

Cobb, Charlie. (1944-   ) (3) (5)
"Ain't That a Groove." First person. In Black Fire, L.
Jones (A. Baraka) and L. Neal, eds.
   The narrator calls for blacks to struggle for libera-
   tion. 69-1.

Coleman, Wanda. (2) (5)
"Watching the Sunset." Third person. In Negro Digest
19(4), February 1970.
   A man - who is racially mixed - reflects on his life.
   70-55.

Collier, Eugenia. (1928-   ) (2) (3) (4) (5)
"Marigolds." First person. In Negro Digest 19(1), November
1969; Brothers and Sisters, A. Adoff, ed.
   A young girl - who is approaching puberty - views an
   old woman as a witch; she taunts and harrasses the old
   woman. 69-22.
"Ricky." Third person. In Black World 24(10), August 1975.
   A woman takes in a homeless and disturbed little boy.
   He sorely tries her patience, and the situation becomes
   very difficult. 75-25.
"Sinbad the Cat." First person. In Black World 20(9),
July 1971.
   A forty year old man relates to a group of rowdy young-
   sters, after he reads one of the youngsters' essay
   about a castrated, clawless cat. 71-47.
"Sweet Potato Pie." First person. In Black World 21(10),
August 1972.

The taxicab driver - whose brother is a college professor - insists that a college professor cannot walk
through the lobby of an exclusive hotel with a brown
paper bag of sweet potato pie. 72-42.

Collins, Paschal.
"Black Bottom." Third person. In Negro Digest 13(6), April
1964.
A poor black man - who is frustrated with his life of
poverty - robs a moonshiner to get money to provide a
better life for his wife and child. 64-3.

Colter, Cyrus. (1910-   ) (2) (3) (4) (5)
"After the Ball." Third person. In The Beach Umbrella,
Colter.
This is a story about a married woman who thinks very
highly of her father. Her father implies that she
should come home and care for him; this creates a
dilemma for her, since she feels her husband will
disapprove. 70-2.
"The Beach Umbrella." Third person. In Soon One Morning,
H. Hill, ed.; The Best Short Stories by Negro Writers,
L. Hughes, ed.; The Beach Umbrella, Colter.
A man - who likes the beach - borrows money from his
son to buy a beach umbrella. He is "henpecked," and he
is afraid his wife will not approve of his buying it.
63-3.
"Black for Dinner." Third person. In Chicago Review, 1966;
The Beach Umbrella, Colter; Out of Our Lives, Q. P.
Stadley, ed.
A wife is preoccupied with a dinner party and upset
because her husband does not appear to like the black
dress she is to wear. She does not realize that he is
concerned about something much more serious. 66-5.
"A Chance Meeting." Third person. In Threshold, 1960;
The Beach Umbrella, Colter.
Two men who once had the same employers meet. An ensu-
ing discussion reveals that they had very different
perceptions of the family for whom they worked. 60-1.
"A Gift." In Northwest Review, Fall-Winter, 1966-67;
The Beach Umbrella, Colter.
A woman with a terminal illness tries to make provi-
sions for her husband after she is dead. She even tries
to find a woman whom gossips have linked to her husband. 66-10.
"Girl Friend." Third person. In The Beach Umbrella, Colter.
A man begins an affair with a married woman shortly
after his wife dies. His daughter is very upset to
learn that he is interested in a woman so soon after
her mother's death. 70-18.
"The Lookout." Third person. In University of Kansas City
Review, 1961; The Beach Umbrella, Colter.
A woman is despondent because some of her friends and
acquaintances have secured higher social stations than
she has. 61-9.

"A Man in the House." Third person. In <u>Prairie Schooner</u>, 1967; <u>The Beach Umbrella</u>, Colter.
   A girl from Memphis, Tennessee finishes high school and goes to Chicago to visit her aunt and her aunt's husband. Her father died when she was very young and she has not lived in a house in which a man also lived since her father died. 67-30.
"The March." Third person. In <u>Black World</u> 20(8), June 1971.
   A woman tries to cope with her son's enlistment in the Army, her husband's callousness, and a neighbor's involvement in anti Vietnam war protests. 71-29.
"Mary's Convert." Third person. In <u>Chicago Review</u> 17(2 & 3), 1964; <u>New Black Voices</u>, A. Chapman, ed.; <u>The Beach Umbrella</u>, Colter.
   A sixteen year old boy - with a drug habit - meets and becomes attracted to a twenty-three year old woman with a drug habit. The woman tries to fight her habit with religious fervor. 64-20.
"Moot." Third person. In <u>The Beach Umbrella</u>, Colter.
   This is the story of an old man and his dog during the last days of their lives. 70-29.
"Overnight Trip." Third person. In <u>Epoch</u>, 1961; <u>The Beach Umbrella</u>, Colter.
   A husband is deeply troubled over his wife's brief trip from Chicago to St. Louis. 61-14.
"Rapport." Third person. In <u>Epoch</u>, 1964; <u>The Beach Umbrella</u>, Colter.
   A lonely widower finds rapport with a little girl in the dining room of a hotel where he lives. 64-26.
"The Rescue." Third person. In <u>Epoch</u>, 1962; <u>The Beach Umbrella</u>, Colter.
   A woman - who has not done a very good job with her own life - tries to advise her sister on how to live. 62-20.
"An Untold Story." Third person. In <u>The Beach Umbrella</u>, Colter.
   A barroom discussion of Shakespeare's <u>Hamlet</u> leads to arguments and violence. 70-50.

Comiskey, Myra Hargrove.
   "Payment on Account." Third person. In <u>Essence</u> 8(8), December 1977.
   A doorman at an elegant hotel has an encounter with an artist. 77-38.

Coombs, Orde. (2) (4) (5)
   "Another Life." First person. In <u>Essence</u> 7(2), June 1976.
   A young boy tells the story of his grandfather's lechery and death and of his pristine grandmother's reactions. 76-3.
   "Silas Cantebury." First person. In <u>Black Review Number 2</u>, M. Watkins, ed.
   This is the story of a man from Saint Vincent - who was born out of wedlock - and of the impact a trip to England has upon his mind. 72-39.

Cooper, Clarence L. (2) (3) (4) (5)

"Not We Many." First person. In Black!; Black Short Story
Anthology, W. King, Jr., ed.
    A man who is interracial - his father is black; his
    mother is white - joins the "Black Muslims." But this
    branch of Islam does not answer his questions. The
    Black Muslim woman he loves views him as a heretic.
    72-32.

Cornwell, Anita R.
"And Save a Round for Jamie Brown." First person. In
Negro Digest 15(6), April 1966.
    A drifter from the South comes to Philadelphia. He
    decides not to get involved in illegal lotteries and
    becomes an elevator operator. He falls in love with a
    woman who belongs to a higher social class. 66-2.
"Between the Summers." Third person. In Phylon 27(3),
Third Quarter, 1966.
    A young woman - who has become liberated - does not
    want to go through with her scheduled wedding. She is
    afraid that breaking her engagement will upset her
    parents. Then she discovers that her parents are more
    liberated than she thought. 66-4.
"A Sound of Crying." Third person. In Negro Digest 13(4),
April 1966; The Afro-American Short Story, J. C. Elam, ed.
    A young man is expelled from school for civil rights
    activity. Much to the consternation of his parents, he
    comes back to his small Mississippi home town. 64-31.

Crawford, Marc. (2) (5)
"Willie T. Washington's Blues." Third person. In Black
World 21(7), May 1972.
    A black American writer is in Mexico; his situation is
    desperate. He remembers how an old friend was once
    unable to write an autobiographical series. 72-49.

Crayton, Pearl. (2) (3) (5)
"Cotton Alley." First person. In Brothers and Sisters, A.
Adoff, ed.
    A black man who has been drinking and disorderly has a
    tragic confrontation with two white policemen. 70-10.
"The Day the World Almost Came to an End." First person.
In Negro Digest 14(10), August 1965; The Best Short Stor-
ies by Negro Writers, L. Hughes, ed.; Tales and Stories
for Black Folks, T. C. Bambara, ed.
    A twelve year old girl - who is thinking about the end
    of the world - hears an airplane for the first time.
    65-7.
"The Gold Fish Monster." Third person. In The Texas Quarterly, Summer, 1967; Out of Our Lives, Q. P. Stadley, ed.
    An old man rows his boat on the river of the planta-
    tion. He tells a skeptical audience that God will
    cause a fish - with a fifty dollar gold piece in its
    mouth - to jump into his boat. 67-20.

Crittenden, Annie R. (2) (5)
"Love Knot." Third person. In Essence 3(2), June 1972.

A girl has a father who is a famous blues singer, but she has never really known him. After she dreams about her father, she decides that she too will become a professional singer. 72-27.

Cumbo, Kattie M. (1938-   ) (5)
"Boy (A Short Story in Allegory Form)." Third person. In *A Galaxy of Black Writing*, R. B. Shuman, ed.
A lion is captured and treated as if he were a pussy-cat. One day he meets a family of lions and his behavior begins to change. 70-8.

Curry, Georgia. (1947-   )
"A Far Piece." First person. In *Essence* 8(1), May 1977.
A little girl tries to cope with her mother's death. 77-14.

Cuthbertson, James O.
"Rag Sally." First person. In *Essence* 6(8), December 1975.
A woman gathers rags to earn money to care for her five children. She hopes her husband - who left ten years earlier - will return and take his family to a better life. 75-22.

Dalton, Fletcher E.
"I Need Your Love So Bad." Third person. In *Negro Digest* 12(7), May 1963.
A black woman is reared by a white family, and she becomes their cook. Later she becomes a successful blues singer. Finally, after twelve years she retires from singing and returns home. 63-14.

Davenport, Sarah B.
"All of Us and None of You." First person. In *Essence* 8(7), November 1977.
A fourteen year old girl talks about her family and about how her father comes for a visit six years after he abandoned the family. 77-3.

Davis, A. I. (2) (5)
"A Black Woman's Monologue." First person. In *Essence* May 1972.
A mother who is a slave, laments having her child sold away from her. 72-6.
"Great God Stebbs." Third person. In *Essence*, 3(12), April 1973.
Stebbs is supposed to be able to tell what numbers will win lotteries when he overeats and talks in his sleep. 73-17.

"Suffer Little Children." Third person. In *Essence* 5(1), May 1974.
A woman is addicted to drugs, and her family resolves to try to help her. 74-15.

Davis, George. (1939-   ) (2) (4) (5)

"Home Is Much Too Far To Go." Third Person. In Black Review Number 1, M. Watkins, ed.
     A Black Man - with a white wife - returns to his alma
     mater in the Northeast with his wife. But his thoughts
     are on his family in Harlem. 72-18.
"Like a Piece of the Blues." First person. In Negro Digest
16(9), July 1967; Black Short Story Anthology, W. King,
Jr., ed.
     A youngster - who is a Christian - engages in a friend-
     ly debate with a man who is a "Black Muslim. 67-26.

Davis, Gloria. (2) (3) (5)
     "The Wall." In Negro Digest 15(10), August 1966.
     A father and son come into conflict when the son wants
     to go south and work in the mines. 66-34.

Demond, Antoinette S.
     "The Need To Understand." First person. In Phylon 18(2),
     Second Quarter, 1957.
     A little girl is concerned about her parents' marital
     problems. 57-1.
     "The Summer of My Sixteenth Year, A Reminscence." First
     person. In Negro Digest 11(6), April 1962.
     A woman remembers her first love. 62-23.

De Ramus, Betty. (2) (5)
     "The Addict." Third person. In Black World 19(8), June
     1970.
     A boy confesses to a dentist that he smokes hashish.
     70-1.
     "The Fake Picasso." Third person. In Black World 21(8),
     June 1972.
     A burglar is not interested in a fake Picasso. 72-12.
     "Waiting for Beale." Third person. In Essence 7(1), May
     1976.
     A forty year old kept woman is frightened by the fact
     that her eighteen year old daughter is growing more and
     more like her. 76-35.

De Veaux, Alexis. (1948-   )
     "Remember Him a Outlaw." First person. In Black Creation,
     Fall, 1972; Midnight Birds, M. H. Washington, ed. 72-35.
     "The Riddles of Egypt Brownstone." Third person. In Essen-
     ce 9(4), August 1978; Midnight Birds, M. H. Washington, ed.
     A girl's parents are not married; she sees her father
     only once a year. When she is a young woman, he dies.
     78-17.

Diggs, Jeff.
     "Both My Girls." First person. In Negro Digest 14(12),
     October 1965.
     When a black couple drowns, a white couple adopts the
     black couple's infant daughter. 65-3.

Dodson, Owen. (1914-1983) (1) (2) (3) (4) (5)
     "Come Home Early Chile." Third person. In Soon One Morning;

H. Hill, ed. <u>The Best Short Stories by Negro Writers</u>, L.
Hughes, ed.
A man discovers that a woman who has caused his family
a lot of misery is dead. 63-7.

Douglass, Geraldine.
"What Are Friends For?" Third person. In <u>Essence</u> 8(6),
1977.
A secretary in the typing pool is the source of a lot
of entertainment. 77-59.

Dumas, Henry. (1934-1968) (2) (3) (4) (5)
"Ark of Bones." First person. In <u>Ark of Bones and Other
Stories</u>, Dumas.
The narrator and "Headeye" go aboard a ship which
contains the bones of everyone in America with African
ancestry. Headeye has been annointed for a mission
having to do with this ark of bones. 70-5.
"A Boll of Roses." Third person. In <u>Ark of Bones and Other
Stories</u>, Dumas.
A poor high school student - who must pick cotton on
school days - tries to cope with his feelings about the
civil rights movement, his family, his desire to have
something, and his "crush" on a young woman - who is a
civil rights worker. 70-7.
"The Crossing." Third person. In <u>Negro Digest</u> 15(1),
November 1965; <u>Ark of Bones and Other Stories</u>, Dumas.
Three black children play and talk about the death of
Emmett Till and the "ways of white folks." 65-5.
"Devil Bird." First person. In <u>Rope of Wind</u>, Dumas.
A young boy - whose grandfather is ill - assumes that
two people who visit and play cards with his parents
are the Devil and God. A bird arrives, and the bird's
actions puzzle the boy. 79-5.
"The Distributors." First person. In <u>The Anthologist</u>
1964-65; <u>Rope of Wind</u>, Dumas.
This is an unusual story about the distribution of a
strange machine. 64-11.
"Double Nigger." First person. In <u>Ark of Bones and Other
Stories</u>, Dumas.
Four young black males have some experiences in the
rural South where whites have a reputation for being
hostile. 70-12.
"The Eagle, the Dove, and the Blackbird." Third person. In
<u>Black Ikon</u>, August 1963; <u>Rope of Wind</u>, Dumas.
An eagle enslaves a blackbird and makes a dove the
blackbird's overseer. 63-11.
"Echo Tree." ("Rain God.") First person. In <u>Ark of Bones
and Other Stories</u>, Dumas. 70-14.
See "Rain God."
"Fon." Third person. In <u>Black Fire</u>, L. Jones (A. Baraka)
and L. Neal, eds.; <u>Ark of Bones and Other Stories</u>, Dumas.
A former deputy sheriff and his friends confront "Fon"
after the ex-deputy's car window is smashed with a
stone. 69-12.
"Harlem." Third person. In <u>Rope of Wind</u>, Dumas.

This is a story of a bombed and burned out Islamic temple, a man who views the ruins daily, a black nationalist, and a riot in Harlem. 79-8.
"A Harlem Game." Third person. In Ark of Bones and Other Stories, Dumas.
　　A boy tries to cope with a meanspirited father. 70-21.
"Invasion." Third person. In Rope of Wind, Dumas.
　　Children's war games escalate into warfare. 79-10.
"The Lake." Third person. In Rope of Wind, Dumas.
　　This is a fantasy about a man's magic lake. 79-11.
"The Marchers." Third person. In Black Ikon, August 1963; Rope of Wind, Dumas.
　　This is a highly symbolic story of a march for freedom, justice, and equality; the march neglects the soul for rhetoric. 63-17.
"Rain God." ("Echo Tree.") First person. In Negro Digest 17(3), January 1968.
　　Boys play in the rain and repeat folklore about the devil and various signs of nature and the supernatural. 68-28.
"Rope of Wind." Third person. In Rope of Wind, Dumas.
　　A black youth witnesses a lynching. 79-17.
"Six Days Shall You Labor." First person. In Rope of Wind, Dumas.
　　A teenage boy works on Sunday, and he and two men steal pecans. 79-18.
"Strike and Fade." First person. In Ark of Bones and Other Stories, Dumas.
　　Young blacks have confrontations with policemen during riots. 70-46.
"Thalia." First person. In The Black Scholar 6(9) June 1975.
　　A man loves Thalia, and he tells her so in a long monologue. 75-32.
"Thrust Counter Thrust." Third person. In Rope of Wind, Dumas.
　　A young man tries to cope with losing an eye. 79-19.
"The University of Man." Third person. In Rope of Wind, Dumas.
　　A watchmaker goes off in search of an education. He finds a man digging a canal who has interseting ideas about education. 79-20.
"The Voice." First person. In Rope of Wind, Dumas.
　　A group of singers tries to cope with the death of a popular and talented member of the group. 79-21.
"Will the Circle Be Unbroken." Third person. In Negro Digest 16(1), November 1966; Ark of Bones and Other Stories, Dumas.
　　Three white people insist upon entering a club for blacks only. It is rumored that the music played in the club is fatal to whites. 66-35.

Duncan, Pearl. (2)
　　"Contact." Third person. In Essence, 6(12), April 1976.
　　A woman - who is a travel agent visiting Jamaica - decides to pick up a man at a bar and to go to his room

with him. 76-6.
"Rendezvous with G. T." First person. In <u>Essence</u> 5(12),
April 1975.
A black American woman is physically attracted to a
Jamaican man. She is frustrated because they view life
very differently. 75-24.
"Still Waters." First person. In <u>Essence</u> 8(5), 1977.
A woman - who is a photographer - goes to a Carribean
island and becomes involved with a married man. 77-48.

Dunham, Katherine. (1912-   ) (2) (3) (5)
"Afternoon into Night." Third person. In <u>The Best Short
Stories by Negro Writers</u>, L. Hughes, ed.
A bullfighter reacts to the death of his mentor; the
mentor is also a close friend. 67-1.
"Audrey." First person. In <u>Phylon</u> 15(2), Second Quarter,
1954.
The friendship between a black girl and a white girl is
affected when the white girl's aunt from Florida
visits. 54-1.

Echewa, T. Obinkaram.
"Inertia." Third person. In <u>Essence</u> 6(9), January 1976.
The values of a school teacher clash with her husband's
values. He is part owner of a service station. 76-14.
"The Return of Tarkwa." Third person. In <u>Essence</u> 7(6),
October 1976.
A black American woman hopes for the return of an
African she has loved thirty years earlier. One day she
sees an African who reminds her of her lost love. 76-25.

Edwards, Junius. (1929-   ) (2) (3) (4) (5)
"Duel with the Clock." Third person. In <u>The Best Short
Stories by Negro Writers</u>, L. Hughes, ed.
A soldier - who is a drug addict - reacts to the death
of a friend from a drug overdose. 67-14.
"Liars Don't Qualify." Third person. In <u>Urbanite</u> 1(4),
June 1961; <u>Black Short Story Anthology</u>, <u>W</u>. King, Jr., ed.
A black man tries to register to vote in a southern
town where there is resistance to blacks registering to
vote. 61-8.
"Mother Dear and Daddy." First person. In <u>The Angry Black</u>,
J. A. Williams, ed; <u>Beyond the Angry Black</u>, J. A. Wil-
liams, ed.; <u>Brothers and Sisters</u>, A. Adoff, ed.; <u>Out of
Our Lives</u>, Q. P. Stadler, ed.
The parents of five children are killed in an accident.
The maternal relatives will take the three light skin-
ned girls, but they do not want the two dark skinned
boys. 62-13.

Ellison, Ralph. (1914-   ) (2) (3) (4) (5)
"A Coupla Scalped Indians." First person. In <u>New World
Writing</u>, March 1956; <u>Black Literature in America</u>, H. Baker,
ed; <u>Black Short Story Anthology</u>, W. King, Jr., ed.
Two boys have been playing Indian scout in the woods
and are on their way to a carnival. Then one of them

has a strange encounter with a woman who is a spiritua-
list and a healer. 56-2.
"Out of the Hospital and Under the Bar." First person. In
Soon One Morning, H. Hill, ed.
  This is a chase and escape story based on material
  edited out of Ellison's novel Invisible Man. 61-13.

Esslinger, Pat M.
  "Desire Is a Bus." First person. In Phylon 27(3), Third
Quarter, 1967.
  A man with African ancestry - who can sometimes pass
  for white - tries to deal with sometimes being perceiv-
  ed as white. 67-13.

Evans, Don. (1935-   ) (2) (5)
  "Love Song on South Street." Third person. In Essence
4(7), November 1973.
  A woman loves a married man. He comes to her from time
  to time, and she always "welcomes" him. 73-22.
  "Youngblood." Third person. In Essence 6(3), July 1975.
  Two youths - with limited sexual experience - brag
  about having considerable sexual experience. They
  double date two girls who are willing to have sexual
  relations. 75-37.

Evans, Henry L.
  "The Coat of Alms." Third person. In Essence, 12(8),
December 1981.
  A boy's parents are divorced; he does not know his
  father well. He goes to visit his father one day, and
  his father buys him a coat. 81-5.

Evans, Mari. (1923-   ) (1) (2) (3) (5)
  "The Third Step in Caraway Park." Third person. In Black
World 24(5), March 1975.
  Whites "program" a black college dropout to murder a
  black leader. 75-34.

Fair, Ronald. (1932-   ) (2) (3) (4) (5)
  "Just a Little More Glass." First person. In Essence 2(3),
July 1971.
  A boy describes his mother's compulsive buying habits
  and her constantly growing collection of wine and
  brandy decanters and glasses. 71-23.
  "Life with Red Top." First person. In Negro Digest 14(9),
July 1965; Black Fire, L. Jones (A. Baraka) and L. Neal,
eds.
  This is the story of the day to day lives of two black
  social rejects. 65-17.
  "Miss Luhester Gives a Party." First person. In The Best
Short Stories by Negro Writers, L. Hughes, ed.
  A very interesting woman throws a wild party. 67-33.

Feelings, Muriel L. (1938-   )
  "Zamani Goes to Market." Third person. In Liberator 10(3),
March 1970.

This is a story of an African boy and his family. 70-60.

Fields, Julia. (1938-   ) (1) (2) (3) (5)
"The Equalizer Supreme." Third person. In Negro Digest
16(10), August 1967.
        A young black woman - who lives in the South - reacts
        to sexual advances from a white optometrist. 67-16.
"The Hypochondriac." Third person. In Negro Digest 17(9),
July 1968.
        An old man - who constantly complains about various
        ailments - becomes seriously ill. 68-17.
"No Great Honor." Third person. In Black World 19(8), June
1970.
        A boy quits school and joins a band of thieves. 70-32.
"Not Your Singing Dancing Spade." Third person. In Negro
Digest 16(4), February 1967; Black Fire, L. Jones (A.
Baraka) and L. Neal, eds.; Black Short Story Anthology,
W. King, Jr., ed.
        A black maid - who works for a black entertainer - has
        an impact on the entertainer. 67-41.
"The Plot To Bring Back Dunking." In Black World 22(10),
August 1973.
        A boy reacts to his parents' separation. 73-27.
"Ten to Seven." Third person. In Negro Digest 15(9), July
1966.
        A man decides to leave his wife of twenty-five years.
        66-29.

Flannery, John S.
"Bottle of Ship." First person. In Negro Digest 13(9),
July 1964.
        A black boy and a white boy are friends. They are
        working to buy a gift for the white boy's brother, but
        they discover that he does not deserve the gift. 64-4.

Fox, Paula.
"Lord Randal." First person. In Negro Digest 14(9), July
1965.
        A mother has a lot of thoughts as she goes to a scene
        of tragedy involving her son. 65-18.

Franklin, J. E. (1937-   ) (2) (3) (5)
"The Enemy." First person. In Black Short Story Anthology,
W. King, Jr. ed.
        A little girl reacts to another little girl's "outcast"
        status. 72-11.

Freeman, Lorraine. (3) (5)
"The Harlem Teacher." In Harlem, J. H. Clarke, ed. 70-22.

Fuller, Charles H., Jr. (1939-   ) (2) (3) (5)
"A Love Song for Seven Little Boys Called Sam." Third
person. In Liberator 6(1), January 1966; Black Fire, L.
Jones (A. Baraka) and L. Neal eds.; Brothers and Sisters,
A. Adoff, ed.
        The seven black boys in a desegregated school have to

fight white boys each day. The lone black teacher will
not help them. 66-18.
"A Love Song for Wing." Third person. In Black Short Story
Anthology, W. King, Jr., ed.
    A fourteen year old boy falls in love with a twelve
year old girl; he names her wing. 72-28.

Fuller, Hoyt W. 1927-1981) (2) (3) (4)
"The Apostle." Third person. In Beyond the Angry Black,
J. A. Williams, ed.
    A white advertising executive seeks the endorsement of
a black religious leader for one of his accounts. 66-3.
"The Senegalese." First person. In American Negro Short
Stories, J. H. Clarke, ed.
    A black American, travelling in Africa, meets a very
interesting native of Senegal. 66-25.

Gaines, Ernest J. (1935-   ) (2) (3) (4) (5)
"Bloodline." First person. In Bloodline, Gaines.
    The interracial son of a white plantation owner and a
black woman who was - of course - born out of wedlock -
has a confrontation with his white uncle - his father's
brother. The uncle has inherited the plantation when
the interracial youth's father died. 63-5.
"Just Like a Tree." First person. In Bloodline, Gaines,
Cavalcade, A. P. Davis and S. Redding, eds.; Black Short
Story Anthology, W. King, Jr., ed.
    This story gives several first person perspectives on
the plight of an old woman - who is being taken from
her life-long home in the South to the North in the
wake of a bombing. 63-15.
"A Long Day in November." First person. In The Texas
Quarterly; The Best Short Stories by Negro Writers, L.
Hughes, ed.; Bloodline, Gaines.
    This story gives a little boy's view of his parents
break-up and reconciliation. 64-19.
"The Sky Is Gray." First person. In Bloodline, Gaines;
Afro-American Writing II, R. Long and E. Collier, eds.;
Black Writers of America, R. K.Barksdale and K. Kinnamon,
eds.; Brothers and Sisters, A. Adoff; Dark Symphony, J. A.
Emanuel and T. Gross, eds.; Negro Digest 12(10), August
1963; Tales and Stories for Black Folks, T. C. Bambara, ed.
    This is a view of people and life in rural Louisiana
seen through the eyes of a little boy with a toothache.
63-27.
"Three Men." First person. In Bloodline, Gaines; New Black
Voices, A. Chapman, ed.; Out of Our Lives, O. P. Stadler,ed.
    A young black man - who is in jail for a homicide -
tries to cope with a jailer - who is a sadistic bigot -
a homosexual, and an older man who represents what the
young man might become. 63-5.

Gant, Lizabeth A. (1933-   ) (2) (3) (5)
"Etta's Mind." Third person. In What We Must See, O.
Coombs, ed.
    This story is an ironic commentary on a black woman

involved in the women's movement for liberation. 71-10.
"You've Come a Long Way Baby." Third person. In <u>We Be Word
Sorcerers</u>, S. Sanchez, ed.
  After her husband's arrest a black woman becomes inter-
  ested in his role in the civil rights movement. 73-46.

Gaskin, Jonee.
  "Widow Woman." Third person. In <u>Essence</u> 12(4), August 1981.
  A young woman tells an old woman her troubles. 81-29.

Giovanni, Nikki. (1943-   ) (1) (2) (3) (5)
  "The Library." First person. In <u>Brothers and Sisters</u>, A.
  Adoff, ed.
    A little girl - who wants to learn about black people -
    is shown a secret room in a library; the room contains
    the "Great Black Book." 70-27.
  "A Revolutionary Tale." First person. In <u>Black World</u> 17(8),
  June 1968; <u>Black Short Story Anthology</u>, W. King, Jr., ed.
    This story pokes fun at a black "revolutionary," be-
    cause the revolutionary is more rhetorical than sub-
    stantive. 68-29.

Gladden, Frank A. (2) (5)
  "Maude." Third person. In <u>Black World</u> 21(8), June 1972.
    A black woman resists efforts of the highway department
    to condemn and purchase her home. 72-29.

Gores, Joe.
  "John Henry on the Mountain." Third person. In <u>Negro
  Digest</u> 10(10), August 1961.
    This story retells the legend of John Henry - the steel
    driving man. 61-7.
  "The Mob." Third person. In <u>Negro Digest</u> 11(2), December
  1961.
    A newspaper editor - who has defended a lynch mob -
    becomes the suspect in a rape and a murder. A lynch mob
    comes for him. 61-11.
  "The One Upstairs." First person. In <u>Negro Digest</u> 12(6),
  April 1963.
    A white man - who thinks he is "liberal" reacts to an
    interracial marriage in which the woman is white. 63-20.

Goss, Clay. (1946-   ) (3) (5)
  "NUT-BROWN: A Soul Psalm." First person. In <u>Liberator</u> 10
  (7), July 1970.
    A black man tries to relate to two women - one on a
    platonic level - and the other on a romantic level.
    70-33.

Gray, Alfred. (1933-   ) (5)
  "Any Other Reason." Third person. In <u>Liberator</u> 5(4), April
  1965.
    A man lives in Harlem with his wife and son. The hus-
    band wants to move, but the wife does not. Her reasons
    for wanting to stay where they are seem invalid to him.
    65-1.

Gray, Darrell. (1933-   ) (5)
"A Harsh Greeting." First person. In A Galaxy of Black
Writing, M. B. Shuman, ed.; Out of Our Lives, Q. P.
Stadler, ed.
     The narrator recalls his first experience with racial
     discrimination. 70-24.

Greene, Burkes G.
"Miriam." Third person. In Essence 9(6), October 1978.
     A woman - who has had a life filled with trying exper-
     iences - meets a sailor and falls in love with him.
     78-15.

Greenfield, Eloise. (1929-   ) (2) (5)
"Dream Panopy." Third person. In Negro Digest 19(3),
January 1970.
     A poor girl fantasizes about a concert and the lead
     singer. The girl's mother is a widow; her sister is
     pregnant with her second out-of-wedlock child. 70-13.
"Intrusion." Third person. In Black World 21(8), June 1972.
     A woman is unable to cope with her husband's illness.
     72-22.
"Karen's Spring." Third person. In Negro Digest 15(3),
January 1966.
     A black woman - who is pregnant - becomes depressed and
     envious of her white friend, who is also pregnant.
     66-16.
"Noblesse Oblige." Third person. In Negro Digest 15(9),
July 1966.
     This is a story about a white woman's hypocritical
     charity and her infidelity. 66-23.
"Not Any More." Third person. In Negro Digest 18(4),
February 1969.
     A young girl learns what "nigger" means by witnessing a
     fight and a shooting. 69-24.
"A Tooth for an Eye." Third person. In Black World 19(9),
July 1970.
     After he writes a letter to the President of the United
     States, a mailman is subjected to surveillance. 70-51.
"Way To Go Home." Third person. In Black World 23(7), May
1974.
     A large black woman tries to cope with her fear of a
     second marriage and with living in a black world and
     working in a white world. 74-16.

Greenlee, Sam. (1930-   ) (2) (3) (4) (5)
"Autumn Leaves." Third person. In Negro Digest 16(3),
January 1967.
     A freshman - who is a football player - tries to adjust
     to the college environment. 67-6.
"Blues for Little Prez." First person. In Black World
12(10), August 1973.
     A boy's inability to emulate Lester Young (Prez) leads
     to the boy's drug addiction. 73-2.
"The Sign." First person. In Negro Digest 15(4), February
1966.

Two soldiers – one black the other white – react to the
segregation which exists in Georgia where they are
stationed. 66-27.
"Sonny' Not Blue." Third person. In Black Short Story
Anthology, W. King, Jr., ed.
A little boy – living in the ghetto – dreams about
becoming a professional basketball player. 72-40.
"Sonny's Seasons." First person. In Black World 19(12),
October 1970; We Be Word Sorcerers, S. Sanchez.
A young boy in Chicago learns about gangs and the gangs'
territories. 70-44.
"Summer Sunday." First person. In Negro Digest 15(11),
September 1966.
A man reacts to the marriage of the woman he loves to
someone else. 66-28.
"Yes We Can Sing." Third person. In Negro Digest 15(2),
December 1965.
A Boy Scout encounters racial attitudes in summer camp.
65-33.

Guardine, Leonard J.
"Never Show Your Feelings, Boy." First person. In Black
World 23(8), June 1974.
A boy discusses his experiences with and attitudes
towards his grandfather/father. The boy's mother and
her father have had an incestuous relationship so that
his grandfather is also his father. 74-11.

Hairston, Loyle. (1926-   ) (2) (3) (5)
"Harlem on the Rocks." First person. In Freedomways 9(2),
Spring 1969; Harlem, J. H. Clarke, ed.
A black militant has a humorous dream. 69-14.
"The Winds of Change." First person. In American Negro
Short Stories, J. H. Clarke, ed.; Harlem USA, J. H.
Clarke, ed.
An aspiring Afro-American musician begins to question
his values and his lifestyle – after he meets an Afri-
can woman and observes Africans at the United Nations.
63-29.

Hamer, Martin J. (1931-   ) (2) (3) (5)
"The Mountain." First person. In Negro Digest 11(8),
June 1962.
A black boy wants his mother to buy him a blue suit for
his graduation from high school. His white principal is
requiring that boys attend the graduation ceremony
in blue suits. 62-14.
"Sarah." Third person. In The Atlantic Monthly; Out of Our
Lives, Q. P. Stadley, ed.; American Negro Short Stories,
J. H. Clarke, ed.
A young woman – who is trying to establish a relation-
ship with a man – invites the man to her apartment for
Thanksgiving dinner. He is surprised to discover that
she has also invited her family. 64-27.

Hamilton, Bobb. (1928-   ) (1) (2) (3) (5)

"Blackberry Pit." First person. In <u>Negro Digest</u> 14(5),
March 1965.
   Tragedy strikes two boys who are picking blackberries
   at an abandoned mine. 65-2.

Hampton, John. (With Bill Mahoney.)
   "A Story for Claustrophobiacs." 67-55.
   See Bill Mahoney.

Hankins, Paula. (2) (3) (5)
   "Testimonial." First person. In <u>Black Short Story Antho-
   logy</u>, W. King, Jr., ed.
      This is a eulogy for a black "militant." 72-44.

Hansen, Joyce.
   "Gift Exchange." First person. In <u>Essence</u> 11(7), November
   1980.
      A woman has an affair with her best friend's husband.
      80-7.

Harris, Peter.
   "Firmly Though Softly." Third person. In <u>Essence</u> 10(2),
   June 1979.
      A young woman learns why a man she met at a conference
      did not seek a greater degree of intimacy. 79-6.

Harrison, Delores. (1938-   ) (2) (3)
   "Clarissa's Problem." First person. In <u>Essence</u> 8(6),
   October 1977.
      A woman - who has problems of her own - writes about a
      friend who has mental problems. 77-10.
   "A Friend for a Season." First person. In <u>Redbook</u> 133(4),
   August 1969; <u>Out of Our Lives</u>, Q. P. Stadler, ed.
      A girl tries to cope with the strained relations bet-
      ween her parents, and she tries to talk about her
      problems with her best girlfriend. 69-13.
   "Going Home." First person. In <u>Redbook</u> 146(2), December
   1975.
      A little girl and her mother - who live in New York
      City - go to Virginia where the mother was reared and
      where the mother's parents and sister are buried. 75-10.

Hart, Newell.
   "Direct Action." Third person. In <u>Negro Digest</u> 13(11),
   September 1964.
      A young white woman - who writes papers on race rela-
      tions - decides to date a young black man. 64-10.

Hawkins, Odie. (1937-   )
   "Ralph's Story." Third person. In <u>Essence</u> 6(10), February
   1976.
      A train driver is attracted to one of his regular
      passengers. But when he is transferred to another
      shift, he has to make other arrangements to see her.
      76-33.

Heard, Nathan C. (1936-   ) (2) (3) (4) (5)
    "Boodie the Player." First person. In <u>We Be Word Sorcer-
    ers</u>, S. Sanchez, ed.
        A young pimp - who is in reform school - writes a
        letter explaining why he was convicted of killing a
        prostitute. 73-3.

Hemsley, Howard.
    "Stuff." First person. In <u>Black World</u> 19(8), June 1970.
        This story reveals the thoughts of a confidence man as
        he bilks a bank of money. 70-47.

Henderson, George. (1942-   ) (1) (2) (5)
    "Taking Grits for Granted." Third person. In <u>Black World</u>
    20(3), January 1971.
        A Korean War soldier cannot remember how his favorite
        breakfast food smells. 71-50.

Henderson, Stephen. (1925-   ) (5)
    "The Magic Word." First person. In <u>Negro Digest</u> 18(8),
    June 1969; <u>The Afro-American Short Story</u>, J. C. Elam, ed.
        The narrator is in the hospital after having been beat-
        en and having one testicle taken out. He talks about a
        professor who looked white and claimed to be black.
        This profesor died after being castrated. 69-21.

Hernton, Calvin C. (1932-   ) (2) (3) (4) (5)
    "Never Alone in the World." Third person. In <u>Freedomways</u>
    3(2), Spring, 1963.
        A fourteen year old girl tries to desegregate a segre-
        gated high school. 63-19.

Herve, Julia Wright. (2) (5)
    "The Forget-for-Peace Program." Third person. In <u>Black
    World</u> 22(7), May 1973.
        A little green pill is devised to tranquilize the
        masses of people. 73-13.

Higgs, E. Van. (2)
    "Sketch in Blue." First person. In <u>Negro Digest</u> 19(5),
    March 1970.
        A young boy speaks - in dialect - about his friends and
        their behavior. 70-42.

Hobbes, Dwight.
    "One Going, One Staying." Third person. In <u>Essence</u> 10(9),
    January 1980.
        A woman wants a man to make a stronger commitment to
        their relationship than he is willing to make. 80-17.

Hodges, Frenchy. (1940-   )
    "Requiem for Willie Lee." First person. In <u>Ms</u>, October
    1979; <u>Midnight Birds</u>, M. H. Washington, ed.
        This is a story of an attempted robbery. 79-16.

Holland, Mignon K. (Mignon Holland Anderson.)

"November." 71-35.
    See Mignon Holland Anderson.

Holmes, R. Ernest. (1943-   ) (2) (3) (5)
    "Cheesy Baby!" Third person. In Liberator 8(4), April
    1968; What We Must See, O. Coombs, ed.
        The interracial son of a black American woman and an
        Italian father has problems relating to the gang of
        black youths to which he wants to belong. 68-4.

Holred, F. Guy.
    "The Confessions of George Washington." First person. In
    Negro Digest 18(9), July 1968.
        The "father" of his country is attracted to a slave
        woman. 68-6.

Holt, Len.
    "The Bug Feeder." Third person. In Liberator 5(3), March
    1965.
        This is the story of a hypocritical minister - who is a
        civil rights leader - the minister's special assistant,
        and a poor white man with low self-esteem. 65-4.

Howard, Vanessa. (1955-   ) (2) (5)
    "Let Me Hang Loose." First person. In Tales and Stories
    for Black Folks, T. C. Bambara, ed. 70-26.

Hudson, Frederick B.
    "The Peach Tree." Third person. In Freedomways 22(2),
    Second Quarter, 1982.
        A black man and his sons work for a white man at his
        plant. When the plant is closed, some of the workers
        picket it. The plant owner also owns a peach orchard,
        and the black man and his sons pick peaches rather
        than picket the plant. 82-8.

Hudson, William. (2)
    "A Credit to the Race." First person. In Black World
    24(3), January 1975.
        A black man talks about his menial job in a swank men's
        store. 75-6.

Hughes, Langston. (1902-1967) (2) (3) (4) (5)
    "African Morning." Third person. In Laughing To Keep From
    Crying, Hughes; Brothers and Sisters, A. Adoff, ed.;
    Something in Common, Hughes.
        A twelve year old interracial child lives with his
        white British father after the death of his black
        African mother. 52-1.
    "Big Meeting." First person. In Laughing To Keep From
    Crying, Hughes; Something in Common, Hughes.
        Two black boys and some white spectators watch a black
        revival meeting being held in a tent. 52-2.
    "Early Autumn." Third person. In Something in Common,
    Hughes.
        Two former lovers meet after many years of not having

seen each other.
"Heaven to Hell." First person. In <u>Laughing To Keep from Crying</u>, Hughes; <u>Something in Common</u>, Hughes.

A woman and her husband have been in an automobile accident. At the hospital the woman reacts to the presence of another woman whom she views as a rival for her husband's affections. 52-6.

"Little Old Spy." First person. In <u>Laughing To Keep from Crying</u>, Hughes; <u>Something in Common</u>, Hughes.

A black American tells of being followed by a government spy in Cuba and of later becoming friendly with the spy. 52-7.

"Mysterious Madame Shanghai." First person. In <u>Laughing To Keep from Crying</u>, Hughes; <u>Something in Common</u>, Hughes.

An aloof boarder, called Madame Shanghai by the other boarders because of her Chinese kimono, has a very interesting past. Her past is revealed when her husband whom she has not seen in a long time, comes to kill her. 52-8.

"Name in the Papers." First person. In <u>Laughing To Keep from Crying</u>, Hughes.

A man gets his name in the papers for being involved in a love triangle. 52-9.

"Never Room with a Couple." First person. In <u>Laughing To Keep from Crying</u>, Hughes; <u>Something in Common</u>, Hughes.

A Love triangle develops when a man boards with a friend and falls in love with the friend's wife. 52-10.

"On the Road." Third person. In <u>Laughing To Keep from Crying</u>, Hughes, <u>Something in Common</u>, Hughes.

During the Great Depression, a poor black man is jailed for trying to break into a church. 52-11.

"On the Way Home." Third person. In <u>Laughing To Keep from Crying</u>, Hughes; <u>The Langston Hughes Reader</u>, Hughes; <u>Something in Common</u>, Hughes.

A man learns of and reacts to his mother's illness and later to her death. 52-12.

"One Friday Morning." Third person. In <u>Laughing To Keep from Crying</u>, Hughes; <u>The Langston Hughes Reader</u>, Hughes.

A black girl looks forward to the Friday morning high school assembly - when it is to be announced that she has won the Artist Club's high school competition. But she is unaware of the Club's bigotry. 52-13.

"Powder-White Faces." Third person. In <u>Laughing To Keep from Crying</u>, Hughes; <u>Something in Common</u>, Hughes.

This is the story of a murder and the causes of the murder. 52-14.

"Professor." Third person. In <u>Laughing To Keep from Crying</u>, Hughes; <u>Something in Common</u>, Hughes; <u>Modern Black Short Stories</u>, M. Mirer, ed.

A black sociology professor compromises his principles to advance his personal ambitions and to promote the financial status of the black southern college where he teaches. 52-15.

"Pushcart Man." Third person. In <u>Laughing To Keep from Crying</u>, Hughes; <u>Something in Common</u>, Hughes.

A number of things happen in the vicinity of a pushcart

vendor in Harlem on a Saturday night. 52-16.
"Rock Church." Third person. In Something in Common,
Hughes; Soon One Morning, H. Hill, ed.
    This is a humorous story about how an ambitious minis-
    ter's scheme to stage a fraudulent crucifiction of
    himself goes awry. 63-23.
"Rouge High." Third person. In Laughing To Keep from
Crying,, Hughes; Something in Common, Hughes.
    This story provides a glimpse at a prostitute and a
    pimp. 52-17.
"Sailor Ashore." Third person. In Laughing To Keep from
Crying, Hughes; Something in Common, Hughes.
    A sailor - disturbed about racial discrimination -
    meets a prostitute at a bar and goes home with her.
    52-19.
"Saratoga Rain." Third person. In Laughing To Keep from
Crying, Hughes; Something in Common, Hughes.
    Two lovers escape from a sordid life for a brief per-
    iod. 52-20.
"Slice Him Down." Third person. In Laughing To Keep from
Crying, Hughes; Something in Common, Hughes.
    Two friends get into a fight over women at a club in
    Reno, Nevada. 52-21.
"Something in Common." Third person. In Laughing To Keep
from Crying, Hughes; The Langston Hughes Reader, Hughes;
Something in Common, Hughes.
    An old black man and an old white man discover that
    they have something in common when they meet in a bar
    in Hong Kong. 52-22.
"Sorrow for a Midget." First person. In Literature Review;
Negro Digest 10(12), October 1961.
    A hospital employee befriends a dying midget and loca-
    tes her "son" for her. 61-15.
"Spanish Blood." Third person. In Laughing To Keep from
Crying, Hughes; The Langston Hughes Reader, Hughes; Some-
thing in Common, Hughes.
    This is a story about the escapades of the son of a
    black American woman and a white Puerto Rican sailor.
    52-23.
"Tain't So." First person. In Laughing To Keep from Cry-
ing, Hughes; The Langston Hughes Reader, Hughes; Something
in Common, Hughes.
    A white woman - who is a prejudiced hypochondriac -
    goes to a black healer. 52-24.
"Thank You M'am." Third person. In The Langston Hughes
Reader, Hughes; The Best Short Stories by Negro Writers,
Hughes, ed.; Black American Literature: Fiction, D. T.
Turner, ed.; Something in Common, Hughes; Tales and Stor-
ies for Black Folks, T. C. Bambara, ed.
    A young boy attempts to snatch a hefty woman's purse.
    She shakes him until his teeth rattle, and she takes
    him home where they learn something about each other.
    58-3.
"Tragedy at the Baths." First person. In Laughing To Keep
from Crying, Hughes; The Langston Hughes Reader, Hughes;
Something in Common, Hughes.

A love triangle leads to a suicide at a bath house in Mexico City. 52-26.

"Trouble with the Angels." First person. In Laughing To Keep from Crying, Hughes; Something in Common, Hughes.

A black actor attempts to get the other blacks in a play to protest the fact that blacks are not allowed to see the play in some places. 52-27.

"Who's Passing for Who?" First person. In Laughing To Keep from Crying, Hughes; Cavalcade, A. P. Davis and S. Redding, eds.; The Langston Hughes Reader, Hughes; Something in Common, Hughes.

A couple convinces some blacks that they are blacks passing for white. After the blacks believe them and they spend some time together, the couple change their story and say they are white after all. The narrator is confused at the end of the story. 52-28.

"Why You Reckon?" First person. In Laughing To Keep from Crying, Hughes; Something in Common, Hughes.

A black man helps a black stranger rob a white stranger. 52-30.

Hunter, Charles.
"Nefertiti." First person. In Liberator 10(1), January 1970.
The narrator kills a policeman; the policeman is beating the narrator's friend. 70-30.

Hunter, Kristin. (1931-   ) (2) (3) (4) (5)
"Debut." Third person. In Negro Digest 17(8), June 1968; Black American Literature: Fiction, D. T. Turner, ed.
A girl is getting ready for a ball at which she will make her debut. 68-7.

"Honor among Thieves." Third person. In Essence 1(12), April 1971.
The actions of a black man - who shines shoes - causes a black woman to gain enough courage to try something new. 71-17.

"How I Got into the Grocery Business." First person. In Black World 21(8), June 1972.
In this two part story - blacks begin to operate a business, and a black man and a German immigrant family have conflicts. 72-19.

"An Interesting Social Study." Third person. In The Best Short Stories by Negro Writers, L. Hughes, ed.
A young woman who is the newest resident of Cape May, New Jersey, visits the home of a long time resident of the town. 67-24.

Hunter, M. Joe.
"A Gift for Mama." First person. In Essence 3(7) December 1972.
A boy lies to help his mother defend her honor. Her honor is threatened by the boy's father who deserted the family eleven years earlier. 72-15.

Ingram, Alyce.
"A Little Ordinary." Third person. In Negro Digest 11(9), July 1962.
A white woman has trouble finding a suitable black maid. 62-11.

Jackson, Franklin. (1940-   ) (2) (5)
"Claudia." Third person. In Black Review Number 1, M. Watkins, ed.
A young black woman living alone in Harlem reflects on past frustrations and prepares for a party. 72-9.

Jackson, Mae. (1946-   ) (1) (2) (3) (5)
  "Cleaning out the Closet." First person. In The Black Scholar 8(5),
  March 1977.
      The narrator observes a woman react to having her love for a
      prisoner frustrated after having lost a previous love to war.
      77-11.
  "I Could Rest Forever." Third person. In Essence 8(12), April 1978.
      A black American woman goes to Africa and has sex with an Afri-
      can on their first meeting. 78-9.
  "I Remember Omar." First person. In Negro Digest 18(8), June 1969.
      This story is a humorous description of a black "revolutionary."
      69-16.
  "These Ain't All My Tears." Third person. In Essence 11(6), October
  1980.
      A woman - in an emotionless marriage - commits adultery, is divor-
      ced loses custody of her children, and has a nervous breakdown.
      80-24.
  "Who's Gonna Tell Wilma?" Third person. In Essence 10(5), September
  1979.
      A woman finds love in her second marriage. 79-22.

Jackson, Norlishia.
  "Bless the Dead." First person. In Essence 8(8), December 1977.
      The narrator talks of trying to get dead people to help her to
      win the Maryland lottery. 77-7.

Jacobs, Marjorie K.
  "Sins of the Fathers." Third person. In Phylon 29(2), Second Quarter,
  1968.
      A little black girl and her mother live in the servants' quarters
      where the mother is the housekeeper for a white family. The little
      girl begins to learn about racial taboos. 68-30.

James, Alan. (Psuedonym for James Alan McPherson.)
  "Beyond Chicago Someone Sleeps." Third person. In Negro Digest 16(5),
  March 1967. 67-7.
      See James Alan McPherson, "On Trains."

James, Rosetta.
  "Giving Honor to God." Third person. In Essence 8(3), July 1977.
      Some scruffily dressed young white adults come to a black church.
      77-17.

Jefferson, Stebbins.
  "Aunt Melia's Visit: Memories from the 40s." First person. In Essence
  6(11), March 1976.
      Aunt Melia is the twin sister of the narrator's mother. She is
      given to interesting antics; she is also willing to have confron-
      tations with white people. 76-4.

Joans, Ted. (1928-   ) (1) (2) (3) (5)
  "A Few Fact Filled Fiction of African Reality." First person. In
  We Be Word Sorcerers, S. Sanchez, ed.
      The narrator discusses Casablanca - which he does not like - a
      horrible experience on a ship carrying migrant workers, and the
      nature of ships on which one can book passage from Casablanca.

73-10.

Johnson, Clifford Vincent. (1936-   ) (2) (4) (5)
"Old Blues Singers Never Die." In The Best Short Stories by Negro
Writers, L. Hughes, ed.
A black youth sees an old blues singer in Chicago. Later when the
youth is an American G. I., he meets the blues singer in Paris.
67-43.

Johnson, Doris. (2) (5)
"Somebody." "Second" person. In Negro Digest 17(1), November 1967.
A little black boy - who wants to be a pianist - is confronted
with a Ku Klux Klan attack. 67-51.

Johnson, James C.
"Just Another Saturday Night." First person. In Essence 11(9), January
1981.
This is a humorous story of a Saturday night on the town. 81-14.

de Joie, Norman.
"'On,' The Charm of Harry Jones." Third person. In Negro Digest
16(10), August 1967.
A black woman goes to Paris. She dates a Frenchman, even though
he is not very appealing to her. 67-44.

Jones, Edward P.
"Harvest." First person. In Essence 7(7), November 1976.
When she was a young girl living in Virginia the narrator's father
insisted that she have an abortion when she became pregnant. 76-13.

Jones, Edward S.
"Luck of the Mestizo." Third person. In Liberator 5(6), June 1965.
A mestizo in a Latin American country wins a lottery and is accus-
ed of robbery and murder. 65-19.

Jones, Gayl. (1949   ) (2) (3) (4) (5)
"Asylum." First person. In White Rat, Jones; Midnight
Birds, M. H. Washington, ed.
The narrator is being treated for abnormal behavior.
77-5.
"The Coke Factory." First person. In White Rat, Jones.
A retarded boy talks about his life. 77-12.
"Jevata" First person. In Essence 4(7), November 1973;
White Rat, Jones; Midnight Birds, M. H. Washington, ed.
This story is about a woman who is fifty - her eighteen
year old bisexual lover, her daughter, her son, and her
grandson. 73-21.
"Legend." Third person. In White Rat, Jones.
This is a brief account of the stories told about a
rape and a lynching. 77-27.
"Persona." First person. In White Rat, Jones.
The narrator speaks of her attractions to other women.
77-39.
"A Quiet Place for the Summer." Third person. In White
Rat, Jones.
A college student rents her professor's home for the

summer - so she can have a place to write and reflect.
77-41.
"The Return: A Fantasy." First person. In Amistad 2, John
A. Williams and Charles F. Harris, eds.; White Rat, Jones.
> A young woman tries to cope with her husband's emotion-
> al/mental/psychological problems. 71-41.
"The Roundhouse." First person. In Panache, R. B. White,
ed.; White Rat, Jones.
> A woman who works in a roundhouse - a shop where trains
> are serviced - meets a man who does not say much. When
> he gets sick, she cares for him. 77-43.
"A Sense of Security." First person. In Essence 4(4),
August 1973.
> A twenty-four year old woman meets a man who dated her
> mother ten years earlier. 73-34.
"Spaces." Third person. In The Black Scholar 6(9), June
1975.
> A man and a woman meet and have an interesting conver-
> sation. 75-28.
"Version 2." In White Rat, Jones.
> "Version 2" is a second version of "The Return: A
> Fantasy." The narrator is a young man with emotional/
> mental/psychological problems. 77-57.
"The Welfare Check." First person. In Essence 1(6), Octo-
ber 1970.
> A welfare office employee meets a welfare recipient.
> 70-58.
"White Rat." First person. In Giant Talk, Quincy Troup and
Rainer Schulte, eds.; White Rat, Jones.
> An Afro-American man looks as if he is white. His wife
> is Afro-American with very light skin. They have a son,
> and they have problems. 75-35.
"The Women." First person. In White Rat, Jones.
> The narrator talks about her mother's homosexual rela-
> tions and about her own early sexual experiences. 77-64.
"Your Poems Have Very Little Color in Them." First person.
In White Rat, Jones.
> This is a brief slice-of-life sketch. 77-65.

Jones, John H. (2) (5)
"The Harlem Rat." Third person. In Harlem USA, J. H.
Clarke, ed.
> A World War II veteran lives in a rat and roach infest-
> ed apartment with his wife and baby. His wife urges him
> to do something about their plight, and a rat bites the
> baby. 64-17.

Jones, Leroi. (Amiri Baraka.)
See Amiri Baraka.

Jones, Silas. (1942-   ) (2) (5)
"Roman Times." Third person. In Black World 21(3), January
1972.
> A little boy's father is a poor example of a man. The
> boy is afraid of being castrated. 72-36.
"The Way of Shadows." First person. In Black World 22(5),

March 1973.
    This is a story of black attitudes, a protest, and of
    policemen killing a black militant. 73-43.

Kalish, Richard A.
"The Democrat." First person. In <u>Negro Digest</u> 12(11),
September 1963.
    The narrator is a white man in the armed services who
    is upset because a Japanese woman he has dated now
    dates a black serviceman. 63-9.

Kelley, William Melvin. (1937-   ) (2) (3) (4) (5)
"Aggie." Third person. In <u>Dancers on the Shore</u>, Kelley.
    A woman - who is considering divorce - sees a lonely,
    single forty-five year old woman respond to a homosex-
    ual advance. 64-1.
"Brother Carlyle." Third person. In <u>Dancers on the Shore</u>,
Kelley.
    A mother worries about the relationship between her two
    sons; the father cannot see any problem. 64-5.
"Bumper's Dream." Third person. In Black World 19(12),
October 1970.
    A man makes the mistake of trying to get friendly with
    a gangster's daughter. 70-9.
"Christmas and the Great Man." Third person. In <u>Dancers on
the Shore</u>, Kelley.
    A college student goes to a classmate's home for Christ-
    mas dinner. He looks forward to talking to the class-
    mate's grandfather; the grandfather is a famous civil
    rights pioneer. 64-6.
"Connie." Third person. In <u>Dancers on the Shore</u>, Kelley.
    A young woman and her family react to her pregnancy
    and to her decision to keep the baby. 64-8.
"Cry for Me." First person. In <u>Dancers on the Shore</u>, Kel-
ley. <u>The Afro-American Short Story</u>, J. C. Elam, ed.; <u>Afro-
American Writing, II</u>, R. Long and E. Collier, eds.; <u>Ameri-
can Negro Short Stories</u>, J. H. Clarke, ed.; <u>Black Litera-
ture in America</u>, H. A. Baker, Jr., ed.; <u>Dark Symphony</u>, J.
A. Emanuel and T. Gross, eds.
    A young man tells the story of his uncle. The uncle
    sang captivating blues songs and he finally got the
    opportunity to sing in Carnegie Hall. 62-5.
"The Dentist's Wife." Third person. In <u>Playboy</u>; <u>Black
Writers of America</u>, R. K. Barksdale and K. Kinamon, eds.
    A dentist wants pictures of his wife in a compromising
    position, so he can get a divorce. 68-8.
"Enemy Territory." First person. In <u>Dancers on the Shore</u>,
Kelley.
    A six year old - who is frightened by the gang of six,
    seven, and eight year olds in the next block - learns
    about his grandfather's courage. 64-13.
"A Good Long Sidewalk." Third person. In <u>Dancers on the
Shore</u>, Kelley; <u>New Black Voices</u>, A. Chapman, ed.; <u>Harlem</u>,
J. H. Clarke, ed; <u>Negro Digest</u> 13(4), February 1964.
    A boy joins in barbershop chatter about interracial
    marriage. He later gets a job shovelling snow for a

lonely middle-aged white woman with a long sidewalk. 64-15.
"The Life You Save." Third person. In <u>Dancers on the Shore</u>, Kelley.
    A college student - who works with disturbed boys - has trouble relating to one of the boys. 64-18.
"The Most Beautiful Legs in the World." First person. In <u>Dancers on the Shore</u>, Kelley.
    The narrator is opposed to the engagement of his close friend and a woman - whose legs are the most beautiful he has ever seen - because the woman only has one arm. 64-22.
"Not exactly Lena Horne." In <u>Dancers on the Shore</u>, Kelley.
    Two retired widowers share a home on Long Island. One talks about his hobby of keeping a record of out of state license plates until the other becomes very upset. 64-23.
"The Only Man on Liberty Street." Third person. In <u>Negro Digest</u> 12(5), March 1963; <u>The Best Short Stories by Negro Writers</u>, L. Hughes, ed.; <u>Black American Literature: Fiction</u>, D. T. Turner, ed.; <u>Cavalcade</u>, A. P. Davis and S. Redding, eds.; <u>Dancers on the Shore</u>, Kelley, <u>On Being Black</u>, C. T. Davis and D. Walden.
    Only black and interracial women - who are the mistresses of white men - and their interracial children live on Liberty Street. When a white man moves to the street to live with his mistress and daughter, he generates considerable concern among the whites in the area. 62-16.
"The Poker Party." First person. In <u>Dancers on the Shore</u>, Kelley; <u>Black Short Story Anthology</u>, W. King, Jr.; ed.; <u>Brothers and Sisters</u>, A. Adoff, ed.
    A little boy gets to watch the Saturday night poker party held in the kitchen of his home. 64-25.
"Saint Paul and the Monkeys." Third person. In <u>The Saturday Evening Post</u> 236, April 13, 1963; <u>Dancers on the Shore</u>, Kelley.
    A man with very ambivalent feelings about his goals and plans, becomes engaged to a woman who wants her future clearly defined. 63-24.
"The Servant Problem." Third person. In <u>Dancers on the Shore</u>, Kelley; <u>Mademoiselle</u> 58(174), March 1964.
    This story is about a white couple, their child, and the couple's black maid. 64-28.
"A Visit to Grandmother." Third person. In <u>Dancers on the Shore</u>, Kelley.
    A successful man takes his son home to meet his family. 64-32.
"What Shall We Do with the Drunken Sailor." Third person. In <u>Dancers on the Shore</u>, Kelley.
    A drunken white sailor insults a black man when he wants the black man to direct him to a black prostitute. 64-34.

Kemp, Arnold. (1938-   ) (2) (3) (4) (5)
"The Blue of Madness." Third person. In <u>What We Must See</u>, O. Coombs, ed.
    This is the story of a man - on a ledge - contemplating suicide. A crowd gathers, and a priest - who has con-

verted from Judahism - comes to talk to the man. 71-4.

Kensey, Barbara L.
   "Talk O' the Town." First person. In Essence 6(11), March
   1977.
      A flirtatious young girl defies predictions that she
      will come to a bad end. 77-51.

Kent, George E. (1920-1982) (2) (3) (4) (5)
   "Intruder." First person. In Black World 23(3), January
   1974.
      The narrator is a little boy who tells about a "love
      triangle" involving himself, another little boy, and
      a little girl. 74-7.

Kilgore, James C. (1928-   ) (2) (5)
   "Cecil." Third person. In Essence 3(3), July 1972.
      A boy - who attends church and school regularly and who
      reads and writes poetry - becomes an "outcast." 72-8.

Killens, John Oliver. (1916-   ) (2) (3) (4) (5)
   "God Bless America." Third person. In American Negro Short
   Stories, J. H. Clarke, ed.; Black Literature in America,
   H. A. Baker, Jr., ed.
      A black soldier has to leave his pregnant wife and go
      to Korea. 52-5.
   "Rough Diamond." In Harlem, J. H. Clarke, ed. 70-40.
   "The Stick-Up." First person. In The Best Short Stories by
   Negro Writers, L. Hughes, ed.
      A white derelict tries to get a black man to give him
      four cents. 67-53.

King, Woodie, Jr. (1937-   ) (2) (3) (4) (5)
   "The Bag Man." First person. In Liberator 8(9), September
   1968.
      A heroin addict - who was once a heroin dealer - dies.
      68-3.
   "Beautiful Light and Black Our Dreams." Third person. In
   Negro Digest 12(8), June 1963; The Best Short Stories by
   Negro Writers, L. Hughes, ed.
      A man and a woman reflect on her decision to accept
      another man's proposal. 63-4.
   "Emancipation." First person. In The Black Scholar 6(9),
   June 1975.
      A white high school student propositions a black woman
      old enough to be his mother. 75-8.
   "The Game." First person. In Liberator 5(8), August 1965;
   Black Short Story Anthology, W. King, Jr., ed.
      A "hipster" talks about the champion of the "hipsters."
      65-8.
   "Listen to the Wind Blow." Third person. In Negro Digest
   17(8), June 1968; We Be Word Sorcerers, S. Sanchez, ed.
      A man comes to Mobile, Alabama from Detroit, Michigan
      to see his dying father. 68-20.

Knight, Etheridge. (1933-   ) (1) (2) (3) (5)

"My Father, My Bottom, My Fleas." First person. In Negro
Digest, 15(10), August 1966.
     This is a story about a youth's relationship with his
     father and about the place where they live. 66-19.
"On the Next Train South." Third person. In Negro Digest
16(8), June 1967.
     A man awaits a train bringing home the body of his
     brother; his brother has been executed. 67-45.
"Reaching Is His Rule." Third person. In Negro Digest
15(2), December 1965.
     A ten year old boy joins a civil rights demonstration.
     65-27.
"A Time To Mourn." Third person. In Black Voices from
Prison, Knight, ed.; New Black Voices, A. Chapman, ed.
     A prisoner reacts to the death of his uncle - his last
     living relative. 70-49.

La Guma, Alex.
     "Coffee for the Road." Third person. In Negro Digest
     12(12), October 1963.
          An Indian woman, driving through South Africa with two
          children, tries to buy coffee at a cafe that only
          whites are allowed to enter. 63-6.

Lauderdale, Beverly.
     "First Comes Touch." First person. In Essence 9(4), August
     1978.
          A mother talks about her daughter's abortion and about
          the mother's difficulty in relating to and communicat-
          ing with the daughter. 78-7.

Lawson, J. M.
     "Roll Call." Third person. In Essence 7(2), June 1976.
          A ten year old reacts to her eighty year old grandfa-
          ther's stroke and to his delusions. 76-27.

Lawson, Jennifer.
     "Early Morning Calls." First person. In Essence 7(4),
     August 1976.
          A former civil rights activist - who has become much
          less militant - learns that a former lover and friend -
          whom she thought was dead - is alive and working in an
          underground movement. 76-8.

Lee, Audrey. (2) (3) (4) (5)
     "Alienation." First person. In Black World 21(12), Novem-
     ber 1971.
          A black woman reflects on the rude treatment she exper-
          ienced while seeking a job in an office where all the
          employees are white. 71-2.
     "Antonio Is a Man." Third person. In Essence 2(9), January
     1972.
          This is a story about an independent, proud, strong
          black man and the cost of his independence, pride, and
          strength. 72-2.
     "The Block." Third person. In Black World 19(12), October

1970.
    This story tells of events that led to a riot. 70-6.
"Eulogy for a Public Servant." Third person. In Black
World 25(3), January 1976.
    A poor black man becomes affluent, and he feels very
    guilty about being affluent. 76-9.
"I'm Going To Move Out of This Emotional Ghetto." First
person. In Negro Digest 19(2), December 1969.
    A woman describes her frustrations as an emotional
    ghetto. 69-17.
"A Man Is a Man." Third person. In Essence 1(10), February
1971.
    A woman's husband is a restless wanderer. 71-28.
"Moma." First person. In Negro Digest 18(4), February 1969.
    A young woman talks about the noble efforts of her
    mother. 69-23.
"The Ride." Third person. In Essence 1(2), June 1970.
    Four children ride a subway train with their mother.
    They think she is asleep, but they are unable to awaken
    her. 70-39.
"To Love a Man." First person. In Essence 1(7), November
1970.
    A woman - who lives in a neighborhood that is being
    torn down - is attracted to her building superintendent.
    The people who do not want to move from the neighbor-
    hood blame the superintendent for their plight. 70-50.
"Waiting for Her Train." Third person. In What We Must
See, O. Coombs, ed.
    A homeless woman tries to survive with dignity. 71-52.

Lester, Julius. (1939-   ) (2) (3) (4) (5)
    "The Valley of the Shadow of Death." Third person. In
    Black Review Number 2, M. Watkins, ed.
        A man who has been a black activist has become involved
        with a white woman. His former lover - who is black -
        informs him of the death of his best friend. 72-46.

Lofton, C. A.
    "With Malice Aforethought." First person. In Black World
    19(8), June 1970.
        This story tells the thoughts of a dying woman. 70-59.

Lomax, S. P.
    "Pollution." Third person. In The Angry Black, J. A.
    Williams, ed.
        A black man believes his white associates are racists.
        62-18.

Lucas, W. Francis. (1927-   )
    "The Firing Squad and the Afterlife." Third person. In
    Liberator 7(9), September 1967.
        A man is condemned to death because he has love in his
        heart. 67-17.

McCluskey, John A. (1944-   )
    "Nairobi Nights." Third person. In Black World 22(3),

January 1973.
   A robbery attempt is made. 73-25.

McCluskey, John M. (2) (4)
   "The Pilgrims." First person. In What We Must See, Coombs,
   ed.
      A man - who is waiting to see if he will get a con-
      struction job for which he has applied - reflects on
      his life and loves. 71-37.

Mack, Donna.
   "If That Mockingbird Don't Sing." Third person. In Essence
   8(3), July 1977.
      A woman tries to cope with being deserted by her hus-
      band, being on welfare, being a single, working mother,
      the death of her son, and alienation from her daughter.
      77-21.

Mack, Tommy L.
   "End of a Rest." First person. In Negro Digest 11(4),
   February 1962.
      Some white youths attack some blacks picketing for
      civil rights, and a black medical social worker tries
      to decide what role he should play in the civil rights
      movement. 62-7.

McKissack, A. G.
   "Coming into Her Own." First person. In Essence 11(7),
   November 1980.
      A young black woman does very well when her opportunity
      comes.80-3.

McKnight, Nathaniel.
   "South from Nowhere." Third person. In Liberator 8(11),
   November 1968.
      A black man and a white woman are the only survivors of
      a plane crash. 68-32.

McMillan, Herman L. (3)
   "The Day Little Mose Spoke." First person. In Black World
   19(8), June 1970.
      A little boy tries to cope with his father's killing
      his mother, with living with his aunt and uncle - who
      are alcoholics - and with his aunt's insults. 70-11.

McPherson, James Alan. (1943-   ) (2) (3) (4) (5)
   "An Act of Prostitution." Third person. In Hue and Cry,
   McPherson.
      This is a story of courtroom incidents involving an
      eccentric judge, a black soldier charged with assault-
      ing a white police officer, a white prostitute - who is
      married to a black man - and the prostitute's unethical
      lawyer. 68-1.
   "All the Lonely People." First person. In Hue and Cry,
   McPherson.
      A man searches for his sexual identity and for the

proper kind of sexual identity. 68-2.
"Elbow Room." First person. In Elbow Room, McPherson.
   Both an editor and a narrator tell a story of an inter-
   racial marriage in this story; McPherson employs an
   experimental approach. 77-13.
"The Faithful." Third person. In Atlantic Monthly 231,
April 1973; Elbow Room, McPherson.
   A minister - who is also a barber - cannot or will not
   change with the times. 73-9.
"Gold Coast." First person. In Hue and Cry, McPherson;
Atlantic Monthly 222, November 1968; The Best American
Short Stories, 1973.
   A young black man - who says he is a writer gathering
   material - tells about his experiences as a janitor.
   68-13.
"Hue and Cry." Third person. In Hue and Cry, McPherson.
   A black woman first tries to have a loving relationship
   with a white man, then she tries to have a loving
   relationship with a black man. 68-15.
"I Am an American." First person. In Elbow Room, McPher-
son.
   A black tourist in London aids two Japanese students
   who have been robbed. 77-19.
"Just Enough for the City." First person. In Elbow Room,
McPherson.
   A man speaks philosophically about his experiences with
   missionaries from a number of religious groups. 77-23.
"A Loaf of Bread." Third person. In Elbow Room, McPherson.
   Black people in a black neighborhood demonstrate, when
   they discover that a white grocer charges more at his
   store in the black neighborhood than he charges at his
   stores in other neighborhoods. 77-28.
"A Matter of Vocabulary." Third person. In Hue and Cry,
McPherson; Atlantic Monthly 223, February 1969.
   A boy tries to understand religion, race relations, and
   the nature of the world. 68-22.
"A New Place." First person. In Hue and Cry, McPherson.
   Two men who share an apartment have a falling out.
   68-23.
"Of Cabbages and Kings." First person In Hue and Cry,
McPherson; Atlantic Monthly 223, April 1969.
   This story tells of the strange relationship between
   two black apartment mates - one of whom is an unortho-
   dox black nationalist. 68-24.
"On Trains." (Alan James, "Beyond Chicago Someone Sleeps.")
Third person. In Hue and Cry, McPherson; Afro-American
Literature: An Introduction, R. Hayden, D. J. Burrows, and
F. R. Lapides, eds.
   This is a story of interactions among some passengers
   on a train and some of the people who work on the
   train. 68-25.
"Private Domain." Third person. In Hue and Cry, McPherson.
   A middle class black man tries to relate to contempo-
   rary notions of black culture. 68-27.
"Problems of Art." Third person. In Elbow Room, McPherson.
   A white lawyer represents a black woman accused of

drunk driving. 70-40.
"A Sense of Story." Third person. In Elbow Room, McPherson.
   A black man is being tried for killing his white super-
   visor, and the trial takes an unusual turn. 73-34.
"The Silver Bullet." Third person. In Playboy; Elbow Room,
McPherson.
   Young black gang members and black militants get much
   more than they bargain for when they try to hold up a
   black owned bar. 77-46.
"A Solo Song for Doc." First person. In Hue and Cry,
McPherson; On Being Black, C. T. Davis and D. Walden, eds.
New Black Voices, A. Chapman, ed.
   An old school waiters' waiter - on a train dining car -
   talks about his experiences and about the tragedy of
   the king of the waiters' waiters. 68-31.
"The Story of a Dead Man." First person. In Elbow Room,
McPherson.
   The narrator talks about his nonconformist cousin.
   77-49.
"Story of a Scar." First person. In Atlantic Monthly 232,
December 1973; Elbow Room, McPherson.
   A man and a woman meet in a doctor's office. Her face
   is badly scarred, and she tells him how she got the
   scar. 73-38.
"Why I Like Country Music." First person. In Elbow Room,
McPherson.
   The narrator likes country music because it reminds him
   of the humorous events that led to his getting to dance
   with a little girl on whom he had a childhood crush.
   77-60.
"Widows and Orphans." Third person. In Elbow Room, McPherson.
   A man attends an awards ceremony for a woman he was
   once engaged to marry. 77-62.

Mahoney, Bill. (5) (With John Hampton.)
"A Story for Claustrophobiacs." First person. In Liberator
7(8), August 1967.
   An Afro-American soldier in Korea interacts with his
   Polish American sergeant. 67-55.

Major, Clarence. (1936-   ) (1) (2) (3) (4) (5)
"A Life Story." First person. In Essence 2(9), January
1972.
   A man relates his life's experiences to the woman he
   loves. 72-25.
"Marilyn." Third person. In The Black Scholar 10(1/2),
November/December 1978.
   This is a very brief sketch about a woman with a pro-
   blem. 78-14.
"Social Work." In The Black Scholar 6(9), June 1975.
   A man has a tonsilectomy. 75-27.
"Ten Pecan Pies." Third person. In Essence 4(7), November
1973.
   A demented, paralyzed, old man finally allows his wife
   to take the pecans she needs for ten pies from his

room. 73-40.

Manns, Adrienne.
"Monday Morning." Third person. In Essence 7(11), March
1977.
A woman with a husband, a son, and a daughter, and a
full time job tries to cope with the problems the
family and the job present. 77-32.

Marcus, Lorraine.
"Bridal Shower." Third person. In Essence 7(4), August
1976.
A young woman gives a bridal shower for her roommate,
and she reflects on the lives of the guests and her own
life. 76-6.

Marshall, Paule. (1929-   ) (2) (3) (4) (5)
"Barbados." ("Soul Clap Hands and Sing.") Third person. In
Soul Clap Hands and Sing, Marshall; The Best Short Stories
by Negro Writers, L. Hughes, ed.; Black Writers of Ameri-
ca, R. K. Barksdale and K. Kinamon, eds.; Reena and Other
Stories, Marshall.
After fifty years in the United States, a man returns
to Barbados relatively wealthy. He reluctantly hires a
servant girl, who shows him that much is lacking in his
life. 61-1.
"Brazil." Third person. In Soul Clap Hands and Sing,
Marshall; Dark Symphony, J. A. Emanuel and T. Gross, eds.
A nightclub comedian - who has a professional name -
has an identity crisis. 61-3.
"British Guiana." Third person. In Soul Clap Hands and
Sing, Marshall.
The first colored man to hold a high position in broad-
casting in the West Indies tries to cope with being old
and dissipated. 61-4.
"Brooklyn." Third person. In Soul Clap Hands and Sing,
Marshall; Cavalcade, A. P. Davis and S. Redding, eds.;
Reena and Other Stories, Marshall.
This is a story of a confrontation between a Jewish
professor and a southern black woman. She has light
skin, and she is a grade school teacher. 61-5.
"Reena." First person. In Harpers 225, October 1962;
American Negro Short Stories, J. H. Clarke, ed.; Black-
eyed Susans, M. H. Washington, ed.; Reena and Other Stor-
ies, Marshall.
A woman - whose parents are West Indian - goes through
several stages of life and tries to cope with several
reverses. 62-19.
"Some Get Wasted." Third person. In Harlem USA, J. H.
Clarke, ed.; Harlem, J. H. Clarke, ed.
This is a story of a gang fight and the death of a
young gang member. 64-30.
"Soul Clap Hands and Sing." ("Barbados.") In Mademoiselle
51, June 1960. 60-3.
See "Barbados," Marshall.
"To Da-duh in Memoriam." First person. In Black Voices,

A. Chapman, ed.; Afro-American Writing, R. Long and E.
Collier, eds.; Reena and Other Stories, Marshall.
   A young girl goes to Barbados - with her mother and
   sister - to visit her grandmother. Grandmother and
   granddaughter make profound impressions on each other.
   67-60.
"The Valley Between." Third person. In The Contemporary
Reader; Reena and Other Stories, Marshall.
   A young woman - who has a young daughter - is trapped
   in an unhappy marriage. 54-2.

Marshall, Sharon R.
   "The Granddaughter." Third person. In Essence 6(10),
   February 1977.
      A fourteen year old girl lives with her grandmother;
      the two of them cannot communicate. 77-18.

Martin, Kenneth K.
   "The End of Jamie." Third person. In Negro Digest 14(2),
   December 1964.
      A sullen, withdrawn boy learns to play the harmonica,
      and it becomes a vital part of his life as he grows
      into a man. Then he marries a woman who does not like
      harmonica playing. 64-12.

Martinez, Joe. (2) (3)
   "Rehabilitation and Treatment." Third person. In Black
   Voices in Prison, E. Knight, ed.; New Black Voices, A.
   Chapman, ed.
      This is a very short story about the frustrations of
      blacks in prison. 70-37.

Marvin X. (1944-   ) (1) (2) (3) (5)
   "Three Parables." Third person. In Black World 19(8),
   June 1970.
      These three sketches reflect the philosophy of the
      Nation of Islam/"Black Muslims" in the 1960s and 1970s.
      70-48.

Mason, Judi Ann. (1955-   )
   "Smells That Go Boom." First person. In Essence 11(4),
   August 1980.
      A teenage girl is determined to marry a man - who has
      fathered three children by three different girls - over
      the objections of her mother. 80-22.

Mathis, Sharon Bell. (1937-   ) (2) (5)
   "Arthur." Third person. In Essence 2(11), March 1972.
      A man cares for his widowed, mentally ill mother and
      reacts to the "black revolution." 72-3.
   "Ernie Father." First person. In Black World 22(8), June
   1973.
      A very young couple is expecting a baby. 73-7.

Mayfield, Julian. (1928-1984) (2) (3) (4) (5)
   "Black on Black; A Political Love Song." First person. In

Black World 21(4), February 1972.
> This is the story of the love of an Afro-American en-
> tertainer and an African political leader; his tradi-
> tions prohibit their being married. 72-5.

Mays, Ramina Y.
"Lerna's Mother, Verda Lee." First person. In Essence
11(11), March 1981.
> A single, unlettered woman struggles to rear her daugh-
> ter. 81-15.

Meaddough, R. J., III. (1935-   ) (2) (3) (5)
"The Death of Tommy Grimes." Third person. In Freedomways
2(3), Summer 1962; The Best Short Stories by Negro Writ-
ers, L. Hughes, ed; Brothers and Sisters, A. Adoff, ed.;
Modern Black Stories, M. Mirer, ed.
> A young white boy kills a black escaped prisoner. 62-6.
"The Other Side of Christmas." Third person. In Freedomways 7(4), Fall 1967; Harlem, J. H. Clarke, ed.
> This is a Story in three parts: A black track star wins
> a mile race and thinks about escorting the white Queen
> of the Christmas Prom to the Prom; the Queen prepares
> for the Prom; racism emerges at the Prom. 67-46.
"Poppa's Story." Third person. In Liberator 9(3), March
1969; Out of Our Lives, Q. P. Stadler, ed.
> This is a story about a black man and his contest with
> machines; the machines are programmed to play the game
> of life. 69-27.

Melford, Larry. (2) (5)
"A Wandorobo Masai." Third person. In Liberator 10(8),
August 1970.
> This is a story about members of two African tribes -
> the Wandorobo Masai and the Wakikuyu. 70-54.

Meriwether, Louise M. (2) (3) (4) (5)
"Daddy Was a Numbers Runner." First person. In The Antioch
Review 27, Fall 1967; Harlem, J. H. Clarke, ed.; Out of
Our Lives, Q. P. Stadler, ed.
> This is a "rites of passage" story. A young girl tries
> to cope with poverty, and she begins to understand why
> some blacks are conditioned to behave negatively. 67-11.
"A Happening in Barbados." First person. In Antioch Review
27(1), Spring 1968; Black-eyed Susans, M. H. Washington,
ed.; Black Short Story Anthology, W. King, Jr., ed; Essen-
ce 2(2), 1971.
> A black woman comes to grips with her biases during a
> trip to Barbados. 68-14.
"The Large End of the Strop." First person. In Negro Digest 18(1), November 1968.
> The narrator tells about life in Harlem during the
> depression. 68-19.
"That Girl from Creektown." Third person. In Black Review
Number 2, M. Watkins, ed.
> A young black woman - who has finished high school and
> who does not want to do domestic work - struggles

against bias in a small town. 72-45.

Mighty, Julia Grimes.
   "Chitterlings for Breakfast." Third person. In <u>Negro Di-</u>
   <u>gest</u> 11(10), August 1962.
      A black woman - living on a military post in Alaska
      with her husband - cooks chitterlings late one night.
      This attracts the attention of her neighbor who is a
      southern white woman. 62-3.

Milner, Ron. (1938-   ) (2) (3) (5)
   "The Flogging." Third person. In <u>Black Short Story Antho-</u>
   <u>logy</u>, W. King, Jr., ed.
      A black busboy experiences discrimination and reacts.
      72-13.
   "Junkie Joe Had Some Money." First person. In <u>The Best</u>
   <u>Short Stories by Negro Writers</u>, L. Hughes, ed.
      A boy reacts to being a witness to a robbery and a
      murder; he also reacts to having been warned not to say
      anything about the incident. 67-25.
   "The Ray." In <u>Urbanite</u>, May 1961; <u>Black Short Story Antho-</u>
   <u>logy</u>, W. King, Jr., ed.
      This is a short sketch about a ray of light at a murder
      scene. 72-34.

Mitchell, Gwen.
   "56 Ravine Avenue." First person. In <u>Essence</u> 6(8), December 1975.
      A little black girl tries to cope with a variety of
      problems. 75-23.

Mitchell, Kathryn J.
   "A Dangerous Thing." First person. In <u>Negro Digest</u> 14(11),
   September 1965.
      A black woman - who is a student at Columbia Univer-
      sity - comes home to Alabama for the summer and decides
      to try to desegregate the town. 65-6.

Mondesire, J. W.
   "Alownne." Third person. In <u>Liberator</u> 10(9), September
   1970.
      A single, black woman thinks about taking cocaine,
      discovers she is pregnant, and makes plans for her
      unborn child. 70-4.

Moore, Christella.
   "Betrayal." Third Person. In <u>Essence</u> 7(9), January 1977.
      A young woman's lover does not marry her because he
      he wants to marry a virgin. 77-6.

Moreland, Charles K., Jr. (1945-   ) (2) (3) (5)
   "The Top Hat Motel." Third person. In <u>Negro Digest</u> 18(8),
   June 1969.
      A black artist for the Los Angeles Police Department
      becomes involved in a series of incidents with a woman
      who is a member of the Black Panther Party. 69-37.

Moss, Grant, Jr.
"I Remember Bessie." First person. In Essence 9(8), December 1978.
    The narrator associates Bessie Smith with people he has known over a number of years. 78-10.
"A Woman's Man." Third person. In Essence 8(2), June 1977.
    A man's infidelity leads to him and his wife having separate bedrooms. 77-63.

Moss, Ivory.
"Not a Tear in Her Eye." Third person. In Essence 6(5), September 1975.
    This story is about the reaction to a black student's suicide; the student has not been very popular with her fellow black students. 75-18.

Motley, Willard. (1912-1965) (2) (3) (4) (5)
"The Almost White Boy." Third person. In The Best Short Stories by Negro Writers, L. Hughes, ed.; The Afro-American Short Story, J. C. Elam, ed.; Soon One Morning, H. Hill, ed.
    The son of a white father and a black mother falls in love with a white girl whose parents are biased. 63-1.

Muller-Thym, Thomas. (1948-   ) (2) (3) (5)
"A Word about Justice." Third person. In What We Must See, O. Coombs, ed.
    A black drug addict - who also sells drugs - makes a sale to a white youth. 71-56.

Munoz, Amina.
"Negra." Third person. In Essence 6(10), February 1976.
    A woman reacts to her abortion. 76-22.

Murray, Albert. (1916-   ) (2) (3) (4) (5)
"Stonewall Jackson's Waterloo." First person. In Harper's, February 1969; Out of Our Lives, Q. P. Stadler, ed.
    Adults gather around the fire to talk about a variety of topics; the young narrator listens. 69-35.
"Train Whistle Guitar." First person. In Dark Symphony, J. A. Emanuel and T. Gross, eds.; American Negro Short Stories, J. H. Clarke, ed.; Tales and Stories for Black Folks, T. C. Bambara, ed.
    Two little boys idolize Luzana Cholly, who is a drifter/hobo/gambler. The boys decide to run away and adopt Cholly's lifestyle. 68-37.

Murray, Samuel M. (2) (5)
"Brooklyn - A Semi-true Story." Third person. In We Be Word Sorcerers, S. Sanchez, ed.
    This story is about gang warfare, several black gangs, a white gang, and some white policemen. 73-4.

Myers, Vivienne.
"I Can Stand a Little Rain." First person. In Essence 7(10), February 1977.

A young divorced mother seeks to cope with her difficult situation. 77-20.

Myers, Walter Dean. (1937-   ) (2) (3) (5)
"Bubba." Third person. In Essence 3(7), November 1972.
    A white soldier escorts the body of a black soldier -
    killed in Vietnam - to the black soldier's home in
    New York. 72-7.
"The Fare to Crown Point." Third person. In What We Must
See, O. Coombs, ed.
    A drug addict breaks into an apartment, and he finds a
    baby of whom he becomes very fond. 71-12.
"The Fighter." Third person. In Liberator 9(1), January
1969.
    A fighter is on his way to becoming a punching bag.
    69-11.
"The Going On." Third person. In Black World 20(5), March
1971.
    A widower is deeply grieved. 71-14.
"Gums." Third person. In We Be Word Sorcerers, S. Sanchez,
ed.
    A nine year old boy and his sixty-nine year old grand-
    father try to ward off death. 73-18.
"Houseboy." Third person. In Liberator 7(11), November
1967.
    A coloured houseboy in South Africa comes to grips with
    the difference between being coloured and being black.
    67-23.
"How Long Is Forever." Third person. In Negro Digest
18(8), June 1969.
    A black prisoner - who wants to be a good prisoner -
    is taunted and brutalized by a sadistic white guard.
    69-15.
"Song of Youth." Third person. In Liberator 7(4), April
1967.
    A youth - who is a good basketball player - is allowed
    to graduate from high school without any academic
    skills. 67-52.
"The Vision of Felipe." Third person. In The Black Scholar
10(1/2), November/December 1978.
    A Peruvian boy - who is part Indian - experiences
    tragedy. 78-22.

Naylor, Gloria.
"The Block Party." Third person. In The Women of Brewster
Place, Naylor.
    A woman dreams about the block party in which she is to
    participate the next day. 82-1.
"Cora Lee." Third person. In The Women of Brewster Place,
Naylor.
    An unmarried woman loves babies and continues to have
    them. Once they grow beyond infancy, she neglects
    them. 82-2.
"Dawn." Third person. In The Women of Brewster Place,
Naylor.
    This is the story of a street. 82-3.

"Etta Mae Johnson. Third person. In <u>The Women of Brewster Place</u>, Naylor.
   A middle-aged woman has had a life of ups and downs. She has an intense need for a man's affection. 82-4.
"Kiswana Brown." ("When Mama Comes To Call.") Third Person. In <u>The Women of Brewster Place</u>, Naylor. 82-5.
   See "When Mama Comes To Call."
"A Life on Beekman Place." ("Lucielia Louise Turner.") Third person. In <u>Essence</u> 10(11), March 1980.
   Two parents react to the death of their child. 80-13.
"Lucielia Louise Turner." ("A Life on Beekman Place.") Third person. In <u>The Women of Brewster Place</u>, Naylor. 82-6.
   See "A Life on Beekman Place."
"Mattie Michael." Third person. In <u>The Women of Brewster Place</u>, Naylor.
   A woman pays a dear price for spoiling her son. 82-7.
"The Two." Third person. In <u>The Women of Brewster Place</u>, Naylor.
   Tragedy strikes the lives of two women who are homosexual lovers. 82-9.
"When Mama Comes to Call." ("Kiswana Brown.") Third Person. In <u>Essence</u> 13(4), August 1982.
   A young woman with a middle class background, moves to a poor section of town - much to her mother's consternation. 82-10.

Neal, Larry. (1937-   ) (1) (2) (3) (4) (5)
"Sinner Man, Where You Gonna Run To?" First person. In <u>Black Fire</u>, L. Jones (A. Baraka) and Neal, eds.
   Blacks - who belong to a secret sect - burn a white man to death on an inverted cross. 69-32.

Neely, Barbara.
"Passing the Word." Third person. In <u>Essence</u> 12(6), October 1981.
   A conversation on a bus causes a woman to break her engagement. 81-20.

Nyx, Melvin.
"Huntin'." Third person. In <u>Black World</u> 2(10), August 1972.
   A man and a woman meet at a bar. 72-20.

O'Brien, Thomas.
"Reunion." First person. In <u>Essence</u> 6(10), February 1976.
   After her marriage fails and her child dies, a woman has to decide if she will return home on her father's terms. 76-26.

Okore, Ode.
"The Mermaid." Third person. In <u>Essence</u> 7(5), September 1976.
   When a poor Nigerian village girl gets pregnant for a wealthy college student he urges her to abort. 76-18.

Oliver, Diane A. (1943-1966) (2) (3) (5)
"Health Service." Third person. In <u>Negro Digest</u> 15(1),
November 1965.
 A mother takes her four children to the clinic and
 reflects on her poverty. 65-11.
"Mint Juleps Not Served Here." Third person. In <u>Negro
Digest</u> 16(5), March 1967.
 A black couple and their son live deep in the Forest
 Preserve. They react very negatively to white people's
 coming to their home. 67-32.
"Neighbors." Third person. In <u>The Sewanee Review</u>, Spring
1966; <u>The Afro-American Short Story</u>, J. C. Elam, ed.;
<u>Black Voices</u>, A. Chapman, ed; <u>Brothers and Sisters</u>, A.
Adoff, ed.
 A black family has problems when a boy in the family is
 scheduled to be the first black student to desegregate
 the town's white elementary school. 62-21.
"Traffic Jam." Third person. In <u>Negro Digest</u> 15(9), July
1966.
 A black man - who has been missing for a long time -
 returns to his surprised wife with a car. 66-30.

Oliver, James B. (2) (5)
"For 'God and Country' Thing, Circa 1940." First person.
In <u>Black World</u> 21(5), March 1972.
 A black soldier converts to Catholicism; he tries to
 relate to a fellow black soldier who is not patriotic.
 72-14.

Oliver, Kitty.
"Mama." Third person. In <u>Essence</u> 7(6), October 1976.
 A woman, who has left her son with her mother - the
 boy's grandmother - for eight years, returns to reclaim
 the son. 76-16.

Olsen, Paul. (3)
"The Line of Duty." Third person. In <u>The Angry Black</u>,
J. A. Williams, ed.
 Two white soldiers threaten a black soldier. The black
 soldier is dating the same woman one of the white
 soldiers dates. 62-10.

O'Neal, Reams.
"Impotence." First person. In <u>Essence</u> 8(6), October 1977.
 A man is upset because his cat is dead, and he feels
 his neighbors have killed it. 77-22.

Pate, Alexs d.
"Gestures." Third person. In <u>Essence</u> 9(5), September 1978.
 A man and a woman struggle to establish a sound rela-
 tionship. 78-8.

Patterson, Lindsay. (2) (3) (5)
"Miss Nora." Third person. In <u>Essence</u> 1(3), July 1970;
<u>What We Must See</u>, O. Coombs, ed.
 A woman is forty-five, unmarried, and pregnant. 70-28.

"The Red Bonnet." First person. In <u>The Best Short Stories by Negro Writers</u>, L. Hughes, ed.
> An old lady - who is thought to be crippled - begins to walk. Later she challenges segregationist practices. 67-48.

"T Baby." First person. In <u>Essence</u> 3(1), May 1972.
> A black underground organization works to build a black nation in Africa. 72-43.

Perry, Richard. (1944-   ) (2) (4) (5)
"For You There Is Only the Dancing." Third person. In <u>Black World</u> 23(8), June 1974.
> A young boy goes on his first fishing trip with his father and a neighbor. 74-5.

"Me and Julius." First person. In <u>Essence</u> 6(6), October 1975.
> A successful black actor - who was once poor - is still very sensitive about his past and about race relations. 75-17.

"Mississippi Remembered." First person. In <u>Freedomways</u> 17(1), First Quarter, 1977.
> A civil rights volunteer in the South tries to get an old man to register to vote. 77-31.

"Moonlight and Mississippi." Third person. In <u>Freedomways</u> 17(1), First Quarter, 1977.
> A man tries to cope with the fear of death in Mississippi during the civil rights struggle. 77-33.

Petry, Ann. 1911-   ) (2) (3) (4) (5)
"Has Anybody Seen Miss Dora Dean." First person. In <u>The New Yorker</u> 34, October 25, 1958; <u>Miss Muriel and Other Stories</u>, Petry.
> The widow of a man who committed suicide many years earlier prepares to die. 58-2.

"The Migrane Workers." Third person. In <u>Redbook</u> 129(1), May 1967; <u>Miss Muriel and Other Stories</u>, Petry.
> An old man - who is a migrant worker - wants to stay at a truck stop. 67-31.

"Miss Muriel." First person. In <u>Soon One Morning</u>, H. Hill, ed.; <u>Miss Muriel and Other Stories</u>, Petry.
> A twelve year old girl - who is a member of the only black family in town - describes the events of one summer when her aunt attracts three suitors. 63-18.

"Mother Africa." Third person. In <u>Miss Muriel and Other Stories</u>, Petry.
> A dirty, ragged, unshaven, junkman acquires a statute which he believes to be the likeness of an African woman. He cleans up, shaves, and buys new clothes. 71-34.

"The New Mirror." First person. In <u>The New Yorker</u> May 29, 1965; <u>Miss Muriel and Other Stories</u>, Petry; <u>Out of Our Lives</u>, Q. P. Stadler, ed.
> A man - who is very dependable and methodical - is missing, and his family is very worried. 65-22.

"The Witness." Third person. In <u>Redbook</u> 136(4), February 1971; <u>Miss Muriel and Other Stories</u>, Petry.

The only black teacher in an all white town becomes the
victim of a group of white juvenile delinquents. 71-55.

Pharr, Robert Dean. (1916-   ) (2) (3) (4) (5)
    "The Numbers Writer." Third person. In New York Magazine
    September 22, 1969; New Black Voices, A. Chapman, ed.
        This story is about the experiences of a numbers writer
        during a thirty-two hour period. 69-25.

Poston, Ted. (1906-1974) (2) (3) (5)
    "Rat Joiner Routs the Klan." First person. In Soon One
    Morning, H. Hill, ed.; Modern Black Stories, M. Mirer, ed.
        Black citizens of a Kentucky town become upset when the
        movie Birth of a Nation is to be shown at the town's
        segregated theater. 63-21.
    "The Revolt of the Evil Fairies." First person. In The
    Best Short Stories by Negro Writers, L. Hughes, ed.
        The good fairies in the grammar school play are always
        light skinned; the evil fairies are always dark skin-
        ned. 67-49.

des Pres, Francois Turenne.
    "Anancy and the Mongoose." In Phylon 17(1), First Quarter,
    1956. 56-1.
    "Djapie and His Magic Dwarf." In Phylon 13(3), Third
    Quarter, 1952. 52-3.
    "How Le Machoquette Was Changed into a Tornado." In Phylon
    13(3), Third Quarter, 1952. 56-3.
    "The Tale - A West Indian Folk Story." In Phylon 13(4),
    Fourth Quarter, 1952. 52-25.
    "The-Valley-Where-the-Sun-Never-Shines." In Phylon 15(1),
    First Quarter, 1954. 54-3.

Price, E. Curmie. (5)
    "The Victims." Third person. In Negro Digest 19(4), Feb-
    ruary 1970.
        A couple's domestic dispute leads to a confrontation
        with a policeman. 70-53.

Priestley, Eric. (1943-   ) (2) (3) (5)
    "The Seed of a Slum's Eternity." First person. In What We
    Must See O. Coombs, ed.
        The narrator views and comments on a black slum. 71-46.

Prior, J. A.
    "Spectator." First person. In Essence 8(1), May 1977.
        A young woman from the South - who has lived in the
        North for a long time - returns home. During her jour-
        ney she thinks about the past. 77-47.

Pritchard, N. H. (1939-   ) (2) (3) (5)
    "Hoom." In 19 Necromancers from Now, I. Reed, ed.
        This is a very modernistic "short story." 70-25.

Randall, Dudley. (1914-   ) (1) (2) (3) (5)
    "The Cut Throat." First person. In Negro Digest 13(9),
    July 1964.

A barber comes to hate one of his customers; he decides to cut the customer's throat. 64-9.
"Incident on a Bus." Third person. In <u>Negro Digest</u> 14(10), August 1965.
Violence comes from a harmless looking man - after buses are desegregated. 65-13.
"Shoe Shine Boy." Third person. In <u>Negro Digest</u> 15(11), September 1966.
A man - who is shining shoes - reacts differently to a white Army sergeant than he does to a black civil rights worker. 66-26.
"Victoria." Third person. In <u>Negro Digest</u> 15(7), May 1966.
A boy falls in love with a girl, but he does not know how to approach her. 66-33.

Rawls, Melanie A.
"Color the World." Third person. In <u>Essence</u> 10(5), September 1979.
A woman who is struggling to cope with a broken relationship and her stepmother's battle with cancer has a traumatic experience. 79-3.
"Going Home on a Long Cord." First person. In <u>Essence</u> 10(8), December 1979.
A successful young woman visits home after being away for a long time. She and the other members of the family seek to cope with family frictions and difficulties. 79-7.

Reams, Christine.
"The Game." First person. In <u>Negro Digest</u> 17(5), March 1968.
A young girl reacts to the infidelity of the mother of another girl in the neighborhood. 68-5.

Reid, Alice. (2)
"And Shed a Murderous Tear." Third person. In <u>Negro Digest</u> 13(2), December 1963.
This story is in two parts. In part one a liberal white woman expresses support of and sympathy for a young black man who desegregates a school in the face of mob violence. In part two the woman's husband resists his company's efforts to hire a black engineer. 63-2.
"Corinna." Third person. In <u>Negro Digest</u> 11(11), August 1962.
This is the sad story of a neglected little girl. 62-4.
"Give Us This Day." Third person. In <u>Black World</u> 23(8), June 1974.
A broke, frustrated, unemployed man has a confrontation with a holdup man. 74-6.
"Jo Jo Banks and the Treble Clef." Third person. In <u>Essence</u> 5(6), October 1974.
A boy falls in love with Ravel's "Bolero," and his life is changed. 74-8.
"A Special Kind of Courage." Third person. In <u>Negro Digest</u> 11(1), November 1961.
A black man takes the white woman he dates home to meet

his family. 61-16.
"The Night of the Senior Ball." First person. In Negro
Digest 12(1), November 1962.
　　A white boy dances with a black girl - the only black
　　person at the high school Senior Ball. 62-15.

Richardson, Alice I. (2) (3) (5)
"A Right Proper Burial." Third person. In What We Must
See, O. Coombs, ed.
　　A deranged man resists the church's efforts to have a
　　funeral ceremony for his daughter. 71-42.

Richardson, Frederick D.
"Four Months in Time." Third person. In Liberator 10(11),
November 1970.
　　I. ARMAGEDDON; II. The old lady; III. The Old Woman in
　　the Supermarket; IV. Father and Son. 70-17.
"Jolof." Third person. In Liberator 8(2), February 1968.
　　Two African tribes fight; a contest is held for the
　　hand of the daughter of a chief. 68-18.

Riley, Clayton. (1935-   ) (2) (3) (5)
"Now That Henry Is Gone." Third person. In Liberator 5(7),
July 1965; Harlem, J. H. Clarke, ed.
　　Several witnesses give their versions of how a man
　　died. 65-23.

Rive, Richard. (3)
"Strike." Third person. In Negro Digest 11(6), April 1962.
　　Coloured men distributing pamphlets in South Africa run
　　into trouble. 62-22.

Rivers, Conrad Kent. (1933-1967) (1) (2) (3) (5)
"Chinese Food." Third person. In Negro Digest 15(12),
October 1966.
　　A black couple's meal is interrupted by a drunk white
　　man. 66-8.
"Goodbye Baby Boy." Third person. In Negro Digest 13(6),
April 1964.
　　A white fight manager is upset because his best black
　　fighter is marrying the manager's daughter. 64-16.
"Mother to Son." Third person. In The Best Short Stories
by Negro Writers, L. Hughes, ed.
　　A mother cannot bring herself to identify her son's
　　body. 67-34.

Roach, Ralph.
"Rufus." Third person. In Black World 21(3), January 1972.
　　This is a story about a poverty stricken little boy.
　　72-37.

Robinson, Billy Hands.
"Carrie: A New World Ritual." Third person. In Essence
10(6), October 1979.
　　Carrie is a legend in her own time, and her most recent
　　lover tries to cope with her "fame." 79-2.

Robinson, Jeffrey.
   "Three Girls." Third person. In <u>Essence</u> 7(12), April 1977.
      A man has had three separate, unusual experiences with
      three unrelated women. Some time later the four of them
      come to the same bar. 77-53.

Robinson, Louie.
   "Jacob's Dilemma." Third person. In <u>Negro Digest</u> 14(6),
   April 1965.
      A man - whose daughter has desegregated a state univer-
      sity - is torn between the conflicting demands of ra-
      cist whites and his wife. 65-14.

Rodgers, Carolyn. (1) (2) (3) (5)
   "Blackbird in a Cage." First person. In <u>Negro Digest</u>
   16(10), August 1967.
      Seeing a blind man causes a young woman to reflect on
      her teenage years. 67-8.
   "Central Standard Time Blues." First person. In <u>Essence</u>
   6(7), November 1975.
      A black woman sits beside a white man on a bus, and she
      reflects on - and reacts to - the history of race
      relations in America. 75-4.
   "One Time." Third person. In <u>Essence</u> 6(7), November 1975.
      A counsellor for a job training program is forced to
      expel two pregnant young women from the program. 75-19.
   "A Statistic Trying To Make It Home." Third person. In
   <u>Negro Digest</u> 18(8), June 1969.
      A man deliberates about what kind of illegal drugs he
      should buy. 69-34.
   "Walk Wid Jesus." Third person. In <u>Essence</u> 2(12), April
   1972.
      A woman wants salvation because she hopes that being
      saved will help her cope with her problems. 72-47.

Russell, Carlos E.
   "The Negrophile." Third person. In <u>Liberator</u> 5(9), September 1965.
      The protagonist of this story is a "militant" black man
      with a white wife. 65-21.

Russell, Charles. (1932-   ) (2) (3) (5)
   "Klacloueedsedstene." First person. In <u>Liberator</u> 5(11),
   November 1965.
      The title of this story is also the title of a musical
      work by the late jazz musician, Charlie Parker. This
      story is about an interracial youth; his black father
      is dead; his white mother rejects him. 65-16.
   "Quietus." Third person. In <u>Liberator</u> 5(11), November
   1965; <u>The Best Short Stories by Negro Writers</u>, L. Hughes,
   ed.
      A black man acts contrary to his conscience for econo-
      mic reasons. 65-26.

Salaam, Kalamu Ya. (Val Ferdinand.) (1947-   ) (2) (3) (5)
   "Sister Bibi." Third person. In <u>We Be Word Sorcerers</u>, S.

Sanchez, ed.
A young, single, black woman tries to deal with black
male and female relationships and with her sexuality.
73-35.
"Second Line/Cutting the Body Loose." First person. In
What We Must See, O. Coombs, ed.
The narrator describes New Orleans funeral processions.
71-45.

Sanchez, Sonia. (1934-   ) (1) (2) (3) (4) (5)
"After Saturday Night Comes Sunday." Third person. In
Black World 20(5), March 1971; What We Must See, O. Coombs,
ed.
A young woman tries to cope with her lover's drug
addiction. 71-1.

Sanders, Maye Byas.
"Randalene Ain't No Baby. "Third person. In Black World
19(10), August 1970.
A poverty stricken woman - who has nine children -
tries to cope with life and the pregnancy of her oldest
daughter. 70-36.

Self, Charles. (2) (5)
"Ndugu from Tougaloo." Third person. In Black Review
Number 2, M. Watkins, ed.
Ndugu means brother in Swahili. A black man saves his
money and goes to Kenya. 72-31.

Shange, Ntozake. (1948-   )
"aw babee, you so pretty." First person. In Essence 9(12),
April 1979; Midnight Birds, M. H. Washington, ed.
The narrator speaks of the plight of black women tra-
velling alone. 79-1.
"comin to terms." Third person. In Midnight Birds, M. H.
Washington, ed.
A woman refuses to have sexual intercourse with her
lover. 80-4.
"oh she gotta head fulla hair." Third person. In The Black
Scholar 10(1/2), November.December 1978.
A woman has an obsession about hair. 78-16.

Shaw, Elaine Smith.
"Unkept Promises." Third person. In Essence 8(2), June
1977.
A man gets out of prison and tries to find a job before
he goes home to his family. 77-55.

Shawn, Karen.
"The Rape." First person. In Essence 10(6), October 1979.
A woman describes being raped. 79-15.

Shelton, Perkins T.
"What Goes Around." Third person. In Essence 7(8), Decem-
ber 1976.
A husband and a wife both have extra-marital affairs.

76-37.

Shepherd, Don.
    "The Hatcher Theory." Third person. In <u>Negro Digest</u> 15(3),
    January 1966.
        A scholar from the fortieth century speculates on
        twentieth century race relations. 66-13.

Sherrod, Lena.
    "Absence." Third person. In <u>Essence</u> 6(10), February 1976.
        A woman - who is having an affair with a married man -
        wants to break off the affair. 76-1.

Shockley, Ann Allen. (1925-   ) (1) (2) (3) (4) (5)
    "Abraham and the Spirit." Third person. In <u>Negro Digest</u>
    8(9), July 1950.
        A little boy is the last "sinner" on the mourners'
        bench; he is waiting to be touched by the Holy Spirit.
        It is July, and the church goers are anxious to leave
        the hot, humid church. 50-1.
    "Ain't No Use in Crying." Third person. In <u>Negro Digest</u>
    17(2), December 1967.
        A white man attempts to rape a black girl in a small,
        rural, racist southern town. 67-1.
    "A Birthday Remembered." Third person. In <u>The Black and
    White of It</u>, Shockley.
        A woman - who is homosexual - is visited by the daugh-
        ter of her late lover. 80-2.
    "Crying for Her Man." Third person. In <u>Liberator</u> 11(1/2),
    January/February 1971.
        An educated black woman is married to a black man who
        has major problems. 71-6.
    "End of the Affair." Third person. In <u>Liberator</u> 9(6),
    June 1969.
        A black woman is pregnant for her married, white lover.
        69-9.
    "The Faculty Party." Third person. In <u>Black World</u> 21(1),
    November 1971.
        One of the two black faculty members at a white college
        tries to cope with the politics of the situation and
        with his wife's infidelity. 71-11.
    "The Funeral." Third person. In <u>Phylon</u> 28(1), Spring,
    1967; <u>Out of Our Lives</u>, Q. P. Stadler, ed.
        A woman arranges to have her grandmother's funeral
        conducted the way her grandmother requested. Then she
        contemplates her own death. 67-18.
    "Holy Craft Isn't Gay." Third person. In <u>The Black and
    White of It</u>, Shockley.
        A woman - who is an entertainer and who is married - is
        plagued by her homosexual tendencies which she wishes
        to suppress. 80-8.
    "Home To Meet the Folks." Third person. In <u>The Black and
    White of It</u>, Shockley.
        A black woman - who is homosexual - takes her white
        lover home at Thanksgiving time. 80-9.
    "Is She Relevant." Third person. In <u>Black World</u> 20(3),

January 1971.
　　A black "militant" tries to deal with his love affair
　　with a white woman. 71-22.
"Love Motion." Third person. In The Black and White of It,
Shockley.
　　A woman imagines that she is having homosexual sex,
　　while she has sexual intercourse with her husband.
　　80-14.
"A Meeting of the Sapphic Daughters." Third person. In
Sinister Wisdom 9, Spring 1979; The Black and White of It,
Shockley.
　　Two black women - who are homosexual lovers - are the
　　only blacks at a meeting of homosexual women. 79-13.
"Monday Will Be Better." Third person. In Negro Digest
13(7), May 1964.
　　A biased white teacher reacts to the desegregation of
　　the school at which she teaches and to the only black
　　student in her class. 64-21.
"The More Things Change." Third person. In Essence 8(6),
October 1977.
　　A college professor - who is having an affair with a
　　student - asks his wife for a divorce, then he discov-
　　ers that his wife is also having an affair. 77-34.
"One More Saturday Night Around." Third person. In The
Black and White of It, Shockley.
　　A woman - who is homosexual - has a lover who is a
　　married woman with children. They try to meet monthly,
　　but their plans are often frustrated. 80-18.
"The Picture Prize." Third person. In Negro Digest 11(12),
October 1962.
　　A black boy's work of art wins an award, but the boy
　　and other blacks are barred from the segregated public
　　art gallery where the awards ceremony is to be held.
　　62-17.
"The Play." Third person. In The Black and White of It,
Shockley.
　　A woman - who is homosexual - is bothered by the fact
　　that her lover is bi-sexual. 80-19.
"Play It, but Don't Say It." Third person. In The Black
and White of It, Shockley.
　　A newly elected black congresswoman discovers that her
　　homosexuality is a potential problem. 80-20.
"The President." Third person. In Freedomways 10(4),
Fall, 1970.
　　A black college president tries to deal with the civil
　　rights demands of black students. 70-35.
"The Saga of Private Julius Cole." Third person. In Black
World 23(5), March 1974.
　　A veteran - who has been wounded in Vietnam - returns
　　to the United States to find that still more combat
　　situations await him. 74-13.
"A Special Evening." Third person. In Sisters, August
1973; The Black and White of It, Shockley.
　　A woman - who is homosexual - has dinner with another
　　woman and wonders if the other woman is homosexual.
　　73-37.

"Spring into Autumn." Third person. In <u>The Black and White of It</u>, Shockley.
    A teacher - who is homosexual - has an affair with a student who works in her office. 80-23.
"To Be a Man." Third person. In <u>Negro Digest</u> 18(9), July 1969.
    A black man is frustrated by his weaknesses. 69-36.

Simmons, B. Charles.
    "James Washburn." Third person. In <u>Negro Digest</u> 14(8), June 1965.
        Two maintenance workers have contrasting ideas about civil rights. 65-15.

Simpson, Janice C.
    "The Anniversary Story." First person. In <u>Essence</u> 8(10), February 1978.
        A sentimental woman talks about her situation in life. 78-2.

Slaughter, Emma.
    "All Because of Emily." Third person. In <u>Essence</u> 9(1), May 1978.
        Two women go to Paris without much money. 78-1.

Sloane, Donald L.
    "Through Leanness and Desire." Third person. In <u>Negro Digest</u> 17(2), December 1967.
        A black man and a white woman have sexual intercourse; then they talk. 67-59.

Smart-Grosvenor, Verta Mae. (1938-   ) (2) (3) (5)
    "For Once in My Life (A Short Statement)." First person. In <u>We Be Word Sorcerers</u>, S. Sanchez, ed.
        A tall woman finds a man on whose shoulders she can lean. 73-12.
    "Send for You Yesterday, Here You Come Today." Third person. In <u>Essence</u> 5(7), November 1974.
        After her fiance leaves to join a group of entertainers a woman becomes a recluse. 74-14.

Smith, Cheryl.
    "Just Give Me a Little Piece of the Sun." Third person. In <u>Essence</u> 9(2), June 1978.
        A little boy has major problems, and his teacher and his uncle try to help him. 78-11.

Smith, C. George.
    "Old Flames Die Hard." Third person. In <u>Essence</u> 10(7), November 1979.
        A woman - who is divorced and whose former husband is remarried - tries to cope with her situation. 79-14.

Smith, Daniel. (2) (4) (5)
    "Lennie." Third person. In <u>Negro Digest</u> 12(2), December 1962.

Racism forces a black fighter to wait too long for a
title match. 62-9.

Smith, Jean Wheeler. (1942-   ) (2) (3) (5)
"Frankie Mae." Third person. In Black World 18(8), June
1968; Black-eyed Susans, M. H. Washington, ed.; Black
Short Story Anthology, W. King, Jr., ed.
A black sharecropper moves towards civil rights activi-
ty because of the impact racism has had on his oldest
daughter. 68-11.
"The Machine." Third person. In Negro Digest 17(1), Novem-
ber 1967.
A group of black men - who are in jail for civil rights
activity - try to present a united front, and the
jailers try to divide and intimidate them. 67-28.
"Something-To-Eat." Third person. In Black World 20(8),
June 1971.
A man returns to the wife he deserted fifteen years
earlier. 71-48.
"That She Would Dance No More." Third person. In Negro
Digest 16(3), January 1967; Black Fire, L. Jones (A.Bara-
ka) and L. Neal, eds.
A powerless, frustrated black man vents his anger on
his defenseless wife. 67-58.

Smith, Rhuberdia K.
"Needin'." Third person. In Essence 7(1), May 1976.
A woman - who is caring for her terminally ill mother -
finally accepts her mother's advice and begins to
date. 76-21.

Smith, Sandy.
"I Wanna Be Sumpin." Third person. In Essence 3(4), August
1972.
A boy - who wants to be someone important when he grows
up - talks about occupations with his teacher. 72-21.

Soloman, Phoebe.
"Reward." Third person. In Essence 8(5), September 1977.
Reading some old letters, revives a woman's fond memo-
ries of a man she once knew. 77-42.

Sondiata, Samuel.
"Night in Chicago." First person. In Liberator 7(5),
May 1967.
This is a story of a gang fight. 67-39.

Spillers, Hortense.
"Brother Isom." ("Isom.") Third person. In Essence 6(1),
May 1975.
A man - who has led a very full life - dies; he is
survived by his wife, fifteen children, and forty-eight
grandchildren. 75-3.
"A Day in the Life of Civil Rights." First person. In The
Black Scholar 9(7/8), May/June 1978.
A nurse cares for a man in a hospital; he has been

injured in riots that occurred shortly before the
assassination of Dr. Martin Luther King, Jr. 78-6.
"Isom." ("Brother Isom.") In Essence 11(1), May 1980.
80-12.
　　See "Brother Isom."
"A Lament." Third person. In The Black Scholar 8(5),
March 1977.
　　A man and a woman are unable to make their relationship
　　work. 77-24.

Steele, Shelby.
"Survivor's Row." Third person. In Black World 25(5),
March 1976.
　　A woman deliberately gets pregnant by a man - who lives
　　in her mother's rooming house - in the hopes that he
　　will marry her. 76-32.

Stewart, John. (2) (4)
"The Americanization of Rhythm." Third person. In The
Black Scholar 6(9), June 1975.
　　A drummer goes to the residence of a woman who likes
　　his drum playing. 75-1.
"Bloodstones." Third person. In Curving Road, Stewart.
　　A woman is unfaithful to her lover while he is in
　　prison. 75-2.
"Blues for Pablo." Third person. In Stanford Short Stor-
ies 1962; Curving Road, Stewart.
　　A man meets a woman at a library, and she moves in with
　　him. 62-1.
"Early Morning." Third person. In Curving Road, Stewart.
　　Only one man has the courage to remove the bodies of
　　people who have hanged themselves from trees in Jai-
　　paul. 76-8.
"In the Winter Of." Third person. In Curving Road, Stewart.
　　A pregnant woman lives with her lover; he has negative
　　feelings about her. 75-13.
"Julia." Third person. In Curving Road, Stewart.
　　A young black woman is at a freedom rally where the
　　rest of the audience is white, and the singers on the
　　stage are black.75-14.
"Letter to a Would-be Prostitute." First person. In Curv-
ving Road, Stewart.
　　The brother of a woman - who has threatened to become a
　　prostitute - writes to tell her about his feelings when
　　he accepted a job he felt to be degrading. 75-15.
"The Pre-Jail Party." Third person. In Curving Road,
Stewart.
　　A party is held for a prostitute who has to begin
　　serving a jail term the next day. 75-20.
"Satin's Dream." Third person. In Curving Road, Stewart.
　　A prostitute dreams that her lover comes to her apart-
　　ment while she is entertaining a customer. 75-26.
"Small Victories." First person. In The Black Scholar
9(3/4), January/February 1978.
　　A Trinidadian woman and a Portugese woman struggle

against each other in Trinidad. 78-18.
"Stick Song." Third person. In Curving Road, Stewart.
    This is a story about a dangerous game played in Trini-
    dad. 75-29.
"That Old Madness - 1974." First person. In Curving Road,
Stewart.
    An educated, employed, black man is, nonetheless, very
    bitter; he insists that in the future he will be mili-
    tant and violent. 75-33.

Stiles, Thelma Jackson. (1939-   ) (2) (5)
"In Light of What Has Happened." Third person. In Essence
10(2), June 1979.
    A woman - who is separated - tries to meet her child-
    ren's needs. She is also torn between her estranged
    husband and her lover. 79-9.
"Juanita." Third person. In Essence 5(3), July 1974.
    A young woman has a number of experiences - some excit-
    ing - some mundane. 74-9.

Sutherland, Ellease.
"Soldiers." Third person. In Black World 22(8), June 1973.
    A soldier is wounded, and thoughts go through his mind.
    73-36.

Sutherland. Naomi.
"The Physics Teacher." First person. In Black World 22(2),
December 1972.
    A young woman talks to the leader of an unusual group,
    and she has an unusual experience. 72-33.

Sutton, Charyn D. (2)
"Sukkie's Song." Third person. In Black World 24(8), June
1975.
    A singer - whose career has had limited success -
    listens to one of her recordings and drinks wine. 75-31.

Sweet, Elizabeth.
"Walker in the Dust." Third person. In Negro Digest 14(4),
February 1965.
    A white man is terribly upset when a black man he
    considers a friend participates in civil rights demon-
    strations. 65-32.

Talley, Marion.
"Thursday Reckoning." First person. In Essence 8(8),
December 1977.
    A woman who is educated - but divorced and unemployed -
    and who has a daughter to support, reflects on a lesson
    she learned as a girl. 77-54.

Taylor, Geraldine. (2)
"Beans." First person. In Essence 4(11), March 1974.
    The three daughters of a poor woman protest against
    their steady diet of beans. 74-1.
"Strength." Third person. In Essence 5(10), February 1975.

A woman has been married for seventeen years, and she has three children. Now she finds that her marriage is not fulfilling. 75-30.

Taylor, Jeanne A. (1934-   ) (2) (3) (5)
"A House Divided." Third person. In The Antioch Review 27(2), Fall 1967; New Black Voices, A. Chapman, ed.
A black man engages in questionable business practices to better his economic status. 67-22.
"Only Clowns Passing Through." Third person. In Essence 5(1), May 1974.
An old woman is a burden on her son-in-law and an embarrassment to her grandchildren, but her daughter resists putting her in a nursing home. 74-12.

Thelwell, Mike. (1938-   ) (2) (3) (5)
"Bright and Mournin' Star." Third person. In The Massachusetts Review 8(4), Autumn, 1966; New Blackc Voices, A. Chapman, ed.; Out of Our Lives, Q. P. Stadler, ed.
A sharecropper in the Mississippi Delta deals with his grandmother's death and with drought. 66-6.
"Community of Victims." Third person. In Negro Digest 13(3), January 1964; Story Magazine.
A middle class black man stops a drunk black man from harassing a white woman. 64-7.
"Direct Action." First person. In Prize Stories 1963; The Best Short Stories by Negro Writers, L. Hughes, ed.; The Afro-American Short Story, J. C. Elam, ed.
This is a humorous story about a unique type of "sit-in" against segregated facilities. 63-10.

Thief, Luana.
"Fly Away Blackbird, Fly Away Home." Third person. In Essence 11(8), December 1980.
A singer - who has made a lot of money - comes home. 80-6.

Thomas, Frederick L.
"The American Dream." First person. In Black World 22(2), December 1972.
A black college student talks about his Jewish sociology teacher. 72-1.

Thomas, Joyce Carol.
"Lubelle Berries." Third person. In The Black Scholar 10(1/2), November/December 1978.
This is a folk tale about an alliance between a little girl and a snake. 78-13.

Thompson, James W. (1935-   ) (1) (2) (5)
"See What Tommorrow Brings." First person. In Black Short Story Anthology, W. King, Jr., ed.; Transatlantic Review.
A boy desegregates a school that is surrounded by large numbers of protesting whites. 72-38.

Thompson, Samuel. (2) (5)

"Bruzz." Third person. In <u>Freedomways</u> 2(2), Spring, 1962;
<u>Modern Black Stories</u>, M. Mirer, ed.
    A black boy - who is minding the family store - falsely
    accuses a white man of attempted robbery. 62-2.

Tibbs, Delbert.
    "Tricks." First person. In <u>Black World</u> 22(9), July 1973.
    A homocide occurs during a robbery attempt. 73-42.

Torres, Brenda. (2)
    "Convergence." Third person. In <u>Black World</u> 24(4), Febru-
    ary 1975.
        This is a story of a murder and a lynching. 75-5.

Toure, Askia Muhammad. (1938-   ) (1) (2) (3) (5)
    "Of Fathers and Sons." Third person. In <u>We Be Word Sorcer-</u>
    <u>ers</u>, S. Sanchez, ed.
        A "revolutionary" black poet converts his "moderate"
    father to his point of view. 73-26.

Vail, Barnabas.
    "Beginning." Third person. In <u>Negro Digest</u> 10(9), July
    1961.
        A little black girl goes to a formerly all white school.
    61-2.

Vickens, Jimmy.
    "Lead Role." First person. In <u>Essence</u> 8(2), June 1977.
        Two aspiring black actors find themselves stranded in
    Hollywood without any money or any way to get home to
    Watts. 77-26.

Vroman, Mary Elizabeth. (1923-1967) (2) (3) (5)
    "See How They Run." Third person. In <u>Ladies Home Journal</u>
    June 1951; <u>The Best Short Stories by Negro Writers</u>, L.
    Hughes, ed.; <u>American Negro Short Stories</u>, J. H. Clarke,
    ed.
        A young idealistic, black school teacher tries hard to
    educate her students. 51-2.

Walker, Alice. (1944-   ) (1) (2) (3) (4) (5)
    "The Abortion." Third person. In <u>You Can't Keep a Good</u>
    <u>Woman Down</u>, Walker.
        A woman - who is married and who has one child - has an
    abortion. 81-1.
    "Advancing Luna - and Ida B. Wells." First person. In <u>You</u>
    <u>Can't Keep a Good Woman Down</u>, Walker; <u>Ms</u> 6(1), July 1977;
    <u>Midnight Birds</u>, M. H. Washington, ed.
        A black woman - who is a civil rights activist - re-
    sponds to being told by a white civil rights activist
    that a black man raped her. Later she reacts when the
    white woman befriends the alleged rapist. 77-1.
    "The Child Who Favored Daughter." Third person. In <u>In Love</u>
    <u>and Trouble</u>, Walker.
        A black man reacts very strongly to his daughter's
    involvement with a married white man. 73-5.

"Coming Apart by Way of Introduction to Lorde, Teish, and Gardner." Third person. In <u>You Can't Keep a Good Woman Down</u>, Walker.
 Alice Walker refers to this work as a fable. It is the introduction to a chapter in the book <u>Take Back the Night</u>. 81-6.
"The Diary of an African Nun." First person. In <u>Freedomways</u> 8(3), Summer, 1968; <u>In Love and Trouble</u>, Walker.
 An African nun reflects on how alienated she is from her African culture. 68-9.
"Elethia." Third person. In <u>You Can't Keep a Good Woman Down</u>, Walker.
 This is a story of a girl's reaction to the image of an old former slave. 81-9.
"Entertaining God." Third person. In <u>In Love and Trouble</u>, Walker.
 A boy is killed by a gorilla that the boy led from the zoo. 73-6.
"Everyday Use." First person. In <u>In Love and Trouble</u>, Walker; <u>Black-eyed Susans</u>, M. H. Washington, ed.
 A mother has two daughters who are very different.73-8.
"Fame." Third person. In <u>You Can't Keep a Good Woman Down</u>, Walker.
 A famous black woman goes to an interview and an awards ceremony. 81-10.
"The First Day (A Fable after Brown)." Third person. In <u>Freedomways</u> 14(4), Fall, 1974.
 A boy's desegregation of a previously all-white school is an ordeal. 74-4.
"The Flowers." Third person. In <u>In Love and Trouble</u>, Walker.
 A ten year old girl comes upon the scene of a hanging. 73-11.
"Her Sweet Jerome." Third person. In <u>In Love and Trouble</u>, Walker.
 A woman goes mad because she believes her husband is unfaithful. 73-20.
"How Did I Get Away with Killing One of the Biggest Lawyers in the State? It Was Easy." First person. In <u>Ms</u> 9(5), November 1980; <u>You Can't Keep a Good Woman Down</u>, Walker.
 A teenage black girl has an affair with the son of a prominent white racist. 80-10.
"Laurel." First person. In <u>Ms</u> 7(5), November 1978; <u>Midnight Birds</u>, M. H. Washington, ed.; <u>You Can't Keep a Good Woman Down</u>, Walker.
 A black woman civil rights worker is attracted to a white male civil rights worker, but they cannot have sexual relations because they are in the South. Later she discovers that he is married. 78-12.
"A Letter of the Times, or Should This Sado-Masochism Be Saved." First person. In <u>You Can't Keep a Good Woman Down</u>, Walker; <u>Ms</u> 10(4), October 1981.
 A black woman reacts to seeing another black woman dressed as Scarlett O'Hara. 81-16.
"The Lover." Third person. In <u>You Can't Keep a Good Woman Down</u>, Walker; <u>Essence</u> 11(12), April 1981.

A young woman - who is a poet - has an affair during a
   summer when she is at a writers' colony. 81-18.
"Nineteen Fifty-five" or "You Can't Keep a Good Woman
Down." First person. In You Can't Keep a Good Woman Down,
Walker; Ms 9(9), March 1981.
   A black woman - who is a blues singer - sells a song to
   a young white singer, and he becomes the king of rock
   and roll. 81-19.
"Petunias." Third person. In You Can't Keep a Good Woman
Down, Walker.
   This is a very short sketch about a woman who got in-
   volved in the civil rights movement. 81-21.
"Porn." Third person. In You Can't Keep a Good Woman Down,
Walker.
   A woman reacts to her lover's collection of pornogra-
   phy. 81-22.
"Really, Doesn't Crime Pay." First person. In In Love and
Trouble, Walker.
   A woman reacts to her husband and to a man who has
   plagiarized her writing. 73-30.
"The Revenge of Hannah Kemhuff." First person. In In Love
and Trouble, Walker.
   This is the story of how a black woman engages a "root
   worker" to seek revenge against a white woman. 73-31.
"Roselily." Third person. In In Love and Trouble, Walker.
   A woman - who has never been married and who has four
   children - marries a Black Muslim. 73-33.
"Source." Third person. In You Can't Keep a Good Woman
Down, Walker.
   Two Afro-American women were college classmates; one's
   African ancestry is obvious; the other can pass for
   white. 81-26.
"Strong Horse Tea." Third person. In Black World 17(8),
June 1968; Black Short Story Anthology, W. King, Jr., ed.;
In Love and Trouble, Walker.
   A poor, black mother of a very sick child wants a doc-
   tor, but she has to settle for an old black woman who
   is a healer. The healer prescribes horse urine." 68-33.
"A Sudden Trip Home in the Spring." Third person. In Es-
sence 2(5), September 1971; Black-eyed Susans, M. H.
Washington, ed.; You Can't Keep a Good Woman Down, Walker.
   A black student - at an exclusive school with only two
   black students - returns home to bury her father. 71-49.
"To Hell with Dying." First person. In The Best Short
Stories by Negro Writers, L. Hughes, ed.; In Love and
Trouble, Walker; Tales and Stories for Black Folks, T. C.
Bambara, ed.
   Mr. Sweet's "dying" is interrupted many times when his
   neighbor says, "To hell with dying, man; my children
   want Mr. Sweet." 67-61.
"We Drink the Wine in France." Third person. In In Love
and Trouble, Walker.
   A male white French teacher and a black college co-ed
   are "attracted" to each other. 73-44.
"The Welcome Table." Third person. In Freedomways 10(3),
Summer 1970; In Love and Trouble, Walker.

An old, black woman is forcibly removed form a white church. 70-57.

Walker, Evan K. (2) (3) (5)
"Harlem Transfer." Third person. In Negro Digest 19(7), May 1970; Black Short Story Anthology, W. King, Jr., ed.; What We Must See, O. Coombs, ed.
A man's son dies from a drug overdose, and the man seeks violent revenge against the drug dealer and the police. 70-23.
"Legacy." First person. In Black World 21(2), December 1971.
A black man moves towards black militancy because of the actions his black militant friend took in the days just before the friend died. 71-25.

Walker, Victor Steven. (1947-   ) (2) (3) (5)
"The Long Sell." Third person. In New Black Voices A. Chapman, ed.
A salesman - who is on the road - meets a sailor who is approximately the age of the salesman's son. 72-26.

Wardlaw, Exavier X. Lowtricia. (2) (5)
"The Gift of Mercilessness." Third person. In We Be Word Sorcerers, S. Sanchez, ed.
A black man kills white people; he sees himself as an avenging angel. 73-15.

Warntz, Chris (2)
"Courtney Go Huntin'." Third person. In Black World 24(2), December 1974.
A boy daydreams about deer hunting - while he is in school - and again - before he represents his gang in an after school fight. 74-2.

Watkins, Gordon R. (1930-   ) (5)
"Wedding Day." Third person. In Freedomways 4(2), Spring, 1964.
A Black soldier - who is stationed in Mississippi - is on the way to his wedding, when he has a confrontation with a mean, white deputy sheriff. 64-33.

Watkins, Odie.
"A Sense of Pride." Third person. In Essence 7(2), June 1976.
This is a story of a homeless couple. They sleep on commuter trains and survive by their wits. 76-28.

Welburn, Ron. (1944-   ) (2) (3) (5)
"Moon Woman, Sunday's Child." First person. In Essence 2(6), October 1971.
This is a story about a very unusual woman. 71-33.

Wells, Oliver Ray.
"A Separate but Equal Heaven." First person. In Black World 19(8), June 1970.

This is a satirical story about a struggle in heaven
between integrationists and segregationists. 70-41.

Welsh, Kariamu.
"God Bless the Cook." Third person. In Essence 12(1),
May 1981.
   A woman - who is having an affair with a married man -
   has dinner with him. 81-11.
"She Was Linda Before She Was Ayesha." Third person. In
Essence 11(6), October 1980.
   A woman - with a lot for which to live - is senselessly
   killed. 80-21.

Wesley, Valerie Wilson.
"Eve." Third person. In Essence 11(8), December 1980.
   A woman is bothered by her husband's compulsion to
   paint. 80-5.

Westbrook, Gerald.
"The Peacemaker." Third person. In Negro Digest 13(10),
August 1964.
   An alien spaceship - with one being aboard - comes to
   the United States. 64-24.

White, Edgar. (1947-   ) (2) (5)
"Loimos." First person. In Liberator 9(12), December 1969;
Black Short Story Anthology, W. King, Jr., ed.
   The narrator speaks of New York City as if it is in
   the grips of a plague. 69-19.
"Of Acidia." First person. In Liberator 9(8), August 1969.
   This is a story about death and dying. 69-26.
"Sursum Corda (Lift Up Your Hearts)." First person. In
Liberator 8(12), December 1968; What We Must See, O.
Coombs, ed.
   This is a story about the experiences of a black boy
   living in Harlem. 68-34.

White, Joseph. (1933-   ) (3) (5)
"O'Grady Says." Third person. In Liberator 5(2), February
1965.
   The only black soldier in an army unit competes with
   white soldiers in a game; the black soldier becomes the
   victim of racism. 65-24.
"The Wise Guy." Third person. In Liberator 7(7), July 1967.
   A bus driver assumes that the passenger who has not
   paid the fare is a young black male. 67-64.

White, Paulette Childress.
"Alice." First person. In Essence 7(9), January 1977;
Midnight Birds, M. H. Washington, ed.
   A middle-aged woman has had three reactions to another
   woman. When she was a girl she liked the other woman;
   as a young woman she disliked her; now she understands
   her. 77-2,
"The Bird Cage." First person. In Redbook 151(2), June
1978; Midnight Birds, M. H. Washington, ed.

A woman - who is unhappy - listens to the sounds coming from a bar that features "exotic" dancing girls. 78-4.

White, Thurman.
"HE & SHE, or LUV Makes You Do Foolish Things." Third person. In Black World 22(8), June 1973.
   Two former lovers meet at a party and decide to try again. 73-19.

White, Wimley.
"Freedom." First person. In Black World 22(4), February 1973.
   A former slave - who is 130 years old - tells about how he and two of his friends were defrauded by a white man who had been a Confederate Army captain. 73-14.

Wideman, John Edgar. (1941-   )
"Across the Wide Missouri." First person. In Damballah, Wideman; The Seattle Review.
   A man talks about his relationship with his father. 81-2.
"The Beginning of Homewood." First person. In Damballah, Wideman.
   A man writes to his brother who is in prison. 81-3.
"The Chinaman." Third person. In Damballah, Wideman; North American Review.
   An ill, old, black woman is superstitious about Chinese men. 81-4.
"Daddy Garbage." Third person. In Damballah, Wideman; North American Review.
   A man's dog finds a dead baby in a garbage can; the man and a friend bury the baby. 81-7.
"Damballah." Third person. In Damballah, Wideman.
   A slave refuses to behave the way slaves are expected to behave, and he is killed. 81-8.
"Hazel." Third person. In Damballah, Wideman.
   A brother causes his sister to become paralyzed. 81-12.
"Lizabeth: The Caterpillar Story." Third person. In Damballah, Wideman.
   A woman goes to great extremes to save her husband's life. 81-17.
"Rashad." Third person. In Damballah, Wideman.
   An old woman reflects on the situations involving her daughter, her granddaughter, and her son-in-law. 81-23.
"Solitary." Third person. In Damballah, Wideman.
   A mother visits her son who is in prison and in solitary confinement. 81-24.
"The Songs of Reba Love Jackson." First and third person. In Damballah, Wideman.
   A famous gospel singer talks about her experiences, and a third person narrator talks about the singer. 81-25.
"Tommy." ("Bobby.") Third person. In Damballah, Wideman; Tri Quarterly Review (As "Bobby.").
   This is a story of a person accused of a crime who is a fugitive. 81-27.
"The Watermelon Story." Third person. In Damballah, Wide-

An old woman tells stories about how an alcoholic lost
an arm and how an old, childless couple found a child.
81-28.

Wiggins, Paula.
"The Island Lover. " Third person. In Essence 10(12),
April 1980.
A woman - who is on a vacation in the Bahamas - falls
in love with a Bahamian man; she hopes he will come
back to the United States with her. 80-11.

Wilkinson, Brenda Scott. (1946-   ) (2) (5)
"Rosa Lee Loves Bennie." Third person. In We Be Word Sor-
cerers, S. Sanchez, ed.
A high school girl fears that she is pregnant. 73-32.

Williams, Dennis A.
"Sunset Boogie." Third person. In The Black Scholar 8(5),
March 1977.
Two men date two prostitutes, and the four of them
have a clash with one of the prostitute's pimp. 77-50.

Williams, Edward G. (1929-   ) (2) (3) (4) (5)
"A Great Day for a Funeral." First person. In A Galaxy of
Black Writing, R. B. Shuman, ed.
A fifteen year old girl talks about her family's reac-
tion to her grandfather's death. 70-19.
"Nightmare." Third person. In A Galaxy of Black Writing,
R. B. Shuman, ed.
A young black man - who cannot escape from his mother's
domination - has nightmares about cockroaches. 70-31.
"Remembrances of a Lost Dream." Third person. In A Galaxy
of Black Writing, M. B. Shuman, ed.
A middle class black man reacts to the assassination of
Dr. Martin Luther King, Jr. 70-38.

Williams, Gerald M.
"Points of Reference." Third person. In Black World 22(8),
June 1973.
A black American - who is visiting Europe - has some
interesting experiences. 73-28.

Williams, John A. (1925-   ) (2) (3) (4) (5)
"The Figure Eight." First person. In Brothers and Sisters,
A. Adoff, ed.
The narrator remembers elementary school and a teacher
he feared and hated. 70-15.
"A Good Season." Third person. In Urbanite, May 1961;
Black Short Story Anthology, W. King, Jr., ed.
Two American women have interesting experiences in
Spain. 61-6.
"Navy Black." Third person. In Beyond the Angry Black,
Williams, ed.
A black sailor plans to adopt a boy from Chamorro, and
another black sailor tells the Chamorroan boy about
American racism. 66-20.

"Son in the Afternoon." First person. In The Angry Black, Williams, ed.; The Best Short Stories by Negro Writers, L. Hughes, ed.; Dark Symphony, J. A. Emanuel and T. Gross, eds.

A black writer - whose mother is a maid - resents his mother's situation. He also resents the fact that his mother pays a great deal of attention to the nine year old white boy in the family for which she works. The writer seeks revenge by compromising the boy's mother. 62-21.

"Tales of Childhood." First person. In Negro Digest 12(3), January 1963.

This story has two parts. In Joey's Sled a boy's name brand, store bought sled is the envy of his friends; most of them have home made sleds. In Father and Son a father chases after a son who has run away. 63-28.

Wiliams, Kellie.
"Why Mother." First person. In Essence 7(10), February 1977.

A fifty year old woman is hostile to every man her twenty-three year old daughter dates. 77-61.

Williams, Leola G.
"Baptism 1945." Third person. In Essence 9(5), September 1978.

A minor confrontation between a black woman and a white woman takes place in the South in the 1940s. 78-3.

Williams, M.
"The Lie." Third person. In Essence 7(7), November 1976.
A woman gets pregnant for a man who has made no real commitment to her. 76-15.

Williams, Ronald.
"Grandma's Game." Third person. In Negro Digest 15(7), May 1966.

A woman - whose husband is a prominent deacon in the church - runs a gambling game in their home on Saturday night, and he appears not to notice. 66-11.

Williams, Sherley Anne. (1944-   ) (2) (3) (4) (5)
"Meditations on History." First person. In Midnight Birds, M. H. Washington, ed.

A man - who writes books on how to control slaves - interviews a slave woman who has participated in an escape attempt. 80-16.

"Tell Martha Not To Moan." First person. In The Massachu-setts Review 9, 1968; Out of Our Lives, Q. P. Stadler, ed.
An unmarried eighteen year old woman has one child; she is pregnant again. She tries to explain her situation to her mother. 68-35.

Williams, Travis.
"Niggers Don't Cry." First person. In Negro Digest 15(11), September 1966.

A southern white man observes scenes in a bar on a
Saturday night; he is amazed to see a black man crying.
66-22.

Wilmore, Stephen R.
"The Committee." First person. In <u>Negro Digest</u> 19(2),
December 1969.
   The only black member of a committee – studying civil
   disorder by blacks – reflects on and reacts to racial
   stereotyping. 69-5.

Wilson, Freddie M.
"Black Daedalus Dreaming." Third person. In <u>Negro Digest</u>
19(1), November 1969; <u>The Afro-American Short Story</u>, J. C.
Elam, ed.
   This is a story about a series of dreams. 69-2.
"The Willie Bob Letters." First person. In <u>Negro Digest</u>
18(3), January 1969.
   Three people write letters about the shooting death of
   a black boy – who was killed by a policeman during
   civil disorders by blacks. 69-38.

Wingate, S. V.
"Manton Street Blues." First person. In <u>Essence</u> 7(8),
December 1976.
   A poor woman – who lives in a slum – has a number of
   problems. 76-17.

Wolf, H. R.
"To the Fair." Third person. In <u>Negro Digest</u> 14(9), July
1965.
   A widow – who lives alone – decides to travel to a fair
   in New York even though she knows her husband would not
   have approved. 65-31.

Wolf, Shirley.
"Terror." Third person. In <u>Essence</u> 7(4), August 1976.
   Three civil rights workers – who are about to be mur-
   dered by whites – think their last thoughts. 76-33.

Woods, Debbie.
"Sunday School. "Third person. In <u>Essence</u> 7(7), November
1976.
   A girl – who is approaching puberty – hears about men-
   struation from her Sunday Schoolmates. She is very
   afraid that it will be unplesant. 76-31.

Wright, Charles. (1932-   ) (2) (3) (4) (5)
"A New Day." Third person. In <u>The Best Short Stories by</u>
<u>Negro Writers</u>, L. Hughes, ed.
   A black butler and chauffeur reacts to and seeks to
   cope with the rich, racist, southern, white woman who
   is his new employer. 67-35.

Young, Al. (1939-   ) (2) (4) (5)
"Chicken Hawk's Dream." First person. In <u>Stanford Short</u>

Stories, 1968; New Black Voices, A. Chapman, ed.
   A high school student - who uses marijuana and alcohol
   - dreams he can play the saxophone. 68-5.

Young, Carrie A. (3)
   "Adjo Means Goodbye." First person. In Beyond the Angry
   Black, J. A. Williams, ed.
      A little girl - who is a recent immigrant to the United
      States from Sweden - invites her best friend - who is
      black - to her party. The parents of the white children
      - who are invited - object to the black girl's being
      invited. 66-1.

TITLE INDEX

"Great God Stebbs." Davis, A. 73-17.
"The Grief." Anderson, M. H. 76-12.
"Gums." Myers, W. 73-18.
"The Hammer Man." Bambara, T. C. 66-12.
"A Happening in Barbados." Meriwether, L. 68-14.
"Happy Birthday." Bambara, T. C. 72-17.
"Harlem." Dumas, H. 79-8.
"Harlem Farewell." Ahmed, A. B. 70-20.
"A Harlem Game." Dumas, H. 70-21.
"The Harlem Mice." Bullins, E. 75-11.
*"Harlem on the Rocks." Hairston, L. 69-14.
*"The Harlem Rat." Jones, J. H. 64-17.
"The Harlem Teacher." Freeman, L. 70-22.
*"Harlem Transfer." Walker, E. K. 70-23.
"A Harsh Greeting." Gray, D. 70-24.
"Harvest." Jones, E. P. 76-13.
"Has Anybody Seen Miss Dora Dean?" Petry, A. 58-2.
"The Hatcher Theory." Shepherd, D. 66-13.
"Hazel." Wideman, J. E. 81-12.
"HE & SHE, or LUV Makes You Do Foolish Things." White, T. 73-19.
"He Couldn't Say Sex." Bullins, E. 71-15.
"Health Service." Oliver, D. A. 65-11.
*"Heaven to Hell." Hughes, L. 52-6.
"The Helper." Bullins, E. 71-16.
"Her Sweet Jerome." Walker, A. 73-20.
"Heroes Are Gang Leaders." Baraka, A. (Jones, L.) 67-21.
"A Hole They Call a Grave." Baldwin, J. A. 75-12.
"Holly Craft Isn't Gay." Shockley, A. A. 80-8.
"Home Is Much Too Far To Go." Davis, G. 72-18.

"Home To Meet the Folks." Shockley, A. A. 80-9.
*"Home X and Me." Bates, A. J. 65-12.
"Honor among Thieves." Hunter, K. 71-17.
"Hoom." Pritchard, N. H. 70-25.
"A House Divided." Taylor, J. A. 67-22.
"Houseboy." Myers, W. 67-23.
"How Did I Get Away with Killing One of the Biggest Lawyers in the State? - It Was Easy." Walker, A. 80-10.
"How I Got into the Grocery Business." Hunter, K. 72-19.
"How Le Machoquette Was Changed into a Tornado." des Pres, F. T. 56-3.
*"How Long Is Forever." Myers, W. 69-15.
"Hue and Cry." McPherson, J. A. 68-15.
"The Hungered One." Bullins, E. 71-18.
"Huntin'." Nyx, M. 72-20.
"The Hypnotist." Bamberg, E. 68-16.
"The Hypochandriac." Fields, J. 68-17.
"I Ain't Playing, I'm Hurtin'." ("Gorilla My Love.") Bambara, T. C. 71-19.
"I Am an American." McPherson, J. A. 77-19.
"I Can Stand a Little Rain." Myers, V. 77-20.
"I Could Rest Forever." Jackson, M. 78-19.
"I Need Your Love So Bad." Dalton, F. E. 63-14.
"I Remember Bessie." Moss, G., Jr. 78-10.
"I Remember Omar." Jackson, M. 69-16.
"I Wanna Be Sumpin'." Smith, S. 72-21.
"I Was Here but I Disappeared." Brown, W. 81-13.
"I'm Going To Move Out of This Emotional Ghetto." Lee, A. 69-17.
"Ice Tea." Adams, A. 66-14.

About the Compiler

PRESTON M. YANCY is Head of the Department of English and Communications and Assistant Professor of English and Humanities at Virginia Union University. He has contributed articles to the *Journal of Afro-American Studies*.